MW00653998

DIVINE HEALING
&
HEALTH

DIVINE HEALING
&
HEALTH

BY

DR. DOUGLAS J. WINGATE

Copyright©2022 by Dr. Douglas J. Wingate.
All rights reserved.

Unless otherwise indicated, all Scripture quotations are taken from *The New King James Version of the Bible*. Copyright © 1982 by Thomas Nelson, Inc. Used by permission. All rights reserved.

Scripture quotations marked AMP are from *The Amplified Bible*. Copyright © 2015 by The Lockman Foundation, La Habra, CA 90631. Used by Permission.

Scripture quotations marked AMPC are from *The Amplified Bible, Classic Edition*. Copyright © 1954, 1958, 1962, 1964, 1965, 1987 by The Lockman Foundation, La Habra, CA 90631. Used by Permission.

Scripture quotations marked PHILLIPS are from *The J.B. Phillips New Testament in Modern English*. Copyright © 1960, 1972 by J. B. Phillips. Administered by The Archbishops' Council of the Church of England. Used by Permission.

Scripture quotations marked MSG are from *The Message*. Copyright © 1993, 2002, 2018 by Eugene H. Peterson. Used by Permission.

Scripture quotations marked MIRROR are from *The Mirror Study Bible*. Copyright © 2012 by Francois du Toit. mirrorword.net. Used by Permission.

Scripture quotations marked TPT are from *The Passion Translation*. Copyright © 2017, 2018, 2020 Passion and Fire Ministries, Inc. ThePassionTranslation.com. Used by Permission.

Scripture quotations marked WUEST are from *The New Testament: An Expanded Translation by Kenneth S. Wuest*. Copyright © 1961 by Wm. B. Eerdmans Publishing Co. All rights reserved.

Scripture quotations marked YLT are from *Young's Literal Translation* YLT. Public Domain.

TABLE OF CONTENTS

CHAPTER ONE

SUPERNATURAL ENCOUNTERS, EXPERIENCES, & INSIGHTS

GROWING UP ON A LAKE near Tampa, Florida, was a great thrill for a young teenager in the 1960s. I had a ski boat – and three of my friends on the lake, who were about the same age as I was, had ski boats, as well. We would spend the whole summer water skiing, every day. Our parents would buy each one of us a five-gallon tank of gas every week, and we would simply switch from boat to boat until all the gas was gone. Gas was 23 cents a gallon back then, if you can believe it! This much activity got us all in very good shape.

Looking back, I realize how invincible healthy teen boys feel. We did so many daring things: I know now that angels protected us from killing ourselves during our fear-less feats. As young, healthy people, we never thought much about sickness or growing old, even though we saw it all around us. It simply seems like the possibility is so far in the distant future that we didn't give it much thought.

But soon, we humans start to feel like time is speed-ing up and flying by. In our twenties, new challenges of hard work, responsibilities, and stress start to slow us down, even if we have been in relatively good health. At age 23, I was a professional rock drummer with a stressful, unhealthy life style. That was when someone challenged me to check out the claims of Jesus, and I had a major encounter with the Lord. After I had finished reading Matthew, Mark, Luke, and half of the gospel of John, Jesus spoke to me in what seemed like an audible voice. He said, "Doug, I'm alive and I AM the Lord."

I got out of my bed, got on my knees, and asked Jesus to take over my life and be my Lord. Within five days, I was delivered of a spirit of drug addiction and alcoholism, and a week after that, I was baptized in the Holy Spirit with the evidence of praying in tongues. All of this happened through simply reading the Word of God and one Christian book, all alone and without consulting with anyone. The following week, I had an epiphany: I thought to myself, "Maybe I should go to church and see if anyone else has had these kinds of experiences."

A year after I was saved, delivered, and Spirit-filled, I started doing evangelistic outreach through a Christian rock band that I had joined. I didn't know that we were in the ministry – we just wanted everyone we could reach to be saved and on their way to heaven.

The church that we all attended was a Spirit-filled Methodist Church (of all things) and the pastor was a great man of God. It was actually the premier Charismatic Church of the Tampa Bay area. I hung out a lot with the college and career group who were mostly my age. Often we would go up to the church on our own to just go inside and pray. Back in those days, it was actually safe to leave churches unlocked for those who desired to come and pray.

One night, one of the young ladies asked for all of us

to pray for her because she wore contact lenses and wanted her vision to be healed. We all laid hands on her – like we had seen the church elders do – and prayed for Jesus to heal her eyes. I suddenly felt something like electricity flow out of my arms and into her. I was so shocked that I opened my eyes – and to my amazement, everyone else had felt the same thing and had opened their eyes. We all asked simultaneously, "Did you feel that?"

Then the young lady we had prayed for opened her eyes and looked around and said, "Oh no! It's worse. I can hardly see anything." Then she said, "Wait a minute!" She took out her contact lenses and then reported she could now see perfectly, with 20-20 vision. No wonder it was worse with the contacts still in her eyes!

This supernatural healing had a tremendous impact on me, and as I look back, I realize that I have been in the healing ministry since that first night, when a few young adults who didn't really know what we were doing, experienced an incredible display of the love of God.

I would like to share the insights on healing that I have gained over the past 49 years of being a Christian and the past 47 years of ministry experience. I trust God that you will be blessed and enhanced in your walk of faith and divine healing and health as you read the following pages filled with supernatural encounters, experiences, and wisdom from God's Word.

CHAPTER TWO

HEALING: A MOST IMPORTANT SUBJECT

DIVINE HEALING is probably one of the most important subjects you will ever study. I say that because
any billionaire dying on their deathbed would tell you
that their money isn't doing them any good. If they are
beyond what doctors can do for them, money can't keep
them alive.

Additionally, as believers, we want to focus on those
things that we need to complete our divine assignments.
As much as we need prosperity to be able to get the Gospel
out, we need health even more. It's obvious that if you
can't even get out of bed, you're not going to be very use-
ful as far as getting the job done!

In this book, we are going to systematically cover
divine healing from many angles. We will examine every
aspect of divine healing and answer all the common questions. Here is a quick preview of what we will cover.

IT'S IN THE REDEMPTION

We will show from the Scriptures that physical

healing has been provided for us in the redemptive work of Christ. People have said that healing has been provided for us in the atonement but Christ didn't give us atonement. He gave us redemption, which means the complete removal of sin, not the covering over of sin.

In that complete removal of sin, He was able to remove the very source of all sickness and disease. None of this was on the planet until Adam and Eve sinned. Ultimately Satan is the source of all sickness and disease, and man's sin was the open door for all such destruction and death to come into the world. Physical healing has been provided for us in the redemptive work of Christ. He redeemed us from poverty, sickness, and spiritual death — separation from God.

GOD'S WILL IS FOR ALL TO BE HEALED

Next, we will discover God's will with respect to healing everyone. A lot of people believe that God *can* heal—they don't doubt His *ability* to heal—but they doubt His *willingness* to heal because they don't think He's willing to heal everyone. We'll give you enough scriptural evidence to prove to you that Jesus was *always* willing to heal *everyone* who came to Him, and *He still is.* It's an important part of our faith connection to know that Jesus desires to heal everyone, including you!

OVERCOMING HINDRANCES TO HEALING

Then we will discover and learn how to overcome common hindrances to healing. If there is any kind of hindrance that would keep us from receiving any of the covenant promises of God and prevent the blessing of God from working in our life, it is vital that we remove it. Again and again, we find that the greatest obstacle is basically ignorance: God's people lack knowledge and understanding of how faith works and how God's kingdom works. Once we are able to establish ourselves in faith, we're well on the way to making sure that we receive in every area. We will be able to receive divine healing if we need it, but also able to walk in divine health as well.

MANY METHODS OF DIVINE HEALING

After that, we will take a look at God's methods of healing. We're going to observe seven distinct methods that can be identified in the Bible. Now, these methods may overlap, and God may use several methods at the same time, *but the exciting thing is that God has provided so many ways to receive healing, that it makes it easy to be healed!*

MINISTERING HEALING TO OTHERS

Last, we are going to look at ways to minister divine healing to others so you will be able to minister to those you will encounter: whether in family situations, in day-to-day circumstances and situations, or in your ministry. You are going to hear of people who need healing: quite often they are going to come to you. We should desire to be obedient and yielded to the Lord, so that if He would like to use us in any way with a special gifting, that we would freely move in it in ministry.

HEALING IS A MOST IMPORTANT SUBJECT

The older we get, the more important healing and divine health is to us. We want to be strong in faith and able to turn back any challenge that comes our way. We want to walk in divine health so we can live long on the earth and fulfill all God has asked us to do.

Section One:

Discovering God's Will in Healing

CHAPTER THREE

HOW TO BEGIN IN FAITH
FEAR NOT - ONLY BELIEVE

I CANNOT TEACH ON FAITH AND HEALING without first zeroing in on the four most-focused words Jesus ever said on the subject: "Fear not; only believe" (Mark 5:36 DARBY). Jesus said this to Jairus immediately after Jairus heard the worst news any parent could ever hear: "Your daughter is dead." Jesus spoke these words with authority, Jairus believed and received them, and his daughter was raised from the dead. It would be unfair for Jesus to command us to stop the fear, if we couldn't. If Jesus told Jairus not to fear in the *worst* of circumstances, *we can also choose not to fear,* no matter what we face. As born-again, Spirit-filled Christians, God has given us the ability to stop the fear.

Later, Jesus told the father of a demon-possessed son in Mark 9:23, "If you can believe, all things are possible to him who believes." I like to put these two statements together like this: "Fear not; only believe; because – if you can believe – all things are possible to those who believe." There is nothing too hard for God: no healing is too difficult; no sickness is greater than the name of Jesus. God can *always* heal.

11

GOD'S PROMISE OF A LONG, HEALTHY LIFE

When learning about divine healing and health, it's also important to know that God's plan for mankind's lifespan is 120 years.

And the Lord said, "My Spirit shall not strive with man forever, for he is indeed flesh; yet his days shall be one hundred and twenty years" (Genesis 6:3).

We will be looking at longevity in much greater depth later in this book, but for now, it's good to realize that we have a divine assignment. The Lord has a purpose for us on the earth, and in order for us to fulfill that purpose, we might need to live that long! This will require divine healing *and* divine health, because what good is it to live long if you are sick in the hospital? God wants us able to receive healing for ourselves, to walk in divine health, and to be able to minister healing to others.

DISCOVERING GOD'S WILL IN HEALING

If the Bible reveals a history of God healing people supernaturally under the old covenant, and Jesus and His disciples healing people supernaturally under the new covenant, then we must examine all scriptural claims providing healing and how to receive healing, as well as examine every hindrance to healing.

Let's look first at how to begin in faith. Since faith begins where the will of God is known, we must establish the will of God concerning healing in Scripture. Then confident faith can be exercised.

SCRIPTURE IS OUR SOURCE

We've got to base everything we do on the Word of

God. It's our source for life, it's our source for action, it's our source for everything! To be able to put total confidence in God's Word, we must understand what His Word says; we need to get the illumination of Scripture in our hearts so that we are absolutely in faith concerning the Word of God.

Jesus said to those who believed in Him:

"If you abide in My word, you are My disciples indeed. And you shall know the truth, and the truth shall make you free" (John 8:31,32).

We hear people quote this passage all the time, "You shall know the truth and the truth shall make you free." But they forget the prerequisite to knowing the truth. Jesus said, "Here's the only way to know the truth: if you abide in My Word then you are My disciples indeed." What does it mean to abide in the Word? To live in it – every day. We need to be reading, studying, and meditating on the Word at some point during the day, every day. As a Christian in a world full of bad news, we need to daily take in a good measure of the good news. So, turn off the TV and the bad news and look into the good news and learn how to overcome this world – including the things that are in the bad news!

A SOLID FOUNDATION FOR DIVINE HEALING & HEALTH

So then faith comes by hearing, and hearing by the word of God (Romans 10:17).

To apply our faith to the specific area of divine healing and divine health, we will be concentrating on specific scriptures. Perhaps you don't need a healing at the moment. That's where divine health comes in. If young

13

people would learn these things early, before they have any health problems, it would be so beneficial! While you're young, you're more likely to be healthy, even with a really lousy diet. But of course, you're sowing bad seeds that will tear down your health if you don't learn better things to do concerning nutrition and exercise. Teenagers think of themselves as invincible. They are so young and so vibrant; they can't even imagine ever slowing down and having any kind of health issues. They can't imagine being old. But believe me, everybody's going to face aging. As much as we can live above it and stay fit, have plenty of energy, and walk in divine health, it gets to be more of a challenge to maintain divine health as we go along.

But if we get a solid foundation when we are young, how much better when we get older! I got started in the Word when I was born again and filled with the Spirit at age 23, but I didn't really understand things concerning healing and divine protection from the Lord until I was 29 and attended a Word of Faith church that taught the truth. Then at age 30, the Lord spoke to me very clearly and said, "I have called you into the ministry; you'll have to go to school."

Just two weeks after the Lord spoke those words to me, I was a student sitting in class at Rhema Bible Training College! This resulted in an opportunity to be mentored in the healing ministry by Dr. Kenneth E. Hagin. While at Rhema, I began attending Healing School every day, and soon started ushering there, working closely with Dr. Hagin. That's when I began walking in divine health.

BOLD FAITH

"It is impossible to boldly claim by faith a blessing which we are not sure God offers,

14

because the blessings of God can be claimed only where the will of God is known, trusted, and acted upon." – T. L. Osborn

It's obvious: if you don't know that God is offering something to you, how can you claim it? It takes knowledge, it takes understanding, and it takes wisdom to apply that knowledge.

T.L. Osborn was a great statesman for the Lord. He walked in strong faith and divine health until his last days. He was still doing huge international campaigns until six months before he went home to be with the Lord at 89 years of age. T.L. knew what he was talking about!

There are three steps to bold faith: first, you need to *know the Word and the promise you are claiming.* Next, you must *have total trust in that Word.* That's where faith comes alive beyond any doubt. Third, you need to *act upon that Word.* This means to take corresponding action, including praying the prayer of faith and whatever else God says to do. This may be something you could not do before because of a restriction caused by the health problem. As you step out in faith, you are positioned to receive God's promise.

CONFIDENCE IN PRAYER

Now this is the confidence that we have in Him, that if we ask anything according to His will, He hears us. And if we know that He hears us, whatever we ask, we know that we have the petitions that we have asked of Him (1 John 5:14,15).

This breakdown is a logical thought process: if we ask anything according to God's will, we can have confidence that He hears us. Praise God! If He hears us, He is paying attention to us. Then we know that whatever we ask, we have those things we're asking for. This is a wonderful passage of Scripture!

We need this confidence. Faith is confidence: confidence in God, confidence in God's Word, confidence in God's will, confidence in God's abilities, confidence in His willingness to make your life whole and blessed – and to make your *health* whole and blessed as well.

CHAPTER FOUR

HOW TO LEARN
GOD'S WILL IN HEALING

G OD WANTS US TO KNOW, UNDERSTAND, AND DO His will! He has provided three ways we can discover what He has planned for us. The first one is through Scripture: we learn God's will from the written Word of God. Second, Jesus sent us the Holy Spirit to teach us and help us remember what Jesus taught us. Third, Jesus sent us ministry gifts to equip us and build us up.

LEARNING THE WILL OF GOD
THROUGH SCRIPTURE

All Scripture is given by inspiration of God, and is profitable for doctrine, for reproof, for correction, for instruction in righteousness, that the man of God may be complete, thoroughly equipped for every good work (2 Timothy 3:16,17).

"Given by inspiration of God" literally means "God-breathed." God has breathed His life into the Scripture, so we know it's important; it is profitable for us. This verse then gives five areas of profitability.

SCRIPTURE IS PROFITABLE FOR DOCTRINE

The first area is for doctrine. "Doctrine" simply means "instruction," in this case, instruction from God's Word. People use the word "dogma" interchangeably with the word "doctrine," as in "What is your doctrine" or "What is your dogma?" People can be dogmatic about the wrong things. They can wrongly divide the Word of God; they get it wrong, but they are dogmatic. It's ridiculous the way people get dogmatic about error. They would fight tooth and toenail for the things they believe, even when the things they believe don't produce anything of benefit. But accurate instruction from God's Word will always produce life: it will produce faith, it will produce a manifestation of the grace of God, and a manifestation of God's blessing in your life. True doctrine is an exposé of the goodness of God and the blessings of God. Perhaps you have been to a counselor who has told you, "There are no guarantees in life." They were wrong! We have a whole book of guarantees!

SCRIPTURE IS PROFITABLE FOR REPROOF

The next area where the Word of God is profitable is reproof. "Reproof" means "evidentiary proof or conviction." If you're in a court of law, you bring forth evidence that would prove your case. God's Word is the evidentiary proof - it's from the throne of God, spoken to men who penned it as God spoke to their hearts. Through God's Word, we can know God's thoughts and intents - we can think His thoughts, follow His intents, and walk according to His ways. It is settled for us. We are not moved by what we see.

SCRIPTURE IS PROFITABLE FOR CORRECTION

The third area is correction. If you've wandered off God's ways, you need to be corrected. "Correction" simply means "to be straightened up again." Everyone remembers when they first started learning to drive. It can be intimidating to realize you're driving this huge machine down the highway. Even if you are only going 35 miles an hour, to a beginner, it seems like a breakneck speed! It can be petrifying! Keeping your car up on the road and in the right place between the lines is a challenge, at first. With practice, you learn to adjust the steering wheel to correct your course – without over correcting it. Now that you are a seasoned driver, you make these little micro-corrections nonstop. You make hundreds of them every hour. You are constantly keeping the vehicle going in the right direction, correcting the course as you go.

That's what this verse is talking about: straightening up again, correcting the course, making sure that you're in the right lane – in God's lane, going God's direction.

SCRIPTURE IS PROFITABLE FOR TRAINING

Area number four is "instruction" which simply means "training." We are trained by repetition. This is how we train children, going over and over the basic fundamentals. As teenagers, we might find ourselves training for a sports team. We train to get our bodies in shape; we go through various exercises to learn the particular moves, whether it's baseball, football, basketball, or hockey. We learn to work with others on our team. To be excellent, it takes repeating these fundamental drills over and over. The team that best masters the fundamentals is usually the team that wins the championship.

It's the same with our training in the Christian faith.

We can't just hear the fundamental truths about faith, finances, and healing one time. We learn so much more by constant repetition. Knowing what God's Word says about faith, finances, and healing is so foundational; we must have these truths cemented in our hearts. It's the key to victory in this life!

Some young people today have nurturing deficits – perhaps both parents worked, or maybe they were raised in single-parent homes. It is good to know that God makes up the difference: He is the ultimate Father who is always there and always ready to train us up!

SCRIPTURE IS PROFITABLE FOR RIGHTEOUSNESS

The final area where the Word of God is profitable is righteousness. "Righteousness" means "self-evident rightness or equitableness." Spiritual Christians who are more mature in the things of God can plainly see from the Word what is "self-evident rightness." But to a lot of people, it is not so obvious! In fact, we have a course at Life Christian University called "Christlike Character." We chose to name it that instead of naming it "Christian Character," because there can be all kinds of misunderstandings of what it is to be a Christian. For some people, it is not a violation of Christian character to tell a "little white lie" now and then. What is a "white lie"? It's a half-truth – but that makes it a half lie. And a half lie is a lie. As believers, we can't mix truth with lies. We have to know the truth.

"Self-evident rightness" is Christlike holiness and righteousness. We walk that out day by day, empowered by the grace of God. You would think that people would know how to treat one another as Christians, and that would carry over into the ethical treatment of other people, but quite often they just don't get it. Sometimes you must really spell righteousness out for people. For example, in our course "Ministerial Ethics," we cover what ethical behavior is in a lot of different circumstances and situations. We are very specific about what the ethical thing to do is, so that people can understand. I don't know why it's not self-evident to more people. As they say, "Common sense is not so common anymore." Yet, when a hungry Christian studies God's Word, it provides instruction in righteousness that becomes self-evident.

LEARNING THE WILL OF GOD BY THE HOLY SPIRIT

So far, we've established that we can learn the will of God for healing - and every other aspect of life - through Scripture. The second primary way to learn the will of God is through the Holy Spirit. Jesus said:

"But the Helper, the Holy Spirit, whom the Father will send in My name, He will teach you all things, and bring to your remembrance all things that I said to you" (John 14:26).

The Holy Spirit is the great teacher. He is the one who takes words that are being spoken or read and reveals them to us. As you are reading the Scriptures, they are just words in your thought life - they process through your mind as you read them. Only the Holy Spirit can cause the revelation of the truth to come to you - then those words become cemented in your conscience. The Holy Spirit illumines the Word to you, so it becomes a life-guiding fact that becomes part of your life. When He is able to do that, this illumination is permanently with you. I like to use this illustration concerning you receiving illumination from God's Word: suppose I invited you over to my house for a steak dinner. You come into my house and sit on my furniture. I put the steaks on my grill to cook. But after I serve it to you and you eat it, whose steak is it? It's yours! I don't want it back!

It's the same with God's truth. He wants you to receive His truth and once you have it, it's yours. You own it; you own the knowledge and the understanding of God's kingdom that's revealed to you by the Word of God as illumination comes into your life. Illumination only comes to you by the Holy Spirit. He's the only one that can do that miraculous process.

The same process happens with the preaching of the simple gospel. The simple gospel is impossible to believe without the supernatural work of the Holy Spirit. He speaks into people's minds and says, "This is the truth: Jesus Christ was born of a virgin. He is the Son of God who came to earth to redeem mankind. He bore our sins on the Cross and was buried in a grave, but He rose from the dead to prove that we can have eternal life just like Him. Now He is seated at the right hand of God the Father, where He lives forever to make intercession for us." This message is supernatural. You can't teach it to people like you can teach reading or arithmetic. This message must be *preached or proclaimed;* then the Holy Spirit can grab the message and illuminate it to people's hearts. They are convicted and suddenly realize Jesus Christ *is* Lord, and that they must do something about Jesus. They realize they must receive Jesus as their own personal Lord and Savior. They get born again and come into God's kingdom.

That's the miracle of illumination by the Holy Spirit. He does the same thing whether it's the preaching of the Word for people to be saved or the teaching of the Word that comes in afterwards, for us to be discipled. The Holy Spirit is the teacher who makes it all understandable in the realm of the spirit. Each illumination is something that becomes part of your life.

PRAY THAT YOU MAY INTERPRET

As a Spirit-filled Christian, the best way I know to learn the will of God is to study the Word of God, and then pray in tongues, because the Holy Spirit is always going to pray the perfect prayer for you. Let Him help you! Romans 8: 27b says:

He makes intercession for the saints according to the will of God.

You have to make time to pray in tongues, and it may take a couple of hours. It's important to pray in tongues, then pray to interpret.

Therefore let him who speaks in a tongue pray that he may interpret (1 Corinthians 14:13).

Pray in tongues and interpret what you prayed in tongues until you gain understanding and feel a release of God's peace.

This is how God's mysteries are revealed to us: the mysteries are in the Word, and the Holy Spirit reveals them to us.

"Eye has not seen, nor ear heard,
Nor have entered into the heart of man
The things which God has prepared for those
who love Him."
But God has revealed them to us through His
Spirit (1 Corinthians 2:9,10).

This is also how a *rhema* word comes alive in us. Once we have a fresh *rhema* word, we agree with it, then stand on it until the symptoms change and the healing is manifested. We need to have the power of God's promises working for us. And, as a Christian, the number one promise that we need working for us is the healing of our body, because if Satan can take our health away, we are neutralized.

BAPTIZED WITH THE HOLY FIRE

Jesus said this concerning John the Baptist:

"Assuredly, I say to you, among those born of women there has not risen one greater than John the Baptist" (Matthew 11:11a).

No Old Testament prophet was greater than John the Baptist. John gave us three insights into who Jesus was as the Son of God, that no other prophet knew or understood. First, the Old Testament prophets could only predict that the Messiah was coming. John could say, "Here He is!"

The next day John saw Jesus coming toward him, and said, "Behold! The Lamb of God who takes away the sin of the world!" (John 1:29).

Next, John knew God anointed Jesus with the Holy Spirit beyond measure:

"For He whom God has sent speaks the words of God, for God does not give the Spirit by measure" (John 3:34).

Finally, John saw prophetically that Jesus would baptize us with the Holy Spirit and with holy fire.

"I indeed baptize you with water unto repentance, but He who is coming after me is mightier than I, whose sandals I am not worthy to carry. He will baptize you with the Holy Spirit and fire" (Matthew 3:11).

The holy fire part often gets missed. People forget to tell you that you will also be baptized in the holy fire! The holy fire is given to refine you and make you a vessel of honor. People don't come into this until they pray in the Spirit enough, because when you pray in the Spirit, you are walking in the holy fire. The more you walk in the holy fire, the more you are refined for the things God has called you to do.

LEARNING THE WILL OF GOD THROUGH THE MINISTRY GIFTS

The final way we learn the will of God is through the ministry gifts.

And He Himself gave some to be apostles, some prophets, some evangelists, and some pastors and teachers, for the equipping of the saints for the work of ministry, for the edifying of the body of Christ, till we all come to the unity of the faith and of the knowledge of the Son of God (Ephesians 4:11-13a).

The Lord Jesus is the one who appointed these ministry gifts: apostles, prophets, evangelists, pastors, and teachers. These five ministry gifts are often referred to as the "fivefold ministry." These gifts are given by the Lord to equip the saints so they can do the work of ministry. Every Christian is called to do the work of ministry. We're all here on purpose, not by accident! God doesn't make any accidents. You are not an accident; He knew exactly what He had in mind when He created you. There is a book already written about you in heaven (Psalm 139:16). Now it's your job, your responsibility, to seek out that purpose. As you seek, it's the Lord's responsibility to reveal these things to you, because He is in covenant, in partnership with you. He will reveal specifically what your calling is.

Every one of us is going to be involved in ministry in some way. We believe that many of the students at LCU will be called to the fivefold ministry to equip the saints to strengthen and build the body of Christ. The result: we will all come to the unity of the faith and of the knowledge of the Son of God. That doesn't mean the entire church is finally going to be "on the same page" before Jesus comes back. If you believe that's what's required, I don't know if Jesus could ever come back, because the body of Christ is still a mess, concerning division and divisive doctrines. It's not likely that we are *all* going to come into the unity of the faith, in the knowledge of the Son of God. But you *can* do that in *groups* of people; you come into great unity of the Spirit and great knowledge. Even now, there are camps of believers who are on the same page with God, concerning what He's doing.

Still, it's God's intent that the whole body would come to unity. Now, there is a day coming when we're all going to know and believe exactly the same things. No matter what you believed here on earth, once you get to heaven,, it's going to change. It's going to get corrected. If you were wrong down here, you're going to be in shock! That's why I believe that we need to diligently study God's Word - and rightly divide it - so that when we get to heaven, we're not in shock. Then, when we see heavenly things, we're going to say, "I knew that in the spirit! I knew that!"

We don't want God to have to say to us, "Your doctrine was horrible! You did more damage to the Church than you did good. I wish I could have stopped you from messing everything up, but you just took it upon yourself to teach this." There is going to be weeping for a time in heaven, probably for the lack of rewards for all the things people won't receive because they did it their own way - like a song made famous by Frank Sinatra, "I Did it My Way." It turns out Sinatra didn't want to record it because he thought it was a completely arrogant song. That song could be the theme song of hell, because that's where people go who have chosen to do life their way and not God's way.

In the Church, we certainly need to do it God's way, with knowledge and understanding. That's why God gives us the fivefold ministry gifts to teach these things, until we come to the unity of faith and knowledge of the Son of God. This will result in a powerful awakening throughout the entire earth.

> ...to a perfect man, to the measure of the stature of the fullness of Christ (Ephesians 4:13b).

This powerful awakening will cause some in the Church to be so anointed that we'll say, "Wow! That's the way it's supposed to be! That's what is supposed to happen." It will be as it was in the early Church, when miracles, signs, and wonders were done through the hands of the apostles, including healing everyone they prayed for and city-wide revivals. These are recorded in the following passages from the Book of Acts:

> Also a multitude gathered from the surrounding cities to Jerusalem, bringing sick people and those who were tormented by unclean spirits, and they were all healed (Acts 5:16).

> And the multitudes with one accord heeded the things spoken by Philip, hearing and seeing the miracles which he did. For unclean spirits, crying with a loud voice, came out of many who were possessed; and many who were paralyzed and lame were healed. And there was great joy in that city (Acts 8:6-8).

> Now it came to pass, as Peter went through all parts of the country, that he also came down to

the saints who dwelt in Lydda. There he found a certain man named Aeneas, who had been bedridden eight years and was paralyzed. And Peter said to him, "Aeneas, Jesus the Christ heals you. Arise and make your bed." Then he arose immediately. So all who dwelt at Lydda and Sharon saw him and turned to the Lord (Acts 9:32-35).

And it happened that the father of Publius lay sick of a fever and dysentery. Paul went in to him and prayed, and he laid his hands on him and healed him. So when this was done, the rest of those on the island who had diseases also came and were healed (Acts 28:8,9).

That was "the measure of the stature of the fullness of Christ." We need to return to that. It was lost over the past 2000 years: in the Dark Ages there were just a handful of Spirit-filled believers. But today, once again we are seeing miracles being poured out through the Church. And one day, when we are all together in heaven with the Lord Jesus Christ, we will be that perfect human being, that perfect entity. Right now, we are the body of Christ, but on that day, we will be the bride of Christ. There will be a great celebration in heaven, the marriage supper of the Lamb.

It will be marvelous to have that kind of unity – but for now, as much as is possible, let's learn those things the Father, Son, and Holy Spirit want to get across to us, so we're not shocked in heaven because we were so wrong in our doctrine.

JESUS IS THE MEDIATOR OF A NEW & BETTER COVENANT

One of the reasons for wrong doctrine is that some

Church leaders fail to differentiate between the requirements and the perspectives of the old and new covenants. Under the old covenant, the Jews of Jesus' day had a distorted picture of God and served Him with a religion based on fear and works. Jesus came to paint a different picture of God, His heavenly Father, as a God who loved the entire world and wanted everyone to be saved, a God who rescues the one who is lost.

Jesus ministered under the old covenant, with the same spiritual gifts but a greater anointing than the Old Testament prophets enjoyed, because He was the Messiah, the Anointed One. Jesus' death on the Cross gave us an even better covenant, based on grace and better promises.

Jesus is, of course, the mediator of this new covenant. We need to understand that the new covenant it is gazillion percent better than the old covenant. It is better in every way. Even though the old covenant had the blessings of the covenant to take care of the people of God, the new covenant is far, far, far better. Scriptures in the new covenant that fulfill Old Testament prophecies, or have some other direct correlation to the Old Testament, are promises of the "better covenant." Hebrews 8:6 talks about this:

But now He has obtained a more excellent ministry, inasmuch as He is also Mediator of a better covenant, which was established on better promises (Hebrews 8:6).

In other words, you could have a covenant cut with a mediator, not just directly between two individuals. Jesus, the mediator between God and man, cut this covenant for us. Everything is better in the New Testament: not only do we have better promises, every office of ministry is also better in the New Testament. So don't think that we fall behind in anything from the Old Testament. Everything is better.

CHAPTER FIVE

KNOWING GOD'S WILL BY SEEING JESUS

IN THIS CHAPTER, WE WILL TAKE A CLOSER LOOK AT Jesus, who is the exact image of God and the Eternal Word of God. He clearly demonstrated God's will to heal as He fulfilled every Old Testament prophesy.

JESUS CAME TO DO GOD'S WILL

Jesus was the personification of the will of God. Jesus was completely and totally submitted to the Father. He fully demonstrated God's will.

> **"Then I said, 'Behold, I have come - In the volume of the book it is written of Me - To do Your will, O God" (Hebrews 10:7).**

> **"For I have come down from heaven, not to do My own will, but the will of Him who sent Me" (John 6:38).**

The Gospels and Epistles show the will of God. Everything Jesus did, He did by direct marching orders from heaven. He said, "I only do what I see the Father doing and I only say what I hear the Father saying."

Then Jesus answered and said to them, "Most assuredly, I say to you, the Son can do nothing of Himself, but what He sees the Father do; for whatever He does, the Son also does in like manner. For the Father loves the Son, and shows Him all things that He Himself does; and He will show Him greater works than these, that you may marvel" (John 5:19,20).

"I do nothing of Myself; but as My Father taught Me, I speak these things" (John 8:28).

Jesus wouldn't demonstrate anything other than the Father's true character. In Old Testament times, people didn't really understand God. They were afraid of God and yes, judgment fell as people disobeyed His Word. That's because His Word describes how the spiritual laws of the universe work, and those who break those laws will bring suffering into their own lives.

It's like an experienced electrician who is training a new apprentice. The electrician shows the apprentice the tools of the trade and gives him a toolbox. Then they head out to their first job. On the job site, the electrician removes the outlet cover for an electric dryer. "See that fat red wire? That carries 220 volts. Don't touch it. A small black or white wire carries 110 volts. If you touch one of these when the electricity is flowing, it will give you a bad jolt. But if you touch the 220-volt wire when the electricity is flowing, it will kill you."

Now, if the apprentice listens to the electrician and obeys, he will have no trouble at all with 220-volt wires. But if he touches it, he will die. He broke one of the physical laws of the universe: don't touch high-voltage wires!

Did the electrician kill the apprentice? No, of course not. He warned him what not to do, but it was the apprentice's violation of the physical law that killed him.

In a similar way, God's Word warns us of the areas of spiritual danger, for example the Ten Commandments. If we break these spiritual laws of the universe, we will suffer greatly. Is God bringing judgment upon us, punishing us? No, it was our violation of the physical law that judged us.

In New Testament times – even until the last day - the Word is judge over all. In John 12:46-48, Jesus tells us:

> **I have come as a light into the world, that whoever believes in Me should not abide in darkness.**

> **And if anyone hears My words and does not believe, I do not judge him; for I did not come to judge the world but to save the world.**

> **He who rejects Me, and does not receive My words, has that which judges him – the word that I have spoken will judge him in the last day.**

Understanding that it is breaking the laws of the universe that causes misery, and not God who is punishing us, helps us understand the true nature of our Heavenly Father. God is good to all, but especially to those who are part of His family, the Father shows all His favor, as well as love and mercy and compassion. Still, He wants to bring His children into all the blessings, so as a Father, He continues to correct us and train us with Scripture as we have already seen. His goal is to rub the "rough edges" off of us and get us smoothed out to be smooth, living stones in the building of God (1 Peter 2:5).

JESUS IS THE EXPRESS IMAGE OF GOD

Basically, if you want to see God, simply look at Jesus. The Apostle Paul tells us that Satan has blinded the minds of the people in the world to prevent them from seeing that Jesus really is the Son of God, that He is the representation sent from the God who created all things – and us.

> **...whose minds the god of this age has blinded, who do not believe, lest the light of the gospel of the glory of Christ, who is the image of God, should shine on them (2 Corinthians 4:4).**

It should make sense to humans that, if we were created by God, that He would have some method by which He would have contacted us to show us about Himself. He did exactly that through Jesus, His only begotten Son. False religions are what Satan authored to keep men's minds blinded from knowing the truth of the glory of Christ.

The Apostle Paul wrote that Jesus is the image of the invisible God and the express image of His person.

> **He is the image of the invisible God, the first-born over all creation (Colossians 1:15).**

> **Who being the brightness of His glory and the express image of His person, and upholding all things by the word of His power, when He had by Himself purged our sins, sat down at the right hand of the Majesty on high (Hebrews 1:3).**

Jesus, the champion, is sitting at the right hand of the Father. There are times in prayer and worship when the Lord's true majesty is manifested. At these times, you can't express yourself to the Lord or can't see Him in any other way except as His true Majesty. There have been times when I've been praying and that was what came out of my mouth, "Your Majesty." I addressed Jesus as, "Your majesty, the King of Kings and Lord of Lords." The Father is the thought – the mind – behind Jesus, and everything He has done and will do. They are both so majestic.

And yet, at the same time, Jesus is our brother! One day, something had come up in my mind and I was thinking – with concern – before praying about it. Then I heard the Lord Jesus say, "Have you talked with Dad about that yet?" I have two sons, and this was like hearing one of them ask the other, "Have you talked to Dad about that?" It was just that familiar, that close.

Isn't it cool that Jesus would talk to you and let you know the Heavenly Father is your Dad just like He is Jesus' Dad? Jesus is our elder brother in the faith. He made a way for us into God's kingdom, and yes, He is Lord and God, but He treats us like brothers and sisters in the faith. He said, "Have you talked to Dad?" Praise God! We have both ends of the spectrum: the Lord Jesus is so completely majestic, that sometimes you can do nothing but bow down and fall on your face before Him in worship. Yet, at the same time, Jesus will say, "Have you talked to Dad about that yet?" and be that close and familiar.

IF YOU HAVE SEEN ME, YOU HAVE SEEN THE FATHER

Jesus Himself made it so clear. Let's look at what He told His disciples the night He was betrayed:

Philip said to Him, "Lord, show us the Father, and it is sufficient for us" (John 14:8).

Philip said the disciples would be satisfied if Jesus would just show them the Father.

Jesus said to him, "Have I been with you so long, and yet you have not known Me, Philip?

35

> **He who has seen Me has seen the Father; so how can you say, 'Show us the Father'? Do you not believe that I am in the Father, and the Father in Me? The words that I speak to you I do not speak on My own authority; but the Father who dwells in Me does the works. Believe Me that I am in the Father and the Father in Me, or else believe Me for the sake of the works themselves" (John 14:9-11).**

In other words, Jesus said, "Believe Me just for the fact that I can do all these miracles. Only God can do miracles like these. The miracles are happening by the hand of God through Me as I'm anointed by the Spirit of the Lord to be able to do these things." Jesus didn't do anything in His deity as the Son of God. He stripped Himself of that authority while coming to the earth to be our mediator and to become a man anointed of the Spirit of God (Philippians 2:6,7).

Yes, Jesus was 100% God and at the same time 100% man. That's an amazing fact to think about, that after all was said and done, there's one of us – a man – at the right hand of the Majesty on High, one of us ruling the universe!

JESUS IS THE ETERNAL WORD OF GOD

Jesus Christ is the Eternal Word of God, and all things were created through Him. When God the Father wanted to create a human family made in His image and likeness, He needed to create a physical universe with one suitable planet upon which to place His family. So, the second person of the Godhead, The Word, spoke what was in the mind of the Father. Then the Holy Spirit – the Holy Power, or as I like to call Him, "The Holy Enforcer" – moved and created the entire universe, exactly as the Father imagined it and exactly as The Word spoke it.

God didn't do anything in the creation of the universe that didn't involve the Son, who was The Word, through whom God spoke it all into existence. The Holy Spirit was the actual agent who did it all. He was the one who actually brought life to the planet.

ONE GOD – IN THREE PERSONS

Jesus was always with the Father – one God manifest in three persons. John 1:1,2 says:

In the beginning was the Word, and the Word was with God, and the Word was God. He was in the beginning with God.

In *The Mirror Study Bible,* this reads:

To go back to the very beginning, is to find the Word already present there, face to face with God. The Word is I am; God's eloquence echoes and concludes in him. The Word equals God. The beginning mirrors the Word face to face with God.

The Father, The Word (who became the Son when He took on human flesh), and the Holy Spirit are three personalities: three manifestations but only one God. That is a mystery that nobody will ever completely understand until we are actually in heaven.

A HEAVENLY EXPERIENCE OF THE TRINITY

Many years ago, I had a heavenly experience that gave me an awareness of the Trinity that changed my life forever. One afternoon while I was at Rhema, ushering at the afternoon Healing School, Brother Hagin stepped up on the platform as he did every day, but instead of ministering, he immediately said, "I believe the Lord wants us to pray today." I turned around to kneel at my chair, and as soon as my knees touched the floor, I was suddenly in a trance. Next to an open vision, a trance is the highest-level vision that you can experience. In a trance, your senses are suspended, and you are only conscious of what you are seeing in the vision, as though you were actually there. Your physical body is in the same place where the trance started, but your spirit and soul actually go wherever the Lord leads you.

In the trance, I was sitting on a couch in what looked like my apartment, simply reading my Bible, when there was a knock at the door. I got up, opened the door, and saw Jesus standing there. I saw His white robes, but when I looked at His face, I could only see the *shekinah* glory. It was like looking into the sun, but it did not hurt my eyes. I looked down at His hands and noticed that He had an envelope in His right hand. I asked, "What is that?"

He answered, "It's a love letter from the Father."

He handed it to me; I opened it and read, "Doug, I love you with an undying love. If you had been the only person on the earth, I would have still sent Jesus just for you." At that point, I began to weep. I can't remember if there was anything else in the letter.

Then the whole scene repeated: me sitting on the couch, the knock at the door, Jesus standing there with the letter, and me reading it and weeping. Then the scene repeated a third time: but this time, when I opened the door, Jesus didn't have a letter in His hand. He simply said, "Are you ready?"

I asked, "Ready for what?"

He said, "Let's go see the Father."

Suddenly I was in heaven, in one of the throne rooms of God. Now I simply call it the dining room. I looked at the walls and they were made of a light-colored stone. There were gold shields leaning up against the walls all the way around the room. They were the size of a buckler, the small shields worn on the left arm, like those worn while in hand-to-hand combat, with a sword.

The next thing I noticed was a long, rectangular wooden table. I could see the head of the table to my right. I saw all the wooden chairs at their places, but I did not look to my left, knowing that the table went on almost forever. I believe that it was long enough that, one day, every saint of heaven will be able to sit down together to eat with the Father and our Lord Jesus.

Jesus had me sit on the chair to the left of the head of the table, then He sat on the other side, directly opposite me. As soon as He was seated, the Father suddenly appeared, sitting at the head of the table. Jesus was naturally at His right hand, and I was seated to His left.

I was in shock as I realized that I was looking at the Father's hands on the table, and I could see His white robes. He looked just like Jesus. When I looked up to see His face, there was the same *shekinah* glory that prevented me from seeing His features at all.

I looked back at Jesus, then back at the Father and was speechless. Then a thought came to my mind. I realized that I could see the Father and Jesus at the same time, but I couldn't see the Holy Spirit. So, I turned back to the Father and said, "Father I see You, and I see my Lord Jesus."

At that time, I looked back at Jesus, and for the first time in the trance, I noticed the nail scars in the wrists of His hands. I began to weep again as I realized that when we get to heaven, Jesus will be the only one there with scars. We will have been given glorified bodies without spot, wrinkle, or blemish. Jesus will forever bear in His body the marks of having paid the price for our sins on the cross, for each and every one of us.

When I was able to compose myself, I asked, "But where is the Holy Spirit?"

The Father's answer to me was the very purpose for which I had been taken to heaven. He reached out His hand and pointed with His finger directly at my chest, and stopped with His finger about six inches away from me. Then He said, "Why, He is right there in you."

The weight of His statement hit me like a ton of bricks. When we get to heaven permanently, we will be able to see Jesus, and we will be able to see the Father, but we won't be able to see the Holy Spirit, because He will still be the invisible One who is living on the inside of each of us.

I also realized that the Father, Jesus, and the Holy Spirit are always in communication, and because the Holy Spirit is in us, we are drawn up to the table to sit with the Father and the Son, by virtue of the One who resides in us and will do so for all eternity.

Our fellowship with the Father and the Son is like that which was expressed by the Apostle John in 1 John 1:3:

> **"That which we have seen and heard we declare to you, that you may also have fellowship with us; and truly our fellowship is with the Father and with His Son Jesus Christ."**

At this point, the trance came to an end, and I was suddenly back in my natural body. My knees ached because I had been kneeling for 45 minutes, but it seemed to me like only 5 minutes had passed. I looked down at the folding metal chair where I had knelt to pray, and there was a pool of tears in the middle of the chair. My physical body must have wept through the entire trance for 45 minutes.

I was in a bit of a distracted fog for the rest of the day. But the next day, I realized that I had a new consciousness of the presence of the Holy Spirit in me. Since that time, I have traveled nearly the whole world by myself, but I have never felt alone. I have never felt fear while being any place, even places that would have caused me to fear in the past, because my God is with me by the presence of the Holy One who resides in my spirit at all times.

One day several years back, the Father revealed to me that He had made the arrangements for that day and had prompted Brother Hagin to pray that day so that I would have that vision in the trance.

I SHOWED YOU MORE THAN I SHOWED MOSES

About 36 years after this spiritual experience, I was praying to the Father and became conscious of how long it had been since that trance. Though I have had many deep encounters with the Lord Jesus as well as with angels, I began to wonder why I had not had any experience quite like it since. The Father's answer shows me that He has a sense of humor.

I asked, "Father, have I failed in some way? I haven't had a trance like that in all these years. Have I missed it?"

He answered me saying, "Wait a minute! I showed you more than I showed Moses. What do you want?"

Then it hit me. Of course! I was born again, and Moses wasn't when he was on the earth. God could only show Moses His back, but as a born-again child of God, I got to see the front side of Him. Still, I could not look upon His face. Apparently, if you encounter the Father in a trance, or if you died physically and went to heaven, once you see the Father's face, you instantly become a permanent citizen of heaven, without the option to come back to earth.

Moses wrote about his conversation with God in Exodus 33:20:

> **But He said, "You cannot see My face; for no man shall see Me, and live."**

As I have searched the Scriptures, it turns out that most people have only one or two experiences of this magnitude in their whole life. Such a dramatic experience is a defining moment that marks you forever. It becomes a guidepost that sets the course of your life.

Now, don't get me wrong: I hear from the Lord often, and certainly more frequently as I pursue Him and His will for my life, every day in prayer. I have much more to teach on concerning deep communion with the Lord than I can put in this book on divine healing and health, but for now, this makes my point.

A CONSCIOUSNESS OF THE HOLY SPIRIT WITHIN US

I do want to share this about the presence of the Holy Spirit on the inside of us, in our spirit. No Christian escapes experiencing some major crisis in life: it can be the death of a loved one; or a divorce, or any other major betrayal in a relationship; or an evil report concerning your own health. At these times, having a consciousness of the Holy Spirit's presence in your spirit can save your life.

I have been through some times of crisis where all I could do was speak to the Holy Spirit while looking at my belly, knowing He was right there to comfort me. And because of my experience in the throne room of God the Father, I have often immediately sensed the presence of the Lord Jesus standing right next to me, while knowing that the Father is listening to our conversation. That is how close They are and how They are all contending for our victory and deliverance from every opposition of the enemy. We are not always as conscious of Their presence, but nonetheless, They are always with us and we are always with Them.

KEEP COMING UP HERE!

In 2021, I was listening to a minister who had died for 45 minutes and went to heaven, then was sent back to earth. I spoke to the Lord Jesus and told Him that I was envious. Jesus immediately spoke to me and said, "Wait a minute! I took you to heaven and introduced you to the Father. Just keep coming up here."

I instantly knew what He was talking about. Most of my greatest encounters with the Lord have come from extended times of praying in the Spirit, in tongues. So, I began praying in tongues an average of two to three hours per day. After nine months of praying this way, I finally was taken back to heaven.

I had been praying in tongues for four hours in the middle of the night. Suddenly, I was back in the dining room of the throne of God, seated at the table with the Father to my right, and Jesus directly across the table from me. This time, I didn't say anything in English. I just allowed the Holy Spirit to pray through my spirit, directly to the Father and to Jesus. I knew the Holy Spirit was pleading my case to Them, concerning everything that I needed to fulfill my divine destiny. The Holy Spirit would stop, and the Father and Jesus would both say, "Well, that is exactly what We have planned from the very beginning." I immediately knew - without words - that what the Holy Spirit had asked for was now activated. The same scene repeated three times, and then the trance came to an end. I fully intend to keep praying through and going back up to heaven as often as I can!

JESUS – "THE WORD" – CREATED EVERYTHING

Jesus created the universe, including humans (spirit, soul, and body). That means Jesus created your body - so Jesus knows how to heal your body! He knows how the human body works. All the discoveries men are now making about our physiology and the complex chemical and electrochemical reactions in our bodies are not new to God. The Father invented all of these. Jesus was that Word who spoke it all into existence, and the Holy Spirit enforced our creation and makes it all continue to work.

Jesus knows everything about your own body - He knows what's wrong with it and He knows how to fix it. He can do the most miraculous things! That's why it's so important to have great faith. We're coming to a place where I believe a lot more people will be returning to faith in God. For years, folks had faith in their insurance plans and their doctors, but in many cases, the doctors have to say, "I'm sorry. We have done all that we can. There is nothing left for us to do." In contrast, true faith in the promises of God, which are actually blood oaths, sworn by the Father - for which Jesus shed His own blood to purchase for us - will produce miraculous healing and health for us every time. *Note: A blood oath is what is promised while two parties are cutting a blood covenant.*

While we're here on this earth and we have these earthly bodies, we need them to function the way that God designed them to function. Jesus knows how to fix our bodies and He has already paid the price for our healing. We must simply learn to receive it by our faith, and then fulfill a long, fruitful life, following Jesus, our Healer and King.

All things were made through Him, and without Him nothing was made that was made. In

Him was life, and the life was the light of men. And the light shines in the darkness, and the darkness did not comprehend it (John 1:3-5).

The world does not comprehend Jesus. They don't know that Jesus is the one who created the entire world. Scientists are trying to prove that we evolved from the primordial soup or ooze, by our own will. But they can't explain why they have never found a transition from one "evolving" species to the next "evolving" species. No, as animals have adapted over the centuries, they each stay within their same species. The great variety of plants and animals could not have "evolved" from a single, living cell.

In fact, if you studied the complexity of a single living cell, you would realize that something this complex could not simply "spring into existence." Besides, what would that first living cell find to eat? There would be no other organic material yet! God had to create all organic life – first plants as a food source, and then animals.

JESUS – "THE WORD" – CAME TO THE EARTH AS A HUMAN

And the Word became flesh and dwelt among us, and we beheld His glory, the glory as of the only begotten of the Father, full of grace and truth (John 1:14).

The *Mirror Study Bible* says it this way:

Suddenly the invisible, eternal Word takes on visible form – the Incarnation, on display in a flesh and blood Person, as in a mirror! In him, and now confirmed in us! The most accurate tangible exhibit of God's eternal thought finds expression in human life! The Word became a

human being; we are his address; he resides in us! He captivates our gaze! The glory we see there is not a religious replica; he is the authentic begotten Son. The glory (that we lost in Adam) returns in fullness! Only grace can communicate truth in such complete context! (John 1:14 MIRROR).

Jesus has always been the means, the manifest presence by which God deals with His created universe and His created man. Jesus was always The Word that God used to communicate with man. So, it stands to reason that The Word would be the one who would take on human flesh – to be one of us and be part of the human race Himself – and then redeem us.

For the law was given through Moses, but grace and truth came through Jesus Christ. No one has seen God at any time. The only begotten Son, who is in the bosom of the Father, He has declared Him (John 1:17,18).

Jesus is the only human who has seen the Father in full manifestation. Moses had a couple good glimpses of Him, but Jesus was the only one who saw Him face-to-face. The new covenant of grace and truth came through Jesus Christ.

JESUS DEMONSTRATED GOD'S WILL TO HEAL ALL

It's vital to have this completely cemented into your belief system: God wants everybody healed! If you don't believe healing includes everyone, you could take yourself out of the equation. You might say, "I'm probably the one that it's not His will to heal."

Jesus demonstrated it was God's will to heal *all,* again and again.

When evening had come, they brought to Him many who were demon-possessed. And He cast out the spirits with a word, and healed all who were sick, that it might be fulfilled which was spoken by Isaiah the prophet, saying: "He Himself took our infirmities, and bore our sicknesses" (Matthew 8:16,17).

This passage is the New Testament fulfillment of Isaiah 53:4-5, which foretells that the Messiah would bear our sicknesses Himself. Notice that Jesus cast out the spirits with a word and healed *all* who were sick. Anyone who was sick, and who came to Jesus, left healed.

But when Jesus knew it, He withdrew Himself from there. And great multitudes followed Him, and He healed them all (Matthew 12:15).

Great multitudes would be thousands and thousands of people who followed Jesus. He took the time to heal every single one of them. This is an actual fact, or it would never have been recorded in the Bible. God makes sure that what is printed out in the Bible is true: Jesus healed everybody who came to Him.

WE HAVE THAT SAME ANOINTING AVAILABLE TO US

Some people say, "Jesus was the Son of God; He could heal anyone." Jesus never did anything as the Son of God. He was given the anointing of the Holy Spirit without measure, and then was able to do it as the Son of Man. He was anointed: that's what made Him the Messiah, the Christ. We have that same anointing available to us. The more we learn to walk in alignment and agreement with the Lord, not only will we be able to apply healing to ourselves so that we can walk in health, but we can see that anointing released into other people and see them set free, delivered, and healed. I don't know about you, but that is exciting to me!

Every time I have seen anyone instantly healed, I knew it didn't have anything to do with me. It was Jesus and the Holy Spirit's anointing showing up and doing a miraculous thing for someone out of the compassion and mercy of God. That's exciting! That same anointing is available to us as we learn to conform our lives to be in compliance with the Lord and His will, so His anointing can be on us and flow through us. I continually pray, "Lord, show me how to yield to that anointing, more and more."

> **And begged Him that they might only touch the hem of His garment. And as many as touched it were made perfectly well (Matthew 14:36).**

> **And the whole multitude sought to touch Him, for power went out from Him and healed them all (Luke 6:19).**

Everyone who touched Jesus with a touch of faith was healed, as His healing power went into them.

LORD, ARE YOU WILLING?

Born-again believers know that our great God, who created the entire universe, can do any kind of miracle He wants to do. Obviously, He has the power to heal. Believers reverence Him and give Him awe. But they don't all believe that He wants to heal them. They believe He *could* heal them but aren't sure He is *willing* to.

It is essential to eliminate all these factors of doubt from our belief system and go by what the Word of God says: Jesus demonstrated His willingness to heal *every single person.*

The Lord's willingness to heal is found in the wonderful story of Jesus healing a leper, which we find in three of the Gospels: Matthew, Mark, and Luke.

When He had come down from the mountain, great multitudes followed Him. And behold, a leper came and worshiped Him, saying, "Lord, if You are willing, You can make me clean." Then Jesus put out His hand and touched him, saying, "I am willing; be cleansed." Immediately his leprosy was cleansed (Matthew 8:1-3).

The leper didn't question the Lord's ability, He questioned His willingness: "*If* You are willing, You *can* make me clean." In other words, "I know You've got the power to make me clean, I just don't know if You want to." Dramatically, Jesus put out His hand and touched the leper saying, "I am willing." It's vital that we each pay attention to these words out of the Messiah's own mouth: "I am willing – be cleansed. I am willing – be healed. I am willing! In every case, if you come to Me in faith, I am willing! Receive your healing! Receive the fullness of strength and complete restoration for your body! I am willing!"

Immediately, the man's leprosy was cleansed. Under the Law of Moses, it was unlawful for a leper to be in a crowd because leprosy is very contagious. People don't go around touching lepers. Yet, the first thing Jesus did was touch the man. Jesus was not afraid of leprosy – the name of Jesus is above every name. It's above the name of leprosy; it's above the name of cancer; it's above the name of heart disease; it's above the name of joint disease; it's above the name of every kind of disease you can name. Jesus was not afraid to touch the leper.

As Mark tells this same story, he adds that Jesus was moved with compassion.

> Now a leper came to Him, imploring Him, kneeling down to Him and saying to Him, "If You are willing, You can make me clean." Then Jesus, moved with compassion, stretched out His hand and touched him, and said to him, "I am willing; be cleansed." As soon as He had spoken, immediately the leprosy left him, and he was cleansed. And He strictly warned him and sent him away at once (Mark 1:40-43).

The concept of being "moved with compassion" is a whole lot more than just saying that Jesus had empathy for the man, that He felt sorry for the man. The Greek word "compassion" is *splagchnizomai*. It means "to have the bowels yearn." It's really talking about a driving yearning from the very core of one's being that moves outward. When Jesus saw the leper, He was moved with compassion from the core of His being that moved outward toward the man. This kind of compassion demands action. Here's what Jesus did for this man: He put a demand on the power of God and caused that power to be channeled into this man's body to completely heal him. Being moved by compassion puts a demand on the power of God to meet the need. Jesus moved in compassion continuously, demonstrating God's power and willingness to heal.

As soon as Jesus spoke, immediately the leprosy left the man, and he was cleansed. Mark tells us Jesus then "strictly warned him and sent him away at once." In Luke's account of the same story, we see what Jesus sent the leper away to do:

> And it happened when He was in a certain city, that behold, a man who was full of leprosy saw Jesus; and he fell on his face and implored Him, saying, "Lord, if You are willing, You can

**make me clean." Then He put out His hand and
touched him, saying, "I am willing; be
cleansed." Immediately the leprosy left him.
And He charged him to tell no one, "But go
and show yourself to the priest, and make an
offering for your cleansing, as a testimony to
them, just as Moses commanded." However,
the report went around concerning Him all the
more; and great multitudes came together to
hear, and to be healed by Him of their infirmities (Luke 5:12-15).**

Jesus ministered under the Law of Moses, and it was
important to Jesus that the law concerning lepers being
healed would be followed. Healed lepers were to show
themselves to the priest so the priest could examine them
and verify that they were now free from leprosy. This
allowed them to leave the isolation of the leper colony
and return to society. Jesus was always telling the lepers,
"Now go back and offer the offerings required by the
Law."

Notice here, that even though Jesus was ushering in
the new covenant, He was still ministering under the old
covenant. He never did anything against the old covenant.
Some people think Jesus broke the Law of Moses, but He
didn't. He didn't break the *Torah*, although He did break
the *Talmud*, which was man's interpretation of the *Torah*.
The *Talmud* was sometimes distorted, because man's
interpretation was often wrong. For example, when the
Pharisees got upset when Jesus healed on the Sabbath,
Jesus told them their traditions were wrong, that God
never intended the Sabbath to be a day when you could
not do good for your fellowman.

Jesus charged the leper to tell no one, however, Luke

tells us the report went around concerning him all the more, and the great multitude came together to hear and be healed by Jesus of their infirmities. The fame of Jesus spread when He demonstrated the will of God and acted the way God would act among the people. These healings drew huge crowds, because people were in great need.

Jesus was the only solution, the only choice, for those being healed of lameness, paralysis, blindness, leprosy, and epilepsy. News of these miraculous healings traveled through every city, every village, and every nook and cranny of the country. People came out to see if they could be healed by the One that some were claiming to be the Messiah.

CHAPTER SIX

HEALING IS PART
OF SALVATION

SOME MAY ASK, "IF IT IS GOD'S WILL TO HEAL ALL, why aren't all healed?

I'm glad you asked! It's like salvation. God clearly demonstrated His will to save everyone, even though all don't receive salvation. Healing is no different: both are available to everyone.

The Lord is not slack concerning His promise, as some count slackness; but is long-suffering to us, not willing that any should perish, but that all should come to repentance (2 Peter 3:9).

God doesn't want a single person to perish and go to hell. He never has and never will want anyone to go to hell, but it is their choice.

God doesn't want anyone – non-believer or believer – to not be healed, either. You know the old adage, "You can lead a horse to water, but you can't make him drink." We can show people this truth, but we can't make them receive it. Yet it's freely given for all to be able to receive the fullness of it.

It is kind of like our freedoms in America: you have freedom to be spiritually ignorant if you want to be. Nobody can *make* you believe the Bible, the Word of God. In fact, I'll fight for someone's freedom and their right to be a spiritual moron if that's what they insist on. It's their choice!

FORGIVEN AND HEALED!

Jesus intentionally tied forgiveness of sins together with the healing of physical illness when He forgave and healed a paralyzed man. Let's take a careful look at this story from Luke 5:17-26.

Now it happened on a certain day, as He was teaching, that there were Pharisees and teachers of the law sitting by, who had come out of every town of Galilee, Judea, and Jerusalem. And the power of the Lord was present to heal them (Luke 5:17).

These Pharisees and teachers of the law who were sitting there had come from distant towns to hear what Jesus had to say, but they're sitting there in doubt and unbelief. The anointing of God was present as Jesus was teaching, but they are not receiving. Suddenly, the healing power of God started flowing through the room. Anyone who was connected to Jesus by faith knew the power was there, but these Pharisees and teachers were in doubt and unbelief. They had no faith to receive healing: they didn't believe Jesus was the Messiah and they didn't believe much of what He was saying.

Then behold, men brought on a bed a man who was paralyzed, whom they sought to bring in and lay before Him. And when they

could not find how they might bring him in, because of the crowd, they went up on the housetop and let him down with his bed through the tiling into the midst before Jesus (Luke 5:18,19).

I call these five "one crazy guy and his four crazy friends" because they had crazy faith and were willing to go to the extreme to get this man healed.

You may ask, "How do you know the man on the bed also had faith?"

Are you kidding me? He had to have some faith to let his friends carry him up onto the roof without screaming, "No, no, no! Don't take me up there! I'll fall and be even worse!" He had faith in his friends, he had faith that there was a reason to be in the presence of Jesus, and his friends had faith. They opened up the tile roof and lowered their friend down.

As an aside, I believe Jesus paid for the repairs to the roof. He wouldn't let someone else suffer loss because of Him and His ministry.

When He saw their faith, He said to him, "Man, your sins are forgiven you."

And the scribes and the Pharisees began to reason, saying, "Who is this who speaks blasphemies? Who can forgive sins but God alone?" (Luke 5:20,21).

Hello, scribes and Pharisees! Hello! *This is God in the flesh!* You need to pay attention! You are right: only God can forgive sins, so when Jesus says, "I forgive your sins," it's because He is the Son of God, God in the flesh, forgiving sins. He not only healed people as the anointed Son of Man, but He could also forgive sins as the Son of Man.

> **But when Jesus perceived their thoughts, He
> answered and said to them, "Why are you rea-
> soning in your hearts? Which is easier, to say,
> 'Your sins are forgiven you,' or to say, 'Rise up
> and walk'"? (Luke 5:22,23).**

In other words, only God can do either one of these
things: only God can forgive sins and only God can cause
a complete cripple to be able to rise up and walk. It's not
possible, of course, for the scribes and Pharisees to see sins
forgiven, but Jesus was about to give them a *visible, unde-
niable* proof that He was the Son of God and the anointed
Son of Man, the Messiah.

> **"But that you may know that the Son of Man has
> power on earth to forgive sins" – He said to the
> man who was paralyzed, "I say to you, arise, take
> up your bed, and go to your house" (Luke 5:24).**

When Jesus said, "Your sins are forgiven you," the paralyzed man must have thought, "Thank God! As soon as
Jesus told me my sins were forgiven, I felt such relief! I
didn't think I'd ever be free of that burden! And now Jesus
is telling me to take up my bed and walk. I *know* God forgave my sins and now I believe I'm also healed. I'm going
to get up and walk out of here, completely healed!"

> **Immediately he rose up before them, took up
> what he had been lying on, and departed to his
> own house, glorifying God (Luke 5:25).**

Isn't it amazing that the crowd was too tight for him
to get into the house, but all of a sudden when Jesus brings
the attention to him and heals him, the crowd parted for
him? The crowd made way for him as he walked out carrying his bed. They would not part before, but they parted
now because the anointing of the Lord was upon him.

And they were all amazed, and they glorified God and were filled with fear, saying, "We have seen strange things today!" (Luke 5:26).

If you were one of these scribes or Pharisees and you were in doubt and unbelief, what else could you do but leave, scratching your head and saying, "What have we seen here today? This was weird!" But they still didn't believe. They didn't put their faith in the fact that Jesus just proved he was the Messiah: "If I can cause the man to be healed, I can also forgive sins. Recognize who is among you. I am the Messiah, the One who came to redeem you from your sins."

It takes a connection of your faith to the power of God to receive. The power of God was present to heal them all, but only this one man got healed because he and his four crazy faith friends did whatever it took to get into the presence of Jesus.

JESUS FULFILLED OLD COVENANT PROMISES

Another proof that Jesus is the Messiah is that He fulfilled old covenant promises and prophesies that only the Messiah could fulfill. There are at least 333 messianic prophecies, and Jesus fulfilled all of them. Dr. D. James Kennedy wrote:

The chances of one person fulfilling just 8 of these prophecies is 1 in 1,000,000,000,000,000,000 (1 in 10 to the 17th power).

Someone suggested a way to illustrate the chances of all eight predictions being fulfilled, as follows: Cover the state of Texas two feet deep with silver dollars. Mark an "X" on one of the silver dollars and stir them all up. Blindfold a person and send him across the state as far as he wishes to go. Instruct him to pick up one of the silver dollars. The chances of his getting the coin marked X would be 1 in 10 to the 17th power (Kennedy 151).

The chances of Jesus fulfilling all 333 prophecies is mind boggling! Jesus was not here by chance.

Fulfilling of these prophecies includes what Jesus did to demonstrate that healing was part and parcel with salvation. As new covenant believers, we now understand that salvation and healing are inextricably connected. You cannot take them apart. They were paid for at the same time – they are part of the same redemption that was provided for us by the work of Jesus on the Cross and by His resurrection from the dead. Your salvation and your healing are a package deal – you can't separate them. Now, you don't have to receive both of them. A lot of people have only received the salvation part and have not received the healing, but healing is just as available as salvation because these are part and parcel together.

THE ENTIRE GOSPEL IN ONE PASSAGE

Let's take a close look at a wonderful old covenant promise from Isaiah 53:3-5. I love this passage: we'll even see the entire gospel in one verse of Scripture, verse 5.

He is despised and rejected by men, A Man of sorrows and acquainted with grief (Isaiah 53:3a).

As Jesus walked the earth, He was not "a man of sorrows and acquainted with grief." There was, however, a point in time that He *became* a man of sorrows and *became* acquainted with grief, but we'll find out that's on the Cross, not while He walked the earth.

And we hid, as it were, our faces from Him (Isaiah 53:3b).

Jesus was a totally innocent man who was dying in place of all of the guilty. That's why we would hide our faces from Him: it was *our* sin that was placed upon Him on the Cross; it was *our* sin for which He was crucified and judged.

> **He was despised, and we did not esteem Him. Surely He has borne our griefs And carried our sorrows; Yet we esteemed Him stricken, Smitten by God, and afflicted (Isaiah 53:3c,4).**

Jesus was smitten by God. This was the Father's plan. God thought this up, and Jesus was willing to go through with it - to become a human man on the earth and experience all of this. The second person of the Godhead said, "I am willing to go and be stricken and smitten by You, Father. When You lay the responsibility and the judgment of all of mankind's sin upon me, I'll accept it so that I can redeem them."

> **But He was wounded for our transgressions, He was bruised for our iniquities; The chastisement for our peace was upon Him, And by His stripes we are healed (Isaiah 53:5).**

To get the full meaning of this powerful passage, let's closely examine eight of the Hebrew words found in it.

"GRIEF"

In most places, the Hebrew word translated here as "grief" is translated "sickness or disease." So, it actually says, "Jesus was a man of sorrows and acquainted with sickness and disease." When did Jesus, while He was walking on earth, ever personally experience sickness or disease? Since nothing about this is recorded in the Bible, Jesus obviously did not get sick. He was the Son of God:

He was perfect in all His ways. No sin was found in Him anywhere – He was tempted in every way like you and I are, yet without sin (Hebrews 4:15). Sickness and disease were attached to Jesus when He who knew no sin was made to be sin for us that we might become the righteousness of God in Him (2 Corinthians 5:21). That's when Jesus became acquainted with sickness and disease.

"SORROWS"

The Hebrew word translated as "sorrows" can also be translated as "pains." Jesus was a man of "pains." Now, Jesus didn't walk around in pain everywhere He went. He had a human body, so just like you and me, He probably hurt when He walked for miles and miles and miles and miles. He had to rest; He had to sleep at night; He had to eat and do all the same things every other human being does. But he didn't have the pains that are the result of sickness or disease or calamity or accidents. He walked head and shoulders high above those things in His complete righteousness. We find out that what was transferred to Him was not only our sickness and disease, but also the *pain* that is caused by the sickness or disease or calamity or accidents. Jesus also bore the emotional pain and the heartbreak that comes into our lives. The price has been paid for our pains, just like the price was paid for our salvation.

"WOUNDED"

The Hebrew word translated as "wounded" means "to be pierced through." Jesus was "pierced through" for our transgressions. We know that His hands, His feet, and His side were pierced through. A crown of thorns was placed on His head and pierced through his skin. Why was He pierced through? He was pierced through for our transgressions.

"TRANSGRESSION"

The Hebrew word for "transgression" refers to the "sins of revolt." It refers to man's original sin. Adam and Eve revolted against the original plan of God, who told them, "You can eat of every tree in the garden except for this one, the tree of the knowledge of good and evil." Adam and Eve were supposed to tend that tree for the Lord and to present its fruit to Him - the same as when we present our tithe. They didn't. Instead, after a conversation with the devil, they decided the fruit would be good to eat. They disobeyed and threw all the blessings of Paradise away.

Adam and Eve led a revolution at that point of time. You may not think of the Fall in those terms, as there were only two of them. Who would they get to join them in this revolution? As it happened, since both of them sinned, that meant one hundred percent of the human race revolted against the plan of God. One hundred percent suddenly fell. The "corporate head" of the human race had now fallen. That means everyone who would be their descendent is in that same fallen state.

Transgression is the sin of siding in with Adam and Eve in this revolt against the plan of God. It's built into every baby born. Eventually, we come of age, the age of accountability, the age of reason. At that point, we know the difference between right and wrong and we choose wrong. We revolt against the truth and willingly do the wrong thing. That's where we step over the line. We are innocent until the point where we know the difference, and then we're suddenly guilty of the sin of revolution against the plan of God. "Transgression" refers to this sin nature that we received from Adam and Eve, being their descendants - and we are *all* their descendants. Jesus was wounded, pierced through, because of the sin nature we got from Adam and Eve's sin of revolt.

"BRUISED"

The Hebrew word translated as "bruised" also means "crushed." Jesus received many bruising, crushing blows.

The night Jesus was betrayed, He was questioned by the chief priests and all of the council. Mark 14:65 tells us:

Then some began to spit on Him, and to blindfold Him, and to beat Him, and to say to Him, "Prophesy!" And the officers struck Him with the palms of their hands.

The next day, Jesus was tied to a post and beaten with a whip. Then the entire cohort (500 Roman soldiers) gathered to watch as the soldiers mocked Him and beat Him on the head with a staff made of a reed, driving the crown of thorns into His skull.

Matthew 27:28-31 says:

And they stripped Him and put a scarlet robe on Him. When they had twisted a crown of thorns, they put it on His head, and a reed in His right hand. And they bowed the knee before Him and mocked Him, saying, "Hail, King of the Jews!" Then they spat on Him, and took the reed and struck Him on the head. And when they had mocked Him, they took the robe off Him, put His own clothes on Him, and led Him away to be crucified.

By far the worse crushing was what He suffered under the weight of our sins. We have all experienced the weight of our own sins and the relief when we confessed them (1 John 1:9). Imagine the weight of *all* of humankind's sin. That includes everyone: those who lived before Jesus, those during His lifetime, and everyone who will live in the future until God finally creates a new heaven and a new earth. Jesus bore the crushing weight of all our sin, for every single one of us, for billions and billions of people. That crushing blow was upon Him.

"INIQUITIES"

"Iniquities" is a completely different Hebrew word from the Hebrew word for "transgressions" that we looked at earlier. "Iniquities" means the "sins of perversion," referring to our *individual* sins. In other words, it's one thing to revolt against the plan of God for mankind, and it's another thing to pervert the plan of God for our individual life. Our own individual sin had to be paid for, as well. Jesus not only paid for the sin nature that we inherited from Adam and Eve – we also had a number of individual sins that we were responsible for. Jesus had to die for those, as well. He was "pierced through" for our rebellious sin nature and crushed for each of our personal sins, taking both types of sin away.

"PEACE"

Isaiah 53:5 goes on to say, "the chastisement of our peace was upon Him." The word "peace" is the Hebrew word *shalom*. It means "absolute peace," as when all spiritual, physical, and emotional needs have been met; where there's nothing broken, nothing missing, and everything is in perfect order. That's the kind of peace that God wants for us. When a Jewish person wishes you *shalom* in a greeting, whether they say *shalom* when they first see you or *shalom* when you leave, they're wishing you the kind of peace that can only come when everything in your life is fixed and perfect. They are wishing you a heaven-on-earth experience. The chastisement for our perfect peace, a complete and total peace with God, and a heaven-on-earth experience was put upon Jesus.

Our new covenant promise is way beyond God's old covenant promises to take care of, heal, and provide for us. In the New Testament, God says I'll take care of you, heal you, provide for you, and infuse you with My Holy Spirit. I will give you gifts of the Spirit to be in operation, to heal, encourage, and deliver. I will also give you a special anointing, so when you preach My Word, the anointing will flow out. People will hear My Word and it will transform their lives! Wow! Praise God! Everything is better in the new covenant!

"BY HIS STRIPES"

"Stripe" is an old English word for "a stroke or blow, as with a whip." These days we would say "lash wounds," or "lacerations." Before Jesus was sent to be crucified, the Roman soldiers "scourged" Him with a whip. The Roman scourge, also called the "flagellum," was a short whip made of three or more leather straps connected to a handle. To make the scourging even more painful, the leather straps each ended with metal balls or sharp bone fragments designed to cut into the skin.

These "stripes" were both physical and spiritual stripes and bruises. At the same time the Roman soldiers were laying the natural stripes on His back, in the realm of the Spirit, God the Father was laying the spiritual stripes on Him. Jesus was paying for our healing with every one of those stripes.

THE HARDEST PART

We have looked at the brutal physical suffering Jesus

experienced at the hands of the Romans. Yet it wasn't just His foreknowledge of the physical crucifixion that caused Jesus to sweat great drops of blood in the Garden of Gethsemane. He saw the spiritual suffering as well: even while He experienced the beatings, the crushing, and the being pierced through of crucifixion, He also experienced the full weight of all the sin, plus all the sickness, disease, and maladies of all mankind, which rested upon Him.

Yet, the hardest part was being punished by, then being forsaken and separated from God the Father and God the Holy Spirit. Isaiah 53:10 makes it clear that it was the Father who bruised Him.

> Yet it pleased the Lord to bruise Him;
> He has put Him to grief.
> When You make His soul an offering for sin He
> shall see His seed, He shall prolong His
>   days,
> And the pleasure of the Lord shall prosper in
>   His hand.

It "pleased the Father" to lay all this suffering upon Jesus, knowing that Jesus was willing to take it all so that He could redeem a family ("His seed"). It pleased the Father to gain a family out of this whole process: Jesus would redeem people from the sin with which Adam and Eve cursed them and from their own individual sins. Once cleansed, people could now be in fellowship with a holy and righteous God, and part of His family for all of eternity.

You can see why it was so important to the Father that Jesus would go through this whole process. Jesus prayed in Matthew 26:39:

> **"O My Father, if it is possible, let this cup pass from Me; nevertheless, not as I will, but as You will."**

Jesus knew and taught "with God all things are possible." Throughout history, the Father had solved impossible situations at the last minute, with amazing, creative solutions. "So, the largest army in the world is chasing you? And you have no army and no weapons? No problem! We'll drown them in the Red Sea!" Or "So you are about to attack the most heavily walled city in all the Promised Land? Still no army and no weapons? No problem! We'll just make that wall fall down." Or "So a giant is defying the army of the Living God and you are a youth with no weapons and no military training? No problem! We'll kill him with your slingshot!"

When Jesus said, "if it is possible," perhaps He thought that there may be another way to accomplish this. Abraham was stopped by the Angel of the Lord seconds before his knife plunged into Isaac, and the Lord provided a ram, caught in a thicket for the sacrifice. But there was no other way, no other sacrifice. Only Jesus could pay the price for our redemption.

TWO DEATHS

The Bible speaks of two deaths: physical death and spiritual death or separation from the Father. Because Jesus never sinned, He had never experienced separation from the Father. Every other human being since Adam and Eve experienced this spiritual death on the day they knowingly and willingly sinned. At that time, they are separated from God and spiritually dead. That's why Jesus said we must be born again.

Jesus died both deaths at the same time on the Cross. His body could not die until He became sin for us. His body couldn't die because it was immortal while He was completely holy and righteous. In other words, death couldn't have any hand grip on Jesus whatsoever when He walked in total perfection, tempted yet without sin. Jesus was immortal. If He never became sin for us, He would never have been able to die! The fact that He was able to die and be separated from His earthly body was a result of the fact that once He took on our sin, He was separated from God the Father and God the Holy Spirit.

If Jesus had never taken on our sin on the Cross, He would be hanging there still today, not able to die almost 2,000 years later! We know that our sins were placed upon Him because He became physically able to die. He became sin for you and me in this miraculous exchange – His right-eousness for our sinfulness.

CHAPTER SEVEN

HEALING IS "PAST TENSE"

W E HAVE TAKEN AN IN-DEPTH LOOK at Isaiah 53, a much-treasured, old covenant prophecy about the coming Messiah. Matthew 8:17 quotes this passage and declares that Jesus fulfilled it in His healing ministry:

That it might be fulfilled which was spoken by Isaiah the prophet, saying, "He Himself took our infirmities and bore our sicknesses."

When Peter quotes this same passage, he is looking back at what Jesus did on the Cross. He changes the tense from "we are healed" to "we were healed."

Who Himself bore our sins in His own body on the tree, that we, having died to sins, might live for righteousness – by whose stripes you were healed (1 Peter 2:24).

The first thing you need to grasp to develop your faith for healing is that healing is a *past-tense* provision of God. It's already happened! Just as your salvation was provided for you almost 2,000 years ago when Jesus hung on the Cross, your healing was provided for you: paid for, purchased, and available to you almost 2,000 years ago. Obviously, you didn't know anything about this until you heard about Jesus. Now, as you grow in the knowledge of Him, you realize, "I can appropriate all these things. I appropriated the *salvation* part that was paid for back then, and now I can appropriate the *healing* part that was paid for back then."

Peter wrote, "...by whose stripes you were healed." It is vital that you understand that you're not *going* to be healed, you *were* healed. You were healed; therefore, you *are going* to receive a manifestation of healing that was completed almost 2,000 years ago. (I say, "almost 2,000 years ago" because Resurrection Day of the year 2030 is *exactly* 2,000 years.)

You are going to see that healing made manifest in your body. You are not *waiting* for that healing to come, the healing is already there, paid for way back then. In the realm of the Spirit, it's like a mass of energy that's been traveling through space and time to get to you. Suddenly, you believe God, and that energy hits your body and your healing manifests. But it was already in existence for all of those centuries.

THIS IS NOT A "SPIRITUAL HEALING"

Some have said that Isaiah 53:5 and 1 Peter 2:24 are only referring to spiritual healing. However, your spirit was not healed, it was recreated. According to the Bible, your spirit was dead, but Jesus gave it new life.

And you He made alive, who were dead in trespasses and sins...even when we were dead in trespasses, made us alive together with Christ (by grace you have been saved) (Ephesians 2:1,5).

And you, being dead in your trespasses and the uncircumcision of your flesh, He has made alive together with Him, having forgiven you all trespasses (Colossians 2:13).

Your spirit existed but was in a deadened state. It was disconnected from God; it needed the new birth. Jesus does not heal your spirit, but He *does* heal your soul. Your soul was alive, in fact, you were living out of your soul. As you were going through the processes of life, all kinds of experiences came your way and wounded your heart. So, you *do* need to have your soul healed. Jesus is able to heal wounded hearts, as well as bodies. But your spirit doesn't get healed, it gets recreated. It goes from the state of being in a dead, coma-like state, to having the Holy Spirit move into it. It comes alive; it becomes a new creation that never existed anywhere in space or time before, because your dormant, comatose spirit never had the Holy Spirit dwelling in it. Once that took place, the real you came alive! That's an exciting concept to think about!

WE ARE MADE NEW

Let's examine evidence from Scripture that shows our spirits are not healed, but recreated.

We have a new covenant. Jeremiah 31:31 says:

"Behold, the days are coming, says the Lord, when I will make a new covenant with the house of Israel and with the house of Judah."

With this new covenant, God is able to give us new, recreated spirits. Ezekiel 11:19 says:

"Then I will give them one heart, and I will put a new spirit within them and take the stony heart out of their flesh, and give them a heart of flesh."

This promise was fulfilled after Jesus died and rose again. We are a new creation, as it says in 2 Corinthians 5:17:

Therefore, if anyone is in Christ, he is a new creation; old things have passed away; behold, all things have become new.

CHAPTER EIGHT

JESUS CAME TO DESTROY THE WORKS OF THE DEVIL

E VERYTHING JESUS DID ABSOLUTELY RATTLED and
shook-up the devil because Jesus undid everything
that Satan had done to ruin peoples' lives. While ministering on earth, Jesus did works that *counteracted* the devil's
works. Jesus knew He would eventually go to the Cross to
completely destroy the works of the devil.

In this chapter, we will be looking at several passages
that identify the devil as the source of all sickness and disease. Even though Satan is the source, that doesn't mean
there is always a spirit of infirmity – a demon of sickness
– involved. Demons are not involved in all sickness.
Sickness and disease are common in humankind because
they were unleashed into the earth from Adam and Eve's
time on. Since then, disease has been spreading. It morphs
and mutates and shows up like it is something new, with
new mutations every year. For example, every flu that
comes is a mutation of a former flu germ. That's because
the creative power of God has been perverted by the
demonic, sick, detestable power of Satan. He is able to
cause these things.

JESUS WAS ANOINTED TO DO THE WORK

"How God anointed Jesus of Nazareth with the Holy Spirit and with power: who went about doing good and healing all who were oppressed by the devil" (Acts 10:38a).

God anointed Jesus of Nazareth with the Holy Spirit and with power. When you're anointed by God, you're anointed with the Holy Spirit and power. You can't separate the power from the Holy Spirit. Now, you might leave the power there lying dormant. But if you have received the Holy Spirit, you have received potential power - *if* you know how to access it and flow with it. If you walk in the Spirit, walk in love, and walk in faith, you can access that power. You can have the Holy Spirit and power just like Jesus did.

Jesus healed all who were "oppressed by the devil." This verse makes it clear that the devil is the one who oppressed those who needed healing; this shows the devil is the source of sickness.

Jesus hates sickness! There is a story in Mark 8:22-26 that tells how Jesus spit on a blind man's eyes. Wow! That seems so unlike Jesus to spit on someone! Pastor Bob Yandian, a Greek scholar, told how this always bothered him, and how he thoroughly researched this passage. Soon after, he had an encounter with the Lord and asked Him, "Why did You spit on the man's eyes?"

Jesus replied, "I didn't spit on the man's eyes."

Pastor Yandian said, "I have studied it in the Greek. I have looked at everyone's commentary on it. The language is clear: the eyewitnesses say You spit on his eyes."

Jesus replied, "I didn't spit on his *eyes,* I spit on his *blindness.*" (If we simply ask, Jesus will explain some things we don't see with our natural eyes!) Jesus hated the blindness so much that He spit on it.

The further you go on in the Lord and the more you receive that refining by the holy fire of God, the more you start hating sin because you see what it does to people and to families. It twists people and makes them miserable: sometimes it makes them do terrible things to other people. After awhile, you start to hate sickness too, just as much as you hate sin, because you see that half of the suffering people go through is because of sickness. For example, most of us have friends or loved ones who have died of cancer, or heart attacks, or who are suffering terribly because of arthritis.

We have hatred for the results of the sin - not a person's individual sin, but the sin pressed into the human race by Satan. So, you do everything you can to undo it: get people saved, get them healed, get them delivered. You want the same thing for yourself, to walk in all the salvation that is available, all the blessings of the Lord, all the "guarantees"- without any sin or sickness, with nothing holding you back.

Peter goes on to say in Acts 10:38b:

"...for God was with Him."

How was God with Jesus? In this case, it wasn't God the Father: Jesus spoke with God the Father non-stop. In this case, God was with Jesus in the anointing without measure, the presence of the Holy Spirit, who descended on Jesus and remained upon Him (John 1:32). It was the anointing of the Holy Spirit - the "Enforcer" - resting on Jesus, who was enforcing wealth, enforcing health and wellness, enforcing everything "good" in peoples' lives through the Lord Jesus.

And God is with us "in the anointing" today. It's no

different. The whole Church can walk in the anointing that Jesus walked in. It might take all of us together walking in the anointing to match the anointing that Jesus walked in. But, praise God, we *are* the Body of Christ, and the same anointing rests on the Body that was on Jesus when He was walking in His own earthly body. Sure, it gets spread out over several billion of us, but, praise God, it's still there! And it is still powerful and it can still produce the same results.

There is no way for us to be able to see in the realm of Spirit how much power it takes for God to work a miracle. It might just take a little "fleck" of His power to absolutely transform someone's body, which would transform their life - perhaps raise them up out of a wheelchair.

The anointing was powerful in the early Church. The first man Peter and John healed through the name of Jesus there at the Gate Beautiful went walking and leaping and praising God. He had never walked a day before in his life! Suddenly, he's walking and leaping and praising God! Now, when people have never used their legs, their leg muscles have atrophied down to nothing. God did a creative miracle to give the man muscles that were large enough and strong enough to instantly be able to walk and leap and praise God.

I've seen videos of people who were healed after they had been crippled for years. They don't walk well at the very beginning, but praise God, they *can* walk, and they have been healed! However, they *are* wobbly. But if you see a video of them a couple months later, their legs are filled out with muscles, and they can walk normally. Because that doesn't always happen right away, lame men who are suddenly walking is not as spectacular as when someone's blind eyes are suddenly opened and they receive their sight. It's amazing to see the look on their face when they see for the first time! That's the miracle experience: something you were never able to do before, but now you can. And you know it is permanent because it came by the hand of God. A miracle is an awesome demonstration of the love of God.

Some modern medical treatments produce extremely emotional responses from those who have received them. Maybe you've seen the *YouTube* video where doctors did a cochlear implant for a lady. She had never heard words before, and when she could suddenly hear, she instantly started weeping. That is also what often happens when folks receive a miraculous healing from God.

JESUS REVEALED THAT SICKNESS IS SATANIC BONDAGE

"So ought not this woman, being a daughter of Abraham, whom Satan has bound – think of it – for eighteen years, be loosed from this bond on the Sabbath?" (Luke 13:16).

Jesus had a word of knowledge telling Him this Jewish woman had been bent over for 18 years. No one told Him her case ahead of time; Jesus didn't need to take her chart out and look at it to see how long this had been going on. No, He knew by the Spirit how long she'd been bent over. He laid His hands on her, and immediately she stood up straight and began to glorify God.

Jesus plainly said Satan had bound this woman for 18 years. We find that sickness and disease is satanic bondage in every case. That doesn't mean that there is *always* a demon spirit of infirmity, and yet, that is sometimes the case. You'll hear doctors say, "Well, we were successful in treating this person who had a specific kind of a cancer and they got healed. We treated another person who had the same kind of cancer in exactly the same way, and they died." The doctors can't figure it out. They say, "It's one of those mysteries of medicine." More than likely, the second person had a spirit of infirmity and chemotherapy doesn't work on a demon spirit. You must cast demon spirits out. So, unless a doctor knows how to cast out spirits of infirmity, they can't really help in such cases.

But, praise God, when a believer with the gift of discerning of spirits sees someone with a spirit of infirmity, the believer can cast that spirit of infirmity out of the one who is sick. Once the spirit of infirmity is out of the way, the healing can come forth. The sick person usually manifests their healing right away. If a person feels they still need medical treatment, now their body can respond to those treatments. Once the spirit of infirmity is gone, the body can receive healing, either supernaturally or by medical treatment.

JESUS CONTRASTED THE SOURCE OF LIFE AND DEATH

"The thief does not come except to steal, and to kill, and to destroy. I have come that they may have life, and that they may have it more abundantly" (John 10:10).

The devil comes to steal, kill, and destroy – that's what he does. If something fits in the category of being stolen, of death, or destruction, it's from Satan's kingdom. Jesus made it plain in this passage: everything that's good and full of life and abundance comes from God, and everything else is from the devil. God doesn't send sickness or disease to teach you something. God would have to steal it from the devil, and He is not going to do that. God is not a thief.

JESUS CAME TO DESTROY SATAN'S WORK

He who sins is of the devil, for the devil has sinned from the beginning. For this purpose the Son of God was manifested, that He might destroy the works of the devil (1 John 3:8).

Jesus came to destroy the works of the devil – *all* of his works. When Jesus went to the Cross, it changed everything. People who say that healing is not part of the New Covenant are, in effect, denying the price Jesus paid to destroy their sickness, disease, misery, and poverty. It's as though God only wanted to make sure they got saved so they could go to heaven, and that He doesn't care if they suffer while on earth. But according to the Word of God, Jesus came to destroy the works of the devil and *everything* that the demonic works of the devil produced. And the Cross of Christ was a complete, 100% success!

This verse is additional proof that the devil is behind sickness. We know that Satan's ultimate work is to cause people to be bound in darkness, to have their minds blinded to the truth of the gospel, to stay in that condition, die in that condition, and finally go to hell with him. Here's what I believe that Satan is really trying to do – he's trying to gain his own redemption. I think he's trying to get so many people cursed to hell with him that it forces God to change His mind and decide, "I can't possibly send multiplied billions of people to the devil's hell."

Satan hopes that God will do a "blanket amnesty." Even though these people never received God's only plan of salvation, which was through His only begotten Son, Jesus, Satan hopes God would just go ahead and redeem them all anyway. To do this, God would have to forgive all sin, whether people repented and received Jesus as Lord, or not. If God did that, He would have to give the blanket amnesty to Satan, as well. Well, guess what! Satan's judgment is already established. It's in the Word; it's not going to change; God's not going to change His mind. Yet Satan is not smart enough to know that. But that's why I believe Satan is hell-bent on causing so many people to go to hell by keeping their minds blinded to the gospel of Christ.

Now that we believe in Jesus, Satan's mind-blinding tactics don't work on us. We've already escaped his grasp. We have been translated from Satan's kingdom of darkness into the kingdom of God's dear Son (Colossians 1:13).

WHO SINNED THAT THIS MAN WAS BORN BLIND?

Is a person's personal sin the cause of their sickness? We have seen that Job's friends thought so. In fact, Jewish thought was that if a person suffers, it was God punishing him for his personal sin. But we have seen in our study of Isaiah 53 that Jesus died for our "iniquities" - our personal sins. Everyone has sin that needs to be forgiven, but is sin the reason someone is sick?

Jesus came to correct man's doctrine concerning this very question: What is the root cause of sickness? In John 9:2, the disciples asked Jesus, "Who sinned that this man was born blind?"

Jesus answered, "No one." In other words, it was no one's iniquity or personal sin. The root cause of all sickness was man's "transgression" - Adam and Eve's revolt against God's plan - that allowed Satan to impose sin and sickness on the whole planet.

Let's take a close look at this very important passage of Scripture.

Now as Jesus passed by, He saw a man who was blind from birth. And His disciples asked Him,

saying, "Rabbi, who sinned, this man or his parents, that he was born blind?" (John 9:1,2).

You see, the Jews had a theology that a person could sin even *in utero,* while still in his mother's womb. This doctrine taught that since this man was *born* blind, he must have sinned *before he was even born!* How stupid is that? How dumb can you be and still be able to breathe? The Jews had that doctrine because they had gotten so far from the true meaning of the Law of Moses. They were spiritually ignorant. The question that Jesus' disciples asked showed that they had also been taught that doctrine.

In the Greek language, there is no punctuation: there is simply a string of words with no commas or periods. This presents problems. For example, when recounting a historical event, and there is a long passage without punctuation, the way you punctuate that passage can change its meaning. In the same way, if somebody mispunctuates the words of Jesus, they can completely change what He meant to say. This is especially harmful if it becomes a false doctrine. I believe this was done in John 9:2.

First, let's read this verse the way it is punctuated in the New King James Version, as well as most other Bibles. Then we'll read it with a slight change of punctuation. It will give you a completely different meaning!

Jesus answered, "Neither this man nor his parents sinned, but that the works of God should be revealed in him. I must work the works of Him who sent Me while it is day; the night is coming when no one can work" (John 9:3-4).

Punctuated like this, it sounds like Jesus was saying, "No, it wasn't this man's sin or his parents' sin, but he was given this blindness from birth so that the works of God could be revealed." In other words, "This is the work of God. The Father planned this so I could come along and show off My power." Jesus never showed off; He simply did the will of the Father. It's certain that fame went out about Jesus, but Jesus didn't heal people just to get folks to pay attention to Him. And certainly, God didn't need to make someone miserably blind their whole life so Jesus could show off His power and be famous. No one would trust a God who would do such a thing. Yet, the way this passage is punctuated, that looks like what Jesus is saying.

Now, let's go back and read this passage again, with what I believe is the right punctuation.

Jesus answered, "Neither this man nor his parents sinned." Period. Not a comma, but a period. "But that the works of God should be revealed in him," - this time a comma, not a period - "I must work the works of Him who sent Me while it is day."

Notice that these are the same words in the same sequence, we just used different punctuation to better fit the whole counsel of God's Word. Doesn't that make more sense? How can we ever think that God would've made the man blind so that Jesus could come along and show off? This has to be a mispunctuation. Moving a period and a comma drastically changes the meaning. Let's look at this repunctuated passage again: "Neither this man nor his parents sinned. But that the works of God should be revealed in him, I must work the works of Him who sent Me." Wow! That's a perfect expression of the love of God.

Jesus was saying, "Listen, you don't need to concern yourself with how this man got this way. It wasn't because he sinned or because his parents sinned. It was because Adam and Eve sinned that all this evil was unleashed on the human race by the devil."

Let me mention here that personal sin *can* be a hindrance that we need to get right before we can be healed. That's because personal sin results in guilt and shame, and shame is a hindrance that keeps you from approaching God by faith.

Jesus continued to tell His disciples:

"As long as I am in the world, I am the light of the world." When He had said these things, He spat on the ground and made clay with the saliva; and He anointed the eyes of the blind man with the clay. And He said to him, "Go, wash in the pool of Siloam" (which is translated, Sent). So he went and washed, and came back seeing (John 9:5-7).

The man was healed; we know that. We know that Jesus made mud from the dust mixed with saliva, and put it on the blind man's eyes. We don't know why God chose to do it this way, but Jesus did exactly what the Holy Spirit said, and it worked. That's what we believe and teach at Life Christian University: whatever the Holy Spirit says to do will work. You hear from God, do what He says, and watch the miracle!

WHILE IT IS DAY

Jesus said, "I must work the works of Him who sent Me while it is day." Then He warned His disciples that there is going to come a time when no one will be able to do these things. As Jesus was training His disciples to heal the sick, He was showing them, "I've got this ability, and I'm going to give this ability to you and to the Church so it can operate all the days from now until the judgment comes."

There is going to be a day of darkness and judgment

when none of these miracles will be taking place. We will be gone from here when judgment happens. After the judgment, it seems we will come back to a new heaven and a new earth.

CHAPTER NINE

PEOPLE CAME TO JESUS TO HEAR & BE HEALED

WHAT DID JESUS TEACH when He "taught the multitudes"? He taught the Word of God. He knew it was important for the people to hear the Word, because "faith comes by hearing and hearing by the Word of God" (Romans 10:17). When Jesus ministered the Word of God, He used Old Testament Scriptures – because the New Testament had not yet been written! I like to call the Gospels "the Mid-Testament."

Jesus actually ministered under the Old Testament as the last Old Testament prophet. The New Testament doesn't start until Jesus was crucified and raised from the dead. Jesus provided the Jewish people of His day the right interpretation and understanding of the Old Testament Scripture so that they could receive healing. He taught them the true spiritual import behind the Scripture, not the twisted interpretation they had learned from the Talmud, man's interpretation of the Torah, the five books of Moses. Jesus had to change their thinking because their thinking was way off.

As Jesus taught the true meaning of the Word, the

people came to hear. As they heard the words of Jesus, faith came alive in their hearts. As their faith increased, it became easy for Jesus to flow in the gifts of the Spirit and provide healing. That's because the people were already at a high level of faith. That's why *all* could be healed: they had listened! As Jesus flowed in the anointing, with the gifts of the Spirit in full operation, He healed every single person there. Jesus taught them first because He wanted to make sure they were able to keep their healing. They could keep what Jesus gave to them because their faith was alive – they had heard the Word of God and faith had come.

> **However, the report went around concerning Him all the more; and great multitudes came together to hear, and to be healed by Him of their infirmities (Luke 5:15).**

His fame went out and more and more people came to "hear and be healed." We see the same wording in Luke 6:17:

> **And He came down with them and stood on a level place with a crowd of His disciples and a great multitude of people from all Judea and Jerusalem, and from the seacoast of Tyre and Sidon, who came to hear Him and be healed of their diseases.**

I find it interesting that Luke, who was a physician, was the one who wrote these two passages. He was drawing attention to the correlation between the essentials of "hearing to gain faith" and "hearing to be healed." Dr. Luke wanted people to get healed and *stay* healed. I believe he had the right motive. Like modern-day physicians, he had taken an oath to "Do no harm." He was motivated to do everything he could to help people. He wanted to bring out this important correlation because he knew the reason the people got blessed and healed was that they came to hear. The first thing Jesus did was teach them – like nobody had ever taught them before! He taught them with authority, their faith came alive, and then He ministered to them. Healing was manifested in their bodies, and because they were taught, they kept their healing.

The following is a collection of passages on healing from the Old Testament, from which Jesus may have taught.

FORGET NOT ALL HIS BENEFITS

One of the most familiar is Psalm 103:2,3:

Bless the Lord, O my soul, and forget not all His benefits: Who forgives all your iniquities; who heals all your diseases.

David, who wrote many of the Psalms, including this one, knew how to receive from God through praise and worship. Here David is commanding his own soul to "Bless the Lord." This is where you get a hold of yourself by the scruff of the neck and say, "Self, bless the Lord."

Think about it! When we start meditating on the wrong things – all the bad things going on in the world – and we stop meditating on the goodness of God, we come out from under God's umbrella of protection. Our soul gets restless, discouraged, and down in the dumps. We stop living in the arena of God's blessing, this protected kingdom that God has given us.

In Psalm 42:5, David asked himself, "Why are you cast down, O my soul?

The Amplified Bible puts it this way:

Why are you in despair, O my soul? And why

have you become restless and disturbed within me? Hope in God and wait expectantly for Him, for I shall again praise Him For the help of His presence (Psalm 42:5 AMPC).

These are the times we must encourage ourselves in the Lord. We must get our soul in the place of blessing God, then we can move into the place of true worship and begin worshiping the Lord in spirit and in truth. We sense "the help of His presence." This is the place where we can receive all of His benefits.

Psalm 103:2 exhorts us, "Forget not all His benefits." The Hebrew word for "benefits" here comes from a root word that means "treatment." One of the best of these benefits is treatment for healing. I look at it as if we are going to Dr. Jesus for treatment. He treats us like no other doctor can. He doesn't even need to take a stethoscope out to listen to our heart. He can hear our heart soon as we get close to Him. He knows everything about us. Dr. Jesus not only heals our *physical* body, but He also heals us the way only He can – He heals us *emotionally* as well. So, don't forget the benefits of all of His treatments. He treats every one of us to healing, and oh, what a treat healing is when you get it!

Verse 3 says, "who forgives all of your iniquities and heals all of your diseases." This is another one of many scriptures where healing is directly tied to the forgiveness of sins. We see the two tied together over and over again, because your healing is part and parcel with your salvation, and forgiveness of your sins is part and parcel with the healing of your body.

LENGTH OF DAYS

Another old covenant scripture that Jesus might have used to teach on healing is found in Proverbs 3:1,2:

My son, do not forget my law, But let your heart keep my commands; For length of days and long life and peace they will add to you.

Now length of days and long life *has* to include walking in good health, because nobody who is in excruciating pain and miserable sickness wants their days to be extended. Most the time, if people can't be healed, they would rather just "get it over with and get out of here." This can be especially true for a Christian who knows where they are going. Their thinking is, "Let me get rid of this body and get on to where I can receive my new, glorified body." That is certainly understandable, but it's better to claim the promise, believe God for healing, and stay on the earth until we have completed our divine assignment. We want to stay close to the Lord in all things.

Jesus might have taught from Proverbs 3:16, as well.

Length of days is in her right hand; in her left hand riches and honor.

No one wants to live to be 105 if the last 50 years are spent in the hospital or a nursing home. What if you were in hospice care and you still couldn't die for 50 years? No, no one wants that. So "length of days" means "length of *healthy* days."

Proverbs 4 is a powerful verse for healing that Jesus might have used in His teaching.

My son, give attention to my words; Incline your ear to my sayings. Do not let them depart from your eyes; Keep them in the midst of your heart; For they are life to those who find them, and health to all their flesh. Keep your heart with all diligence, for out of it spring the issues of life (Proverbs 4:20-23).

This verse instructs us to keep the Word in our heart. Jesus said in Matthew 12:34, "...out of the abundance of the heart the mouth speaks." That's why we want to make sure that the right thing is in our heart so when we speak, that's what comes out. We want healing power to start flowing out, rather than, "Oh my God, why did this happen to me?" If you hit your thumb with a hammer, you say, "By His stripes, I am healed," instead of a string of bad words. We want to keep God's Word in our heart in abundance, so that the first thing we say is beneficial. That way, we get the results of the heart filled with the Word of God: life and health.

Other verses on long life that Jesus might have used in His teaching are:

"The fear of the Lord is the beginning of wisdom, and the knowledge of the Holy One is understanding.

"For by me your days will be multiplied, and years of life will be added to you" (Proverbs 9:10,11).

The fear of the Lord prolongs days, but the years of the wicked will be shortened (Proverbs 10:27).

If you want your days to be long, healthy days, you must have reverence and respect for the Father and His Word and for His Son and His Word.

Jesus might have also used the fifth commandment, which is found in both Deuteronomy 5:16 and Exodus 20:12:

"Honor your father and your mother, as the Lord your God has commanded you; that your days may be long, and that it may be well with

**you in the land which the Lord your God is giv-
ing you."**

This fifth commandment is also quoted in the New
Testament in Ephesians 6:2,3, where Paul wrote:

**"Honor your father and mother," which is the
first commandment with promise: "that it may
be well with you and you may live long on the
earth."**

DAYS OF HEAVEN ON EARTH

**"That you may prolong your days in the land
which the Lord swore to give your fathers, to
them and their descendants, 'a land flowing
with milk and honey.'"**

**"That your days and the days of your children
may be multiplied in the land of which the
Lord swore to your fathers to give them, like
the days of the heavens above the earth"
(Deuteronomy 11:9,21).**

Is this like having heaven just hovering above the
earth? No, it's that kind of "heaven-on earth-experience"
where we experience everything we hope to have in
heaven. The King James Version says, "as the days of heav-
en upon the earth." God is able to manifest that experience
here and now: health, prosperity, and being worry-free,
simply because you've got total trust in the Lord. Does that
mean you will have no problems ever coming your way?
No, you will have problems, but you remain worry free,
because you know God's already got a plan. If something
comes into your life, it didn't catch God by surprise. He's
not suddenly caught off guard. When opposition comes

your way, it's never like God says, "Wow! I didn't see that coming! What am I going to do now? Jesus, what are We going to do?" God doesn't say that! The Father, Jesus, and the Holy Spirit already know what's coming against you; they've already got the plan, the deliverance, the way of escape, the healing, the restoration, the provision, and the miracles. Whatever it is going to take, it's already been planned for, so we can just walk in faith, with a great trust in the Lord, and great peace.

GOD'S GUARANTEE OF PROTECTION

Another old covenant scripture that Jesus might have used to teach on healing is found in Psalm 91. Most scholars agree that Moses wrote both Psalm 90 and Psalm 91 while in the wilderness. However, we will see how Moses was speaking not only to the nation of Israel in the desert. He was also speaking prophetically for the Lord Jesus Christ. We saw how Isaiah prophesied about the Messiah in Isaiah 53. David also prophesied in Psalm 22 exactly what Jesus would be going through as He paid the price for our sin. Moses was doing a similar thing here, speaking for the One who was coming in the future.

I believe Psalm 91 is a psalm from the Lord Jesus, Himself, to you and me, to His Church, His Body. I call this Psalm "God's guarantee of protection from terrorism, accidents, sickness, disease, and premature death." Some people think these amazing promises are kind of a figurative, poetic thing, like a fairy tale from the past. No, this is real. This is concrete. The Lord wants us to receive the full measure of everything that's in Psalm 91. We are going to hear the words of Jesus in these words and realize Jesus is speaking to us, the Church. I'll make the case for that as we go along.

THE SECRET PLACE OF THE MOST HIGH

Verse 1 is a general observation:

**He who dwells in the secret place of the Most
  High
Shall abide under the shadow of the Almighty.**

This is for anyone: it's an open invitation. We can
choose to dwell in the secret place of the Most High God or
we can choose not to. It's a choice – we are invited by the
Lord Jesus to get up close to the Father and abide under the
shadow of the Almighty. Picture it like this: the hot sun
comes out, and you're standing next to God. He casts a
shadow. Don't you want to be under that shadow?

The Hebrew word "dwell" here means "to have one's
abode." In other words, to sit down, settle, and dwell there.
It reminds us of pioneers who find their dream spot, a plot
of land that will provide all they need. They stake a claim
and settle there. In a similar way, we make our home in
the secret place. We settle in.

Several other psalms have similar images: they speak
about those who want to dwell in God's presence, who
place their life in God's trust, in His hands. They understand that their life is in Christ. Let's take a look at these
psalms.

Psalm 31:19, 20 says:

**Oh, how great is Your goodness,
Which You have laid up for those who fear You,
Which You have prepared for those who trust in
  You
In the presence of the sons of men!
You shall hide them in the secret place of Your
  presence
From the plots of man;**

**You shall keep them secretly in a pavilion
From the strife of tongues.**

The secret place of God's presence is where He hides you. There's no better place to be when the devil is on your trail than to be hidden with Christ in God (Colossians 3:3); to be hidden in the secret place of God where the devil can't find you. If you walk close enough to the Lord and stay in the secret place, the devil might have been on your trail, but no longer because he can't find you to get near you. You've run to the secret place of the Most High. God's secret pavilion is where just He and you can meet. Being in the pavilion of God means hanging out just with God. This is an awesome concept!

This secret place where we can hide is also mentioned in Psalm 119, the longest psalm in the Bible. Every verse in Psalm 119 references the Word of God. Let's look at verse 114:

**You are my hiding place and my shield;
I hope in Your word.**

Psalm 32:7 says:

**You are my hiding place;
You shall preserve me from trouble;
You shall surround me with songs of
   deliverance. Selah**

I love the version of this psalm made famous in 2004 by the group "Selah." God *is* our hiding place. Jesus *is* our hiding place. This is pointed out to us again and again in these Old Testament psalms.

Psalm 27:4,5 says:

**One thing I have desired of the Lord,
That will I seek:
That I may dwell in the house of the Lord**

All the days of my life,
To behold the beauty of the Lord,
And to inquire in His temple.

For in the time of trouble
He shall hide me in His pavilion;
In the secret place of His tabernacle
He shall hide me;
He shall set me high upon a rock.

In this psalm, David brings out another aspect of being in the "secret place." We can "behold the beauty of the Lord and inquire in His temple." This shows that the secret place isn't just a place to hide from the devil. It is also a place to see the Lord and ask Him questions!

Whenever a scripture speaks to you about being in the presence of God and hearing His voice, take the time to stop and meditate on it. Make it one of those *selah* moments. Become comfortable with the fact that our number one assignment is to spend time with God – and that's only done in the secret place of the Most High God.

This is talking about our prayer life and our praise and worship life. True worship doesn't necessarily include singing; rather it's communing with God one-on-one. We use worship and praise in church to train people to go into the presence of God in their own personal prayer life and worship time. As we spend time with the Father and with the Son, our relationship with them grows.

A QUICK VISION OF MY FUTURE FROM THE SECRET PLACE

A few months after being born again and baptized in the Holy Spirit, while I was still on tour with the secular rock 'n roll group, I was sitting alone in the band's rented apartment. The other band members had been gone for about an hour. I had been reading the Word and then I started praying. As I was praying, I started having this vision experience. I was sitting on the floor cross-legged, with my eyes closed, when I suddenly felt like I was floating upward. It was so real: I felt weightless. As I was floating upward, I started seeing all these fluffy, white clouds in a blue sky. As I passed through the clouds, I could actually feel the moisture from the clouds hitting me in the face. I wondered, "What's this all about?"

All of a sudden, I saw a bright light coming through the clouds. The closer I got, the more I could see it was the Lord Jesus. There was a radiant glory coming from His robe. I could just barely make out His face because the light was so bright, and He was still pretty far away. As I was floating up and He was coming down, I kept getting closer and closer to Him. I thought, "Oh, good! I'll be able to see His face up close." Suddenly, He turned around and started going back up to heaven. I was following Him up into the clouds.

Then I knew what the Lord was revealing to me: "I'm just telling you to keep following Me and I'll lead you all the way to heaven." Ever since then, I've had this concrete picture in my mind: I'm right behind Jesus going up into the clouds, following Him all the way to heaven.

Right before the vision quit, I started floating back down to earth. Then I suddenly saw myself playing drums in a huge Christian concert. This was in 1973: I was still in a secular rock band. There were no Christian rock bands back then! A year later, I joined a Christian rock band and we played in a few churches where we were accepted. But a lot of churches thought we were "definitely of the devil." Mainly, we would play at beaches, coffee houses, and prisons and get people saved. We were constantly winning people to the Lord!

Then I was called to the ministry to teach and preach God's Word. I went to Rhema, then came back to Tampa, Florida, and was pastoring my first church. One day, the leader of that first Christian rock band I joined came to our church with his wife. We didn't have a worship leader, so he started leading worship for us. Then he and I got this radical idea: "Let's get the band back together." He entered one of the songs we recorded into a competition for a Christian "Battle of the Bands." This was in 1986, and contemporary Christian music was much more accepted by then. Our group won the "Battle of the Bands"! One of the prizes was to play for a huge "Jesus Festival" in Orlando, Florida. We would be the opening band on the main stage, right before the renowned "Mylon LeFevre and Broken Heart."

We got there, we set up, and we started praying. Then I looked out and saw a huge crowd: it was exactly the same scene that I'd seen all those years before in the vision! It was cool how God brought this to pass. Remember, I'm not touring with a Christian group; I'm the pastor of a church! But God set up this unique opportunity – just as He had shown me.

It is awesome to see how God has these experiences in the Spirit for us. As you are seeking the Lord in the secret place, you can have visions: you can have times when God shows you things in your future. So, the secret place is not only a good place to go hide from the devil. It is also a place to hang out with God and let Him reveal everything that He wants to reveal to you.

HE IS MY REFUGE AND MY FORTRESS

We have seen that Psalm 91:1 makes a general statement, giving an open invitation into God's secret place.

This secret place is repeated throughout the Bible, and is sometimes called a "secret pavilion" or a "hiding place." Now, in Psalm 91:2, the tone suddenly switches from a general statement to a declaration made in first person:

> **I will say of the Lord, "He is my refuge and**
> **my fortress;**
> **My God, in Him I will trust."**

Who is speaking here? I believe Jesus is making this declaration. He is speaking to His Church. We know that Jesus was always dependent on the Father. From the lips of Jesus, His declaration is, "I will say of the Lord, My Father, 'He is My refuge and My fortress, My high tower; My God, My Father, in Him will I trust.'"

Jesus looked to the Father to be His refuge and the high tower that He would run to. The Father was the one Jesus trusted. If the Son of God, who was anointed by the Holy Spirit with the fullest anointing that anyone ever had, had to trust constantly in the Father and run to Him in the secret place, how much more do we need to run to the Father in the secret place? We need to learn from Jesus about how to trust the Father. Sometimes He would pray all night, getting instructions from the Father.

When we understand that Psalm 91 is Jesus speaking prophetically to all of us, we are going to see how real these promises are. It's as though Jesus is saying, "Follow the Father the way I did. And because you love Me, this is what you are going to receive."

COVENANT PROMISES OF PROTECTION FROM JESUS

The Lord Jesus continues to speak in verses 3 through 8, making covenant promises to His Church. I like to visualize Jesus speaking these promises directly to me. These promises are His blood oath: His promises to protect me.

These promises cannot fail.

Surely He shall deliver you from the snare of the fowler [bird catcher], and from the perilous pestilence (Psalm 91:3).

The "snare of the fowler" is the trap of the predator, Satan, who tries to trap you in your sin, tries to trap you with your words, tries to get you to tell lies, or tries to trap you in many other ways. We're going to be smarter than he is! Jesus says He will deliver us from Satan, who is that predator trying to trap us. Jesus says He will also deliver us from the "perilous pestilence." The Hebrew here denotes "a rushing calamity," such as a tornado, flash flood, or tsunami, or other destructive event of nature.

UNDER HIS WINGS

He shall cover you with His feathers, And under His wings you shall take refuge (Psalm 91:4a).

"Covered with His feathers" refers to protection like a mother hen gives, when she covers her chicks with her wings in times of danger. Once, in a TV special on forest fires, I saw the ultimate story of this type of protection. After the forest fire was out, the firefighters went walking back through the forest, looking for smoldering embers that could start the fire up again. They wanted to make sure everything was completely put out. As I watched, a firefighter came upon the burned-up, blackened body of a large bird. As the fire-fighter nudged the charred remains of the bird with his boot, a whole bunch of little chicks ran out from underneath it. The fireman gathered up the chicks to take them to safety.

It's amazing to think how this mother had protected her little chicks under her wings. She could easily have flown off, away from all danger. But instead, she sat there in that scorching heat and let her own life be consumed by the flames. Her feathers were such a protective covering that those babies could survive the deadly heat of the forest-fire.

God says we are covered over with His feathers and take refuge under His wings. This kind of protection may very well be angelic.

HIS TRUTH IS A SHIELD

His truth shall be your shield and buckler (Psalm 91:4b).

The "buckler" mentioned here is actually a small, round shield that soldiers would either carry, or wear strapped to their arm. In hand-to-hand combat, it was used to block blows from their enemy's sword or ax. The "shield" mentioned here refers to a shield that is almost door-sized – big enough to protect the whole body. In Roman days, they locked these large shields together, making a formation called "the tortoise." The men in the front of the formation would lock their shields together, as would the men on the sides. The men in the middle would lift their shields overhead and lock them, to make a "roof." All that was visible was the shields! This would protect the Roman attackers especially well when they came upon a fortress defended by archers on the wall. A common tactic was for the enemy archers to shoot arrows up in the air so the arrows would rain straight down on their attackers. While in this tortoise formation, the Roman soldiers were protected from above and on all sides. The psalmist is saying here that God's truth is a shield that protects us from attacks coming from any direction. We are safe! Hallelujah!

YOU SHALL NOT BE AFRAID

**You shall not be afraid of the terror by night,
Nor of the arrow that flies by day (Psalm 91:5).**

"Terror" is defined as "a sudden, startling alarm producing great fear."

I don't understand why people enjoy Halloween. Satan has made them think that the adrenalin rush of being terrorized by horror movies and spook houses is fun. It is so demonic; people have no idea what they are doing. These things plant fear in their minds; the fear gets lodged in their consciousness and keeps growing. As a result, they start carrying fear with them all the rest of their lives.

That's what terrorism is designed to do: put people in panic and fear. That's why we have to rise up above terrorism and realize God has given us authority over these things. I believe that if we had a nation that was spiritually where it was supposed to be, we would never have had a terrorist attack like we experienced on September 11, 2001.

Our nation is slipping into a place of godlessness, even though the Church is still here and the Church is still pure. But we were not occupying that position of authority and dominion necessary to prevent such things. If the Church was truly on fire, and more believers were filled with the Spirit and prayed in tongues at least an hour a day, there would not have been an open door for the devil to be able to come in with terrorism. So, now we know from experience what terrorism is all about – it's what Israel has been experiencing with terrorism at their doorstep all these years. We finally understand.

But remember, Psalm 91 is also God's guarantee of protection from terrorism. I know I can experience it personally, but if enough Christians bind ourselves together in faith and unity, we can have more of an impact on our homeland, despite the unbelievers.

We can certainly do some things in the natural that are simply common sense. For example, we had to change everything concerning our air transportation security. I remember I was on a flight coming back from Norway in August, right before September 11, 2001. On this flight, I was very close to the front of the plane, right behind first class. They had the door to the pilots' cockpit completely open and flight attendants were walking back and forth, just chatting with the pilots. I was sitting there the whole time thinking, "That is really not safe! What are they thinking? Why don't they have that door closed? Don't they know people could hijack the plane? (At that time, people *had* hijacked planes to Cuba.) I don't know why the airlines didn't have the insight that I had, as a mere passenger. But we certainly did not have the proper security protocols in place on September 11.

"Terror by night" refers to dreams or imagined harm. We can be terrorized when it is not even real. "An arrow that flies by day" is a real threat, something we can see with our eyes. This is when it's absolutely the real thing. But whether it's *imagined* harm or *real* harm, we don't have to be afraid, according to this Word prophesied to us, the Church, by the Lord Jesus.

**Nor of the pestilence that walks in darkness,
Nor of the destruction that lays waste** at
noonday (Psalm 91:6).

"Pestilence that walks in darkness" are night attacks, which are a strategic element of warfare. "Destruction that lays waste at noonday" are day attacks. These are genuine, real things that would come against us, but we don't need to be afraid of either one when we're in the secret place of the Most High, when God is our refuge, our shield, and our buckler. God is all of these things for us: we have His spiritual protection.

IT SHALL NOT COME NEAR YOU

A thousand may fall at your side,
And **ten thousand at your right hand**;
But **it shall not come near you (Psalm 91:7).**

The "thousand at your side" are your comrades in arms, those fighting the battle on your side, against the enemy. This verse says a thousand of those fighting with you could actually fall by your side if they are in ignorance of the protection of the Lord: that He is your shield and your buckler; that He is your hiding place; that He is your pavilion and your fortress; that you are in the high watch tower of the Lord. If they are in total ignorance concerning the secret place of the Most High God, they *could* be taken out. A thousand of your fellow soldiers *could* die at your side.

This next part of this verse puzzled me for a long time until I started studying some historical and cultural references. I wondered, "What's the difference between your side and your right hand?" I discovered that in the Bible, the reference to the "right hand" was always in reference to your sword hand, the hand you use to attack your enemy. The "ten thousand at your right hand" are enemies slain by you with your sword.

As new covenant believers, we realize that "flesh and blood" are not our enemies (Ephesians 6:12). As we minister healing, sometimes we must first cast out the spirits of infirmity to get people healed. We can run off tens of thousands of demon spirits when we minister God's Word in a large gathering and people take hold of that Word. We ruin the devil's plan to bring people to an early, untimely death. Praise God! Jesus destroyed the works of the devil, and now we're called to enforce His victory. That's the disruption of Satan's kingdom that we want to continue to enforce!

Next, Jesus promises, "It shall not come near you." Satan is our enemy, and he tries to put sickness on us. We fight the good fight of faith against sickness with the sword of the Spirit and the shield of faith until we put the devil back in his place. No matter what happens to others, it doesn't have to happen to us!

Some people say it's arrogant to think that we can have faith that will protect us when it's so obvious that other Christians aren't protected. They ask, "So what makes you think that you are holier them, that they would be taken out and not you?" It has nothing to do with holiness! Every person who is born-again is holy and righteous before God. "So, you think *your walk* is that much holier and more righteous than theirs?" No, those things have nothing to do with it. It has to do with faith. You can be truly holy, righteous, and pious and still be ignorant of how to stand in faith for God's protection. But when you believe, rely, and trust on the covenant of God, you will have favor and the blessings of the covenant working in your life.

I believe that ignorance in this area is one of the big stumbling blocks for people concerning healing. It's also one of the misunderstandings that causes preachers to believe that maybe it's *not* God's will to heal everyone. Maybe their mother or their grandmother was the holiest, most righteous person they knew, who prayed every day. But she didn't know the first thing about faith, and she got taken out with sickness and disease. God didn't heal her, and it was painful and horrible to watch. The preacher had to come to the conclusion it must *not* be God's will to heal everyone because He didn't heal her, and she was the most righteous and holy person you could imagine.

We must understand that it is going to require *faith* on people's part in addition to their righteous, holy walk – faith in God's delivering power to protect them, heal them, and keep them from getting any sickness or disease that would take them out early. No, you don't have to die of sickness or disease; not die of sickness, but just die because I'm done – I've finished my race and completed my earthly assignment. I believe this is what the Apostle Paul was telling Timothy in 2 Timothy 4:6-8.

People say, "God's will can't be to heal everybody, or He would heal these most wonderful people we've ever known!" No, it's not an indictment against how wonderful they were. It is simply the explanation that without faith in God for His divine healing, it's impossible to receive the healing that you need.

You can't tell what that person really believed. Much of the time they've attended churches that told them, "Now, God blessed you with this sickness to teach you something. So, when you finally come out of the hospital, tell us what you learned from it."

And the one who is sick will say, "Aw, man, when I was in the hospital, I read the Bible so much. I learned so much. That's why God let me be sick. Maybe He even sent that sickness to me so that I could learn." You know, you could learn those same things by getting in the Bible just as much *without being in the hospital!* It's called self-discipline. It's called being a disciple. If you are a disciplined disciple, you will get your faith built up so you don't have to learn things because you're flat on your back in a bed in the hospital.

Maybe the person who died was a person of faith, yet they died. Was it God's will to heal them? Again, you can't tell what that person really believed. Maybe they were a believer and had great faith, but their unbelief counter-balanced it. Unbelief is when a person is overwhelmed by the way things look and takes their eyes off the Lord and His promise. Once, when Oral Roberts was struggling with the death of someone close to him, God said, "Don't touch this with your thought life." In other words, don't try to figure this out with your mind. That's good advice! Reasoning can take you out of faith.

No matter what happens to others, it does not have to happen to you! You have favor and the blessing of the covenant. The blessing of the covenant is working: it's your rearguard. It's that shield around you on all sides. If you have true faith in God's protection, God will make sure you're not going to go out and be killed in a terrorist attack; you're not going to be killed in an airplane crash. If you're going someplace serving the Lord, you're going out on divine assignment. That means you're going to go there successfully and come back successfully.

THE REWARD OF THE WICKED

Only with your eyes shall you look, And see the reward of the wicked (Psalm 91:8).

Your eyes will eventually see every sin and rebellion reap a negative reward. You will eventually see judgment poured out on the earth.

Everyone has their own picture of "the wicked." For some, it is personal: it's someone who has attacked them, whether verbally, psychologically, or physically. When this happens, the human tendency is to recall the scene over and over again. The Bible calls this "fretting" and says not to do it:

Do not fret because of evildoers,
Nor be envious of the workers of iniquity.
For they shall soon be cut down like the grass,
And wither as the green herb (Psalm 37:1,2).

Fretting over our wounds is definitely not good for our health! Jesus promises us we will "see the reward of the wicked"!

Some people picture "the wicked" as the ungodly leaders in government. As the LCU staff prays for our government, we pray that truth would be revealed, lies would be exposed, and justice would be administered. If we have "snakes in the grass" in our government – as truth is revealed, lies exposed, and justice administered – their plans will fail, they will fall on their faces, their administration will be a disaster, and finally they will be thrown out of office. Then we will get good, righteous people in office, who will make good choices and do the right things. We do not need ungodly, communistic people in a democratic republic's government anymore.

The Bible tells us:

When the righteous are in authority, the peo-
ple rejoice; But when a wicked man rules, the
people groan (Proverbs 29:2).

We pray for those in authority, so that we can live a quiet and peaceful life (1 Timothy 2:1,2) – which contributes to our health! It's far healthier to rejoice than it is to groan!

In addition to praying that truth be revealed, lies exposed, and justice administered, we're also praying for God to raise up righteous rulers to take their place. Some Christians say, "All politics are corrupt. I'd never think about getting into politics." Politics will stay corrupt until some really committed Christians "get into politics" and take their God-ordained places in the government. Then we will have godly leadership. So, we pray that the Lord would administer justice. One day we will see ultimate justice, but we can pray and see justice administered, even now.

The Bible makes it clear, whether "the wicked" are personal enemies or governmental ones, we are not to take any vengeance ourselves. Romans 12:19 says:

"Vengeance is Mine, I will repay," says the Lord."

We're not in a war against people, but against "principalities, powers, the rulers of the darkness of this age, and against spiritual hosts of wickedness in the heavenly places" (Ephesians 6:12). These are the spiritual forces operating behind the scenes, motivating the people to do the evil they do. We war against these spiritual forces in the realm of the Spirit, in prayer.

THERE SHALL NO EVIL BEFALL YOU

Verse 9 shifts in tone again: it is suddenly personalized by Jesus as He speaks directly to us, the individuals who choose to follow His every word.

Because you have made the Lord, who is my refuge, Even the Most High, your dwelling place, No evil shall befall you (Psalm 91:9,10a).

Jesus is telling us that His Father is now our Father, and His God is now our God. In John 20:17, the resurrected Jesus said to Mary Magdalene, "...Go to My brethren and say to them, 'I am ascending to My Father and your Father, and to My God and your God.'" Here in Psalm 91, we see Jesus talking to us from His heavenly position saying, "Because you've made the Lord who is My refuge, even the Most High your dwelling place," that no evil, adversity, affliction, or calamity shall befall us. In fact, many good things are going to happen to us!

NO "STRIKING BLOWS"

Nor shall any plague come near your dwelling (Psalm 91:10b).

I know a lot of people would just immediately say a plague means a sickness that's running rampant through the land. The Hebrew word "plague" used here means "a striking blow or infliction of a wound." The blood covenant promise is that no striking blow shall come near your dwelling or your body.

Doesn't a striking blow or affliction describe car accidents, airplane accidents, or terrorist attacks? An infliction of a wound can come from any one of these things. When people asked me, "Do you think God would protect us from accidents?" I say, "Absolutely!" This is why it is really important for us to understand divine protection. The Word of God is saying here: no striking blow or accident can come near your dwelling. What is your dwelling? Your dwelling is not your house, it's your "earth suit," it's your body! That is your dwelling: that is where you live! The real you is your spirit, you have a soul, and you live in a body. Just as a turtle carries around his house with him at all times, the reality is that your spirit man considers you carrying around your house at all times. You're carrying your body around as you walk through life every single day; going to bed, waking up, going places.

The Gospel of John tells us:

The Word (Christ) became flesh (human, incarnate) and tabernacled (fixed His tent of flesh, lived awhile) among us.... (John 1:14a AMPC).

Just as Jesus tabernacled among us, our body is the temple of the Holy Spirit; it is our temporary dwelling place. I believe this is the part covered in Psalm 91:10, that none of these striking blows will come near our bodies. That doesn't mean that we haven't had these things happen, but we're learning that we can put up a guard through meditation and belief of the Scripture, to actually stop the opposition against our bodies.

If my car is ever in a wreck, I have full faith in God that no striking blow will ever get all the way to my body. I may have a dented fender, but no striking blow will injure my body. This is a covenant promise of protection from accidents and untimely death.

"BEFORE" AND "AFTER" TESTIMONIES

I didn't always know this. I haven't been in a car wreck since I've understood these Scriptures and meditated on them. Before I discovered these promises, I did suffer "a striking blow." Back then, I didn't know the protective covenant of God like I needed to. I was a spirit-filled Christian; I just didn't know the Word of Faith yet, and I certainly didn't know Psalm 91.

I was in a Christian rock band. We were coming home from a concert we played at Crystal Springs. We had been out serving the Lord and ministering to people. My roommate and another buddy were in my Volvo station wagon. This was in 1977, and although most cars had seat belts by then, there weren't any laws yet that said you had to wear them. Nobody I knew wore seatbelts, and none of us had our seat belts on. I was driving along the highway, minding my own business and listening to Christian music. It was raining, but I wasn't paying that much attention to the rain.

All of a sudden, I saw a big, flat-bed truck jack-knife on the highway. I slammed on the brakes. We're going about 40 miles an hour, and the truck was coming at us about 40 miles an hour. Both vehicles were sliding on the wet pavement. All I had time to do was call out, "Jesus!" The next thing I know, I hear this incredible crunch, followed by a horrible crash. If our car would have gone under that flatbed truck, it would've taken the top of the car off and we would have all been instantly decapitated. I thank God that didn't happen!

As it turned out, the truck was a sod truck pulling a trailer with a forklift on it. The truck slid enough so that my bumper hit the tongue of the trailer head-on. The Volvo did what it was designed to do to protect the passengers. The bumper and the whole front of the car absorbed much of the impact and crumpled up to the windshield. The motor mounts snapped, and the motor went underneath the car, instead of into the front seat. This was good. But then, the chain holding the forklift onto the trailer snapped, and the forklift landed on top of our car and rolled off.

We were really messed up.

I never really lost consciousness, but my face had hit the steering wheel so hard that it bent it flat! That's why my nose is the way it is. My friend in the back seat hit the front seat so hard, it ripped the seat bolts out of the floor. His head was gashed open, and he went into convulsions.

Meanwhile, in the front seat, my roommate's head broke the windshield, even though his lower body was trapped in the wreckage between the dashboard and the floorboard. A bunch of people ran up to help me pull the seat back, and my roommate got out. When he and I saw our other friend having convulsions, we didn't care who was there. We laid hands on him and started praying in tongues out loud, calling on God...and his convulsions stopped! He was medivacked to a larger hospital because of his severe head wounds.

While we were waiting for the ambulance, I overheard the wrecker driver ask the sheriff, "Did anybody live through this?" It looked that bad! I knew that God had protected us.

My roommate and I were taken to the closest emergency room. The doctors treated my roommate first, because of his head injuries. I was sitting there waiting for several hours and finally needed to go to the bathroom. As I walked through the lobby of the emergency room to the bathroom, a couple of kids took one look at me and screamed. I hadn't seen myself yet, but when I looked in the mirror, I almost passed out. My nose was underneath my right eye, there were cuts and blood everywhere, plus lots of big, swollen lumps.

Fortunately, all three of us recovered. But I can attest that having a striking blow against your body is a real thing. I didn't know about God's protection the way I do now. It wasn't until I went to Rhema, that I understood the power of Psalm 91.

The reason I told you about that first head-on collision – the "before" story – is so that I could tell you the "after" testimony. There was another time the devil tried to kill me with another head-on collision, but I was miraculously spared. Here's what happened:

After my wife graduated from Rhema, we were helping my parents build a house in the Panhandle of Florida. Her parents were in Tampa, and she was visiting with them for a week. As I was driving back to get her, I was on the interstate behind a big semitruck. It was in the right lane, when it suddenly swerved into the left lane. I wondered why he changed lanes so abruptly. We were approaching an exit ramp, and as soon as the truck moved out of the way, I saw there was somebody coming up the exit ramp the wrong direction, right into our lane! The headlights of this car were coming right at me! I don't know how it missed me – it must have been the hand of God!

The next thing I knew, my car was driving on the median of the interstate, to the left. It miraculously happened to be at a place where the ground was completely flat. I was still going about 70 miles an hour – my car never even slowed down! It went off the highway, onto the grass, and then veered right back up onto the highway. I looked back and wondered, "What just happened?" I wondered if the other vehicle had hit anyone else. By this time, I was a ways down the interstate with no way to get back to help. All I knew to do was to "keep on trucking."

About 10 miles later, I got off the interstate at a rest area. I got out of the car to walk a bit and immediately slumped down. My knees were knocking so hard I could not stand up! Even though I was delivered by the hand of God and "no striking blow came against my dwelling," as I thought about it afterwards, I realized, "I just escaped death!" That kind of wears on your nerves! Was I ever grateful to get all the way to Tampa after that, and grateful that God's Word works. I've never had anything anywhere remotely like that other accident again. I know and can testify that these promises of God's protection work!

HE SHALL GIVE HIS ANGELS CHARGE OVER YOU

**For He shall give His angels charge over you,
To keep you in all your ways (Psalm 91:11).**

This verse carries an additional aspect of God's divine protection: the angels protect us! Jesus told us in Matthew 18:10:

"Take heed that you do not despise one of these little ones, for I say to you that in heaven their angels always see the face of My Father who is in heaven."

The angelic involvement is a whole lot more than we ever imagined, because there is no indication that the guardian angels who are assigned to us as children ever leave us when we become ornery teenagers, or - even worse - when we become even more ornery adults! They are with us our whole life.

Psalm 34:7 expands upon this thought:

**The angel of the Lord encamps all around
    those who fear Him,
And delivers them.**

I love this verse of Scripture. Think about it! The angel of the Lord camps with us if we fear the Lord. This fear of the Lord is not about being afraid that God might do something bad to you. No, the reverential fear of the Lord is that positive fear of wanting the knowledge and understanding of God's Word manifest in your life, of becoming a true worshiper who wants the presence of God in your life. You fear missing out on the fullness of what God has for your life and not fulfilling what God has called you to do. As we enter into the secret place of true worship and enjoy God's presence, these things will unfold for us.

This idea of us being in the will of God is not hard for us. Throughout the Bible, we see that if people are obedient to the Lord, miracles always follow. Yet, obedience isn't hard for a person who wants to be in the will of the Lord. It's not like God is saying, "You obey! You do this!" and we say, "I don't want to do that, but I'll do it anyway, because God says to." No, we want to live for the Lord and have His presence in our lives and have His Word at work in our lives. So, we find ourselves in the perfect will of God, and we wind up doing what is asked of us. Obedience is always followed by promises and provision - quite often miraculous things - as a blessing that comes from being in God's perfect will.

THE ANGELS WILL BEAR YOU UP

**In their hands they shall bear you up,
Lest you dash your foot against a stone
(Psalm 91:12).**

Satan quoted Psalm 91:11,12 when he tempted Jesus in the wilderness.

Then he brought Him to Jerusalem, set Him on the pinnacle of the temple, and said to Him, "If You are the Son of God, throw Yourself down from here.

**For it is written:
"'He shall give His angels charge over you,
    To keep you,' and,**

**'In their hands they shall bear you up,
Lest you dash your foot against a stone'"
(Luke 4:9-11).**

Satan told Jesus, "Throw Yourself off this ledge and a great miracle will happen for You. Everyone will know You are the Son of God because they'll see the Scripture fulfilled. Angels will obviously rush in and catch You. You won't be dashed to the ground." Satan was tempting Jesus to use His deity instead of walking in the Spirit, doing everything the Father asked Him to do by the anointing of the Holy Spirit, and thus teaching His disciples and leading them into the place of understanding that God will use them in the same way. Jesus didn't work the miracles He did as the Son of God, but as the anointed Son of Man. He was anointed by the same Holy Spirit that anoints you and me, and used the same gifts of the Spirit that are available now to be in operation in the Church today, almost 2,000 years later.

Satan quoted this psalm to Jesus, but this psalm is obviously not only for Jesus. We saw that although this was a psalm written by Moses, it's also Jesus speaking this to us, the Church, His Body. I like to picture Jesus looking at me face-to-face and telling me, "The Father has given His angels special orders to guard you, protecting you from all harm, wherever you go. If you stumble, they'll catch you; their job is to keep you from falling."

Whenever I teach the course on angelology, we talk about all the different types of assignments the angels have: there are guardian angels, angels that protect you from harm, healing angels, provision angels, and messenger angels. Even during the first night of class, I have people immediately start realizing, "Gosh, I was delivered by angels at least half a dozen times in my life!"

The more you start spending your time studying and focusing on spiritual matters, the more you become aware of the realm of the spirit. When you study and meditate on angels, you become more aware of their operation in your life. Almost all of us can think of times we could have been killed. When it happened, you might have thought it was just the luck of the draw. But now that you know more about the kingdom of God and the protection His angels provide, you realize how often angels have been involved in your life. God knew you were going to answer the call to be born again. He knew you would answer the call to be used by Him in ministry, so He was at work on your behalf. God was able to tap into that little bit of faith you had that He was out there and that some-how these things were going to work out.

ANGELS AND AIRPLANES

I always pray Psalm 91 before I get on an airplane. I travel all over the world by divine assignment, and I think it's right to assume that if the Lord is sending me some-where, He intends for me to arrive there, get my job done, and arrive back home. That's just the way God's kingdom works, but I always remind Him: "I know, Lord, that even if there was a problem with the airplane and the engines went out, that the angels would bear the entire airplane up in their arms and deliver it safely where it was sup-posed to go." One time, I was praying that on the airplane, and God said, "You know, I don't need to send the angels to hold the airplane up."

I said, "Lord, You could."

He said, "But I don't have to."

I asked, "Why don't You have to?"

He answered, "I know your schedule better than you do. I know what plane you're going to be flying on, and I make sure that you are flying on the best serviced, most trustworthy aircraft possible, so don't worry about it. The engines are not going to go out. I won't need the angels to hold up it up."

I said, "Thank You, Lord, that's good to know. I would be willing to preach the gospel to everybody on the plane should that happen, but I really don't want to go through all the trauma of a near-death experience in a divinely-prevented plane crash!" Then I asked the Lord, "Is it okay that I still pray Psalm 91 before a flight?"

He answered, "Yes, but I won't be using the angels!"

Praise God, we can look back and realize there were

many times the angels have been involved in saving our lives. I can give you half a dozen instances in my own life before I was even born again. After being saved, I recognized that's what God was doing.

YOU SHALL TREAD UPON THE LION AND THE COBRA

You shall tread upon the lion and the cobra, The young lion and the serpent you shall trample underfoot (Psalm 91:13).

The lion, cobra, young lion, and serpent all refer to aspects of Satan's power. These are four different Hebrew words. The "lion" represents the roaring, noisy, in-your-face manifestations of the devil. These come on strong, with plenty of warning, and seem like they will tear you apart with instant death. The "young lions" represent emerging problems that can't roar yet, but will grow bigger over time. It's best to trample on these manifestations of the devil while they are still small.

You may wonder what the difference is between the "cobra" and the "serpent." The King James makes the following distinction between these two Hebrew words:

Thou shalt tread upon the lion and adder: the young lion and the dragon shalt thou trample under feet (Psalm 91:13 KJV).

The "adder" represents the more subtle manifestations of the devil, those that remain quiet until it's too late. These are devious, but deadly. "Dragon" is an interesting word in Hebrew. It is used 28 times in the Old Testament; the King James Version differentiates it from "serpent," translating it most often as "dragon," but also as "whale," and "sea monster." Some have said it represents large,

118

scary, unknown – perhaps even imaginary – problems that the devil tries to implant in our minds. Nice to know we can trample on these as well!

The lion, serpent, young lion, and dragon all refer to aspects of Satan's power that Jesus, Himself, trampled underfoot and defeated. In Luke 10, Jesus was speaking to His disciples after they returned from ministering. The disciples were amazed to find out that even the devils were subject to them in Jesus' name. They were able to cast devils out of people who were tormented. They were able to cast out spirits of infirmity, and people would get healed. Let's take a closer look at this passage:

> **Then the seventy returned with joy, saying, "Lord, even the demons are subject to us in Your name."**
>
> **And He said to them, "I saw Satan fall like lightning from heaven. Behold, I give you the authority to trample on serpents and scorpions, and over all the power of the enemy, and nothing shall by any means hurt you" (Luke 10:17-19).**

Serpents and scorpions are symbolic terms used throughout the Bible when talking about evil. Here, Jesus was telling His disciples, "I've got complete authority over evil and I'm giving it to you." These were the Lord's first disciples; they were not even born again at this point, yet they were given the authority to use Jesus' name and minister great deliverance to others.

We have seen that Satan quoted verse 11 and 12 when he tempted Jesus in the wilderness. It's interesting to note that Satan failed to mention verse 13, with the promise of treading on the lion, serpent, young lion, and dragon.

These things foretold the Lord Jesus' total victory over the devil. Satan was certainly not going to quote that part and confirm his future destruction - his own doom - out of his own mouth!

I WILL SET YOU ON HIGH

"Because he has set his love upon Me, therefore I will deliver him;
I will set him on high, because he has known My name" (Psalm 91:14).

This verse changes again to the first person. This time, it clearly identifies the one speaking as deity. We see it is Jesus, The Word of God, the second person of the Godhead, who has been magnifying God the Father as His refuge. Here, Jesus is speaking about you and me! We could apply these verses personally by saying, "Because I have set my love upon Jesus, therefore Jesus will deliver me: Jesus will set me on high, because I have known His name."

In Old Testament times, the Jews had a great, reverential fear of the Lord's covenant name, which English translations show as *"Jehovah"* or *"Yahweh."* The Jews never spoke the covenant name out loud, but instead, they would say "the Lord." When the scribes were copying the scrolls, they were very careful about handling God's name - they would use a kind of shorthand, without including all the vowels needed to pronounce it. It didn't really need to be that way, but the Jews assumed that was the way it was. They didn't really know His covenant name or speak that name.

Yet, as the Body of Christ, we do everything in the name of Jesus. Jesus told us to ask the Father for everything in His name. We lay hands on the sick in Jesus' name; we cast out demons in His name. As New Testament believers, we know the name of the Son of God, the deliverer for all mankind, and we use His name. We are "delivered" and "set on high," and we are exalted because we know the power in the name of Jesus, the name above every name!

I WILL BE WITH YOU IN TROUBLE...
AND HONOR YOU

"He shall call upon Me, and I will answer him;
I will be with him in trouble;
I will deliver him and honor him" (Psalm
91:15).

Jesus continues here in the first person and promises to answer our prayers for deliverance and provision. He promises to be with us to deliver us from trouble and harm. That's awesome: if you're in trouble and Jesus is with you, you don't need to fear. Jesus said, "I will deliver you." His hand of deliverance is upon us – even if He has to use angels.

God says, "I want to honor you. One of the ways I honor you is by protecting you. When other people's lives are being snuffed out, you still survive; you keep going on and fulfilling My destiny for you.

The Hebrew word for "honor" here means "to make heavy" – in other words, "to add more weight to." God says, "I honor you by adding more years to you and giving you success at what I've called you to do. I give you success at representing Me and being a living witness everywhere you go. People notice something different about your life; your witness is anointed. Your words cut through, and people want to know the same God that you know.

We could personalize this verse by saying, "I will call upon Jesus, and Jesus will answer me; Jesus will be with

121

me in trouble; He will deliver me and honor me."

I WILL SATISFY YOU WITH LONG LIFE

**"With long life I will satisfy him,
And show him My salvation" (Psalm 91:16).**

We have seen that this means being satisfied with a long, *healthy* life, because it's the *zoe* life, the abundant life of God, which would be the only kind of life that God would give us. The idea of us having a long life, but being in the hospital, racked with pain and miserable, does not make any sense. So, we walk closely with God and renew our minds, so that we are in that place of divine health. Then we can expect our life to be extended and it would be an enjoyable, fruitful life.

Next, God says He will show us His salvation. God's salvation is His deliverance, His aid, His victory, His prosperity, His health, and His help. All this was purchased by Jesus - in its fullest measure.

The Hebrew word for "salvation" here is *"Yeshuah,"* which is closely related to *"Yehoshua,"* the name Jesus heard every single day of His life. We translate that into "Jesus" in our English Bibles, but *"Yehoshua"* was what everyone called Him: His name means *"Jehovah is salvation."* His name represents God's salvation in its fullest sense. When God wants to "show us His salvation," He shows us Jesus!

We could personalize Psalm 91:16 by saying, "With a long, healthy life, Jesus will satisfy me, and show me His complete deliverance."

I AM THE LORD WHO HEALS YOU

A final Old Testament scripture that deals with healing is found in Exodus 15:26:

"If you diligently heed the voice of the Lord your God and do what is right in His sight, give ear to His commandments and keep all His statutes, I will put none of the diseases on you which I have brought on the Egyptians. For I am the Lord who heals you."

This is the verse from which we get one of the most important of the Lord's covenant names: *Jehovah Rapha*, the Lord Who Heals.

That's huge to me: God says, "I am the God who heals you, I am the God who saved you, I am the God who blesses you. I am the God who manifests My blessing that I've proclaimed over you in every way to a greater measure, every single day." As a staff here, we believe we are in our best year ever. Every day we proclaim, "This is it: the best year ever! God is giving us the biggest turnaround in ministry and finances and the biggest turnaround in our personal lives: in our health, families, and everything else. It's the best year ever!" We understand the God we serve: He is a God who heals us, saved us, and blesses us in every way.

"PUT" OR "PERMITTED"?

The Hebrew word translated both "put on" and "brought on" in this passage would be better translated as "permitted." Here's the difference between "put on you" and "permitted to come on you": When God told Moses what plagues to prophesy, God didn't have to invent these plagues for them to come upon the Egyptians. The lice, flies, and boils were already available on the earth. All

God had to do was take the umbrella of His protection away from the Egyptians. Then when Moses declared each plague, it happened. The Egyptians got what God had been protecting them from. Once God took His protection out of the way, whoosh! It was bad news! But God doesn't have sickness and disease in His kingdom to put on anyone. He's the Lord who heals!

In his book, *Seven Things You Should Know about Divine Healing*, Brother Hagin wrote: "The Hebrew literally reads, 'I will *permit* none of these diseases upon thee, which I *permitted* upon the Egyptians'" (Hagin 17).

Dr. Michael Maffucci expands on this in his book, *No Darkness at All:*

> This interpretation would change the verb usage from causative to permissive. Causation puts the action and the source of disease as coming from God...What God permits because of free will shows the results of people making wrong choices....
>
> He [God] was not the cause, but He permitted them to choose (Maffucci 21,22,24).

What about the sign God gave Moses in Exodus 4:6-7, where, at God's instruction, Moses' hand turned leprous after he put it inside his cloak? How did God do this if God doesn't have sickness and disease to put on people? God simply took His umbrella of protection away from Moses, and because the curse of leprosy was already on the earth, the leprosy could instantly attach to Moses' hand. Then God told Moses to put his hand back inside his cloak and God instantly healed it. God didn't "put leprosy" on Moses, but He "permitted" it.

A GOD OF LOVE...AND JUSTICE

Dr. Maffucci continues:

Why does God seem so loving in the New Testament and so angry in the Old Testament? Since Jesus and the Father are exactly one in purpose and method, why the difference in appearance? The truth is that both testaments are in complete agreement with each other....

First, there is love in the Old Testament. God does not present Himself *first and foremost* as a God of judgment, but as a God of love. For example, look at Exodus 34:6,7:

And the Lord passed before him and proclaimed, "The Lord, the Lord God, merciful and gracious, longsuffering, and abounding in goodness and truth, keeping mercy for thousands, forgiving iniquity and transgression and sin, by no means clearing the guilty, visiting the iniquity of the fathers upon the children and the children's children to the third and the fourth generation."

Second, there *is* judgment in the New Testament. A word count on "judge" or "judgment" in the New Testament comes up with 108 verses. Even more significant is the fact that Jesus is the one who warns most about judgment.

Third, there is a difference between the testaments in their portrayal of judgment. In the Old Testament, judgment normally happens within history. When Israel sins, they are not told that they will go to hell when they are raised from the dead but that they will be punished by the Midianites or Assyrians.

So, does the Old Testament reveal a God of judgment and the New Testament a God of love? Emphatically, no. Both of the testaments reveal a God of love who is also a God of justice. God offers men and women His love and forgiveness, urging us to repent and escape the terrible and eternal judgments at the end of history (Maffucci 24,25).

As believers, we don't need to concern ourselves with the judgment of the wicked. We are already in that place where God thinks only love thoughts about us. He only thinks blessing thoughts towards us. We have this position because we are in Christ, in heavenly places.

CHAPTER TEN

BUILDING A CASE FOR LIVING TO BE 120

WE HAVE SEEN IN PSALM 91, that Jesus promises to satisfy us with long life. How long it takes for each of us to be "satisfied" will vary: some may be satisfied at 82; some at 95. In this chapter, I will be making a case that according to the Bible, you could live to be 120, if it takes that long for you to be satisfied! It's your choice! If you have a lot of kids, grandkids, and great grandkids and are enjoying robust, wonderful health even at 110, you might just want to stick around!

As one called to the ministry, I am looking forward to a long, healthy life. T. L. Osborn said, "I have preacher friends that want to retire. I'm thinking, 'What? You finally get up to 70 years and you finally have gained some real wisdom. You're finally worth something to God, and now you want to pucker up and quit?'" I think God may require some of us to live to be 120, just to prove that His Word is true! But once we have run our race and accomplished everything on the planet that we need to do, we would be free to go home. God wants us to be "satisfied." The Apostle Paul was satisfied: at the end of his life, he wrote to Timothy:

> **The time of my departure is at hand. I have fought the good fight, I have finished the race, I have kept the faith. Finally, there is laid up for me the crown of righteousness, which the Lord, the righteous Judge, will give to me on that Day, and not to me only but also to all who have loved His appearing (2 Timothy 4:6b-8).**

AN IN-DEPTH STUDY OF LONGEVITY

"He is your life and the length of your days" (Deuteronomy 30:20).

God's definition of the length of our days is what we want to discover: not what man has experienced, nor what seems to be the average – which seems to be on the increase because of "modern medical advancement." This verse says that God is not only our life, but He is also the length of our days. In other words, God is the one who would set the number of man's days – and whatever *He* says is what our potential is! Let's do an in-depth study on what the Bible actually says, and how some verses have historically been misunderstood.

That we would live the full number of our days is promised in Exodus 23:26. God says:

"I will fulfill the number of your days."

Some say that we are promised only 70 to 80 years as stated by Moses in Psalm 90:10. But keep in mind that Psalm 90 precedes Psalm 91 with all the wonderful blessings (including long life) in store for those who dwell in the secret place with God. In contrast to Psalm 91, Psalm 90 is like looking at the curse that comes from disobedience, because Psalm 90 was written to the backslidden, rebellious, stiff-necked generation, whose "carcasses fell in the wilderness" (Numbers 14:29). Psalm 90:1-9 says:

> Lord, You have been our dwelling place in all
>   generations.
> Before the mountains were brought forth,
> Or ever You had formed the earth and the world,
> Even from everlasting to everlasting, You are God.
>
> You turn man to destruction,
> And say, "Return, O children of men."
> For a thousand years in Your sight
> Are like yesterday when it is past,
> And like a watch in the night.
> You carry them away like a flood;
> They are like a sleep.
> In the morning they are like grass which
>   grows up:
> In the morning it flourishes and grows up;
> In the evening it is cut down and withers.
>
> For we have been consumed by Your anger,
> And by Your wrath we are terrified.
> You have set our iniquities before You,
> Our secret sins in the light of Your countenance.
> For all our days have passed away in Your wrath;
> We finish our years like a sigh.

This is a really sad, negative statement about the judgment of God because of Israel's sin which is set before Him.

Now, look at verse 10. People quote this verse of Scripture as though it was "gospel" for born-again believers who are serving God, doing everything He's called them to do. No! What Moses is saying here is in the context of the murmuring, complaining generation in the desert who brought God's wrath upon themselves because of their sin.

> **The days of our lives are seventy years;**
> **And if by reason of strength they are eighty**
> **years,**
> **Yet their boast is only labor and sorrow;**
> **For it is soon cut off, and we fly away.**
>
> **Who knows the power of Your anger?**
> **For as the fear of You, so is Your wrath.**
>
> **So teach us to number our days,**
> **That we may gain a heart of wisdom**
> **(Psalm 90:10-12).**

So, this idea of life being limited to 70 years – 80 at the most – is for those who are under the curse. It's living under the wrath of God that would cause a man's life to be shortened to that length of time. Even so, there are a lot of Christians, who after a surface-level reading of the Bible, grow up their whole life with this expectation: "Man, if you get to 70, that's good. If you go beyond 70, everything else is on borrowed time because you can't really expect to go much beyond 70." This thinking is built into their subconscious; they believe that's the best we can expect and do. Still, they know that some people just miraculously happen to live to be way older than that. Nobody can explain why.

As those who diligently study the Bible with the goal of rightly dividing the Word of truth (2 Timothy 2:15), we're not going to let a misapplication of this scripture limit our faith for a long, healthy life. We are the ones who determine the number of our days by whether or not we are in God's perfect will for our lives. It's all about being yielded.

HIS DAYS SHALL BE 120 YEARS

In Genesis 6, God sets man's days at 120 years:

"My Spirit shall not strive with man forever, for he is indeed flesh; yet his days shall be one hundred and twenty years" (Genesis 6:3).

We know that Moses himself lived to be 120 years old - exactly! He died on his birthday. Moses declared to all of Israel:

"I am one hundred and twenty years old today" (Deuteronomy 31:2).

That same day, Moses wrote a prophetic song concerning the future, and taught it to the children of Israel....Then God said to Moses, that very same day, saying: "Go up to...Mount Nebo...and die...and be gathered to your people" (Deuteronomy 31:22; 32:48-50).

Remember, Moses is the prophet who wrote both Genesis 6:3 and Psalm 90 by hearing God's Word from the Holy Spirit and writing those words down (2 Peter 1:21). If Moses heard God say man's years would be 120 and Moses lived to be exactly 120, I'd say Moses' expectation was to live to be 120; not 70 or 80!

It is also interesting to note that Moses was not sick when he died:

Moses was one hundred and twenty years old when he died. His eyes were not dim nor his natural vigor diminished (Deuteronomy 34:7).

God had to actually show up and say, "Moses, here you are in perfect health: your natural vigor is not diminished, and your eyes have not grown dim. But it is time for you to die." Moses had completed his divine assignment.

A similar thing happened with Brother Hagin. He wanted to live as long as Smith Wigglesworth, who lived to be 87. Brother Hagin died in his 87th year - but he accomplished three times as much in his life as most ministers do! He finished his race! He would quote Psalm 91:16 and then say, "Whenever you hear that I have gone, you can rest assured that I was satisfied." He died at home: he had just finished breakfast - and then he slumped over. He was gone.

They took him to the hospital, but he never regained consciousness. The family could sense his spirit was gone: they finally had to gather around him and command his heart to stop beating! That is especially astonishing, because Brother Hagin had been born with an incurable blood disease and a deformed heart, and yet, at the end of his life, his heart would not quit beating. That was one healed heart! When Brother Hagin had done everything God had asked Him to do, he simply left.

On the day Moses turned 120, God took him up to Mount Nebo and showed him all the lands promised to Israel. Then Moses died. No one saw this but God; God Himself buried Moses.

So Moses the servant of the Lord died there in the land of Moab, according to the word of the Lord. And He buried him in a valley in the land of Moab, opposite Beth Peor; but no one knows his grave to this day (Deuteronomy 34:5,6).

Moses was so revered by the nation of Israel, that God wanted Moses' body to be hidden so that the people would not start worshipping his body.

IS THERE AN APPOINTED TIME TO DIE?

Another verse that is misunderstood by a lot of people

is Hebrews 9:27, which says:

And as it is appointed for men to die once, but after this the judgment.

Some people take this to mean you have an appointment on the day that you're going to die and there's nothing you can do about it. They believe that God has determined your date, and that's it – as though God says, "I'm going to take you out on such and such a date." That's not what Hebrews 9:27 is saying. It says that each one of us *will die once,* one time. That's unless we are here when Jesus comes back, and we go up in the Rapture. In that case, we will not die, but will get a glorified body instantly upon His return. But if we are not still alive when the Rapture occurs, then we are going to die. No one leaves planet Earth alive in their body. Those of us who are born again will "graduate to heaven" and we will leave this earth suit behind. We all have to go through that veil of death; we will die, but this verse is *not* saying we have a God-appointed time to die.

Ecclesiastes 7:17 backs up the thought that there is no preset time for our death. It says:

**Do not be overly wicked,
Nor be foolish:
Why should you die before your time?**

Think about it: If God *did* have an appointed time for you to die, this verse says that it's possible for you to show up for that appointment "early" – if you are wicked or foolish. No, there is no preset appointment with death.

Looking at this another way: if God is giving you a promise of a certain length of days, don't let anybody beat you out of that! Live out the full days of your life! Run your race to the end and be satisfied, knowing you have accomplished all God asked you to do. Don't let the devil rob you ahead of time.

I'm sure the Lord rewards all of us according to our heart's intent. He'd like for us to have enough faith to establish our health and go the distance, but if we don't - as long as our *intent* is to do everything God planned - He's still going to reward us as though we had done it all! There will be students in Bible schools, preparing for the ministry when Jesus comes back. They will get their full reward.

Ecclesiastes 3:1,2 talks about seasons in our lives:

To everything there is a season,
A time for every purpose under heaven:
A time to be born,
And a time to die.

Some have used this verse as an argument for an appointed time for death: "See! There is a time to die!" But is a "season" the same as an "appointment"? God *does* choose the times and geographic boundaries of each person's life (Acts 17:25-26), but not necessarily the exact date of their birth and death. As we keep on reading in Ecclesiastes 3, the meaning of "season" becomes clear:

...A time to weep,
And a time to laugh;
A time to mourn,
And a time to dance (Ecclesiastes 3:4).

Solomon, who wrote Ecclesiastes, is not saying that at 10 a.m. on Tuesday morning, you are scheduled to weep, but on Wednesday afternoon by 4 p.m. you will be able to laugh again. No, not dates, not appointments, but seasons.

I find it interesting that Solomon died at age 60. God gave Solomon great, supernatural wisdom and knowledge, "such as none of the kings have had who were before you, nor shall any after you have the like" (2 Chronicles 1:12). But remember what Jesus said: "To whom much is given, from him much will be required" (Luke 12:48). God wanted Solomon to walk in the wisdom and knowledge he was given, but he didn't. He started off well: he wrote the book of Proverbs, which is full of wisdom. But by the end of his life, he had walked so far away from godly wisdom that he built large altars so his foreign wives could burn incense and sacrifice to their idols (1 Kings 11:7-9).

Solomon died young. Psalm 55:23b gives us some insight into this:

Bloodthirsty and deceitful men shall not live out half their days.

If indeed we have the promise of 120 years, and Solomon died at age 60, that's exactly half of what the promise would have been.

Solomon missed out on the many blessings of living a godly life. In Ecclesiastes, he mentions "vanity" 33 times! By the end of his life, he has concluded: "All is vanity" (Ecclesiastes 1:2). Basically, he is saying, "I have done everything, and it is all just vanity, emptiness, wind." It's true that just being with God is really all that matters. But there were a lot of things that Solomon could have enjoyed that he's calling vanity, such as: enjoying life and laughter (Ecclesiastes 2:1), enjoying satisfaction in the work of his hands (2:11), enjoying the beauty around him (6:9), enjoying abundance (5:10), as well as enjoying riches, wealth, and honor (6:2). When I read about all Solomon could have enjoyed, I say, "I'll take that! That looks like a promise of God to me! I receive it!"

A FASCINATING LOOK AT LIFE SPANS IN THE BIBLE

The Bible carefully records the genealogies of the Patriarchs and their ages. Before the Flood, they lived a long, long time. Even after the Flood, they lived a long time. Let's take a look at this in detail: I find it fascinating!

The record of life spans begins, of course, with Adam, who lived to be 930.

So all the days that Adam lived were nine hundred and thirty years; and he died (Genesis 5:5).

Adam had a son named Seth, who lived to be 912.

So all the days of Seth were nine hundred and twelve years; and he died (Genesis 5:8).

Seth had a son named Enosh, who lived to be 905.

So all the days of Enosh were nine hundred and five years; and he died (Genesis 5:11).

Enosh had a son named Cainan, who lived to be 910.

So all the days of Cainan were nine hundred and ten years; and he died (Genesis 5:14).

Cainan had a son named Mahalalel, who lived to be 895.

So all the days of Mahalalel were eight hundred and ninety-five years; and he died (Genesis 5:17).

Mahalalel had a son named Jared, who lived to be 962.

So all the days of Jared were nine hundred and sixty-two years; and he died (Genesis 5:20).

Jared had a son named Enoch. Enoch was a special case.

So all the days of Enoch were three hundred and sixty-five years.

And Enoch walked with God; and he was not, for God took him (Genesis 5:23,24).

Enoch knew Adam: Adam was Enoch's great, great, great, great-grandfather. Adam was 622 when Enoch was born, and he lived 308 more years. Adam lived long enough to be able to tell Enoch what it was like to walk with God. I can imagine Adam telling Enoch all the stories about walking with God in the cool of the day in the Garden of Eden. Enoch heard about the conversations Adam had with God. Adam had to tell Enoch the whole story: how he and Eve fell, how they did the wrong thing. Enoch began to think, "Why can't I walk with God the same way Grandfather Adam did?" The Bible says, "Enoch walked with God, and then he was not, for God took him." I used to picture it like this: Enoch got so used to walking with God, that one day, when he was out walking with God, God said, "Enoch, you're a whole lot closer to My place than yours right now. Why don't you just come home with Me?"

But then I realized that it didn't happen that way. Hebrews 11:5 says, "By faith, Enoch was taken away." It was "by faith." Whose faith? Enoch's. In other words, Enoch initiated his own departure. I believe that while walking with God one day, Enoch said, "God, I'm closer to Your place than mine. If it is pleasing to You, I'll just go home with You." So, Enoch got translated into heaven. That's why he's the only one of the patriarchs with a shorter life: he stepped right over into glory!

Enoch had a son named Methuselah, who lived to be 969.

So all the days of Methuselah were nine hundred and sixty-nine years; and he died (Genesis 5:27).

Methuselah had a son named Lamech, who lived to be 777.

So all the days of Lamech were seven hundred and seventy-seven years; and he died (Genesis 5:31).

Lamech had a son named Noah, who lived to be 950.

So all the days of Noah were nine hundred and fifty years; and he died (Genesis 9:29).

It's interesting to note that right after God proclaimed mankind's days to be 120 years (Genesis 6:3), their ages started dwindling down. Noah's son, Shem, lived 600 years; nine generations later, Terah, Abraham's father, lived to be 205. Abraham only lived to be 175.

This is the sum of the years of Abraham's life which he lived: one hundred and seventy-five years (Genesis 25:7).

That's a considerable drop from the 900-plus range the patriarchs were experiencing before the Flood.

Abraham had a son named Isaac, who lived to be 180.

Now the days of Isaac were one hundred and eighty years (Genesis 35:28).

Isaac had a son named Jacob, who lived to be 147.

And Jacob lived in the land of Egypt seventeen years. So the length of Jacob's life was one hundred and forty-seven years (Genesis 47:28).

Jacob, whom God renamed "Israel," had 12 sons who became the 12 tribes of Israel. Joseph, the next to the youngest son of Jacob, lived to be 110.

So Joseph dwelt in Egypt, he and his father's household. And Joseph lived one hundred and ten years (Genesis 50:22).

See how quickly it keeps dropping? In just four generations, it goes from 175 to 110. Then, for about 500 years of recorded Bible history, we see the maximum age remaining somewhere around 110 to 120 years.

STATISTICS ON LONGEVITY

Let me give you some current information on longevity. According to statisticians, well over 100,000 people are over the age of 100 today. They call them "centenarians." You can go online and search for "centenarians" and find all kinds of information. The oldest people that are alive right now are around 117 maximum, for the women, while the men are usually in the range 107 to 110.

Historically, we have records of a lot of other people who also lived more that 120 years. Brother Keith Moore, who worked with Brother Hagin at Rhema, later on, taught at healing school. The more Brother Keith taught on healing, the more he received an understanding concerning longevity in the Bible. He also discovered some fascinating records of long-lived people listed in the *Adam Clarke Bible Commentary*. These are records of people who lived between 1400 and 1700. Here are some of the statistics that Adam Clarke recorded:

There was a woman named Agnes Schooner, who died in 1499 at the age of 119.

There was a woman named the "Countess of Desmond" who died in 1612 at the age of 145. The interesting thing about her is that she claimed her teeth renewed themselves three times! We all get two sets of teeth: our baby teeth and our permanent teeth, but she grew a *third* set of teeth. I guess her permanent teeth fell out in her older years, and she grew more. Maybe God knew she was going to live that long and just gave her an extra set of teeth!

There was an interesting fellow named Thomas Parr, from England. He was married at age 88 and had two children with his first wife. Unfortunately, he had an affair when he was 102 years old and had an illegitimate child. But then, apparently his wife died, and he married a widow at 120. At 130, he still ran his own farm. The records show he died at 152. He had testimony of having lived through 10 kings and queens in his lifetime. To outlive 10 kings and queens is pretty awesome.

There was another fellow named Thomas Dumais, who died in 1648 at the age of 145.

Henry Jenkins swam in cold rivers at the age of 102. He said that kept him full of vitality. Jenkins died in 1670 at the age of 169.

These facts can seem like a crazy stretch for us to believe, except we saw people in the Bible who lived to be around 900, until God said, "No, the human life span will be 120." But if, even after God said that, some people pushed the upper limits – like Abraham at 175 and Isaac at 180. Who's to say that these men and women were not doing this same thing in more modern times?

In 1991, there was a guy named Jackson Pollock in Milledgeville, Georgia, who lived to be 124. They asked him, "To what do you attribute your longevity?"

He answered, "Number one: trust in God and He will pull you through." That's a direct quote. Then he said, "I trust God and I only smoke Prince Albert tobacco in a can!" I don't recommend that you smoke Prince Albert or any other kind of tobacco, but Mr. Pollock lived to be 124! He also said, "How you think and believe affects you. Refuse to worry; be at peace."

There is so much wisdom in that saying. Worry and fear bring stress on your body; it was not designed to carry these things. Your body will adjust to stress, but usually in a very negative way. If you can, find godly ways to release stress. My recommendation is to pray in tongues for an hour a day. That will give you the peace of God! It's the best meditation I know of; the best way to produce peace. Plus, of course, you're being a tool of the Lord: you're praying the perfect prayer about all kinds of things, while at the same time you're staying in perfect peace.

Let's look at just a few more people:

Carey White of Palatka, Florida, died in 1991 at the age of 116.

Walter Williams of Texas, died in 1978 at the age of 125.

This next one is unique. In 1994, there was an unnamed 112-year-old woman in Detroit, Michigan whose story was printed in the Detroit newspaper. A burglar broke into her house, and she attacked him. He threw her on the floor, and she grabbed him. The newspaper never said where she grabbed him, but she held him off. The burglar was quoted as saying he was really happy when she had to turn loose! Her son said the burglar was lucky that his mother didn't have her gun. At 112, she was usually carrying a weapon. Her neighbor said she would still ride her motorcycle when she was 80 years of age. They asked what her secret to longevity was. She said, "I don't hate anybody, I'm not bitter at anybody, and I serve God." That's really simple advice: don't hate anybody, don't be bitter, and serve God!

If the Lord tarries His coming again, we know we are going to die. This shouldn't be a surprise to us, and we don't need to fear it. But we *do* need to expect what is promised in Psalm 103:5, that our youth will be renewed like the eagles.

My plan for ministry in my later years is this: when I am 105, if nobody wants to listen to me preach on anything else, if I delivered this message on longevity, I could probably get a crowd! They would say, "You must know something that we need to know about living so long!"

MY FAMILY'S NATURAL LONGEVITY

I like showing a photo to my students of my family reunion at Hillsborough River State Park, near Tampa. In this photo are three great aunts of mine from my dad's side of the family, who always came. Actually, they were the reason we had the reunion at the park. When they were young girls, they lived in Zephyrhills, and they had their family reunion there. They have since graduated to heaven; one lived to be 99, one lived to be 100, and my grandfather's baby sister lived to be 101. My mother's mother - of the Spooner family - lived to be 101. She didn't get saved until she was 96. I don't suggest anyone put off getting saved that long! My great-grandmother on my dad's side passed away soon after her 98th birthday party. I was at the party, and at 98, she was just as sharp mentally as she was at 58.

These family members are all wonderful Christian people, who never really thought that they were shooting for longevity. But they never bought into the idea that we were only promised 70 or 80 years, because they had family members who lived way beyond that. They just assumed that they would live as long as they were supposed to.

CHAPTER ELEVEN

JESUS CHANGES THE WAY PEOPLE THINK

WHEN JESUS TAUGHT, He had to change the way the people thought about God and how His Kingdom works. Under the new covenant, the Apostle Paul tells us:

Do not be conformed to this world, but be transformed by the renewing of your mind, that you may prove what is that good and acceptable and perfect will of God (Romans 12:2).

The Jewish people at the time of Jesus had a lot of wrong knowledge and misunderstanding concerning the Word of God. Most people still do! Of course, anyone who does not have the Holy Spirit residing in their spirit - because they are not born again - will be subject to a lot of wicked thoughts and ways.

THE THOUGHTS OF THE WICKED VS THE THOUGHTS OF THE RIGHTEOUS

Here's a passage of Scripture that most people - even Christians - take out of context and apply to Christians.

But it is talking about wicked people and their ways and unrighteous people and their thoughts.

> **Seek the Lord while He may be found,**
> **Call upon Him while He is near.**
>
> **Let the wicked forsake his way, and the**
> **unrighteous man his thoughts**
> **(Isaiah 55:6,7a).**

Who is God identifying here? The wicked person who has their ways of wickedness and the unrighteous man who has unrighteous thoughts.

> **Let him return to the Lord, and He will have**
> **mercy on him; And to our God, for He will**
> **abundantly pardon.**
>
> **"For My thoughts are not your thoughts, nor**
> **are your ways My ways," says the Lord.**
>
> **"For as the heavens are higher than the earth,**
> **So are My ways higher than your ways, and**
> **My thoughts than your thoughts"**
> **(Isaiah 55:7b-9).**

Christians quote this all the time! I don't how many misguided preachers I've heard say, "God's ways are higher than our ways, and His thoughts are a lot higher than ours." In saying this, they are putting themselves in the category of being a wicked person with wicked ways and an unrighteous person with unrighteous thoughts because, in context, that's who God is referring to. I'm not going to claim being one of them! I want to say, "Wait a minute! I want to draw near to the Lord! I'm trying to absorb His thoughts. I'm trying to absorb His ways; therefore, His thoughts will become my thoughts and His ways will become my ways." That's what God says is available to us as Christians. But God is not talking to believers in the above verses; He's talking to the wicked and to the unrighteous.

The tone changes in the next passage:

"**For as the rain comes down, and the snow from heaven, and do not return there, But water the earth, And make it bring forth and bud, That it may give seed to the sower, and bread to the eater,**

So shall My word be that goes forth from My mouth; It shall not return to Me void, But it shall accomplish what I please, And it shall prosper in the thing for which I sent it" **(Isaiah 55:10,11).**

Our words will do exactly the same thing if it's God's Word that we're declaring out of our mouths!

"**For you shall go out with joy, and be led out with peace; The mountains and the hills shall break forth into singing before you, And all the trees of the field shall clap their hands.**

Instead of the thorn shall come up the cyprus tree, and instead of the brier shall come up the myrtle tree, And it shall be to the Lord for a name, for an everlasting sign that shall not be cut off."

Thus says the Lord: "Keep justice, and do righteousness, For My salvation is about to come, And My righteousness to be revealed" **(Isaiah 55:12-13, 56:1).**

What a completely different experience for the people

who walk in God's ways and think His thoughts! God says wherever we go, everybody will rejoice; even nature is going to rejoice! The trees will be clapping their hands as we come by! If God could say that to His people under the old covenant, how much more in the new covenant will God do these things for those who are born again, filled with the Spirit, and walking in faith? We have abandoned the wicked ways and the unrighteous thoughts, and we're adopting what God has for us. Jesus is changing our thoughts and renewing our minds.

WRITTEN ON OUR HEARTS

With the new covenant, God's thoughts are now written on our hearts. Jeremiah 31:31-33a says:

> **"Behold, the days are coming," says the Lord, "when I will make a new covenant with the house of Israel and with the house of Judah – not according to the covenant that I made with their fathers in the day that I took them by the hand to lead them out of the land of Egypt, My covenant which they broke, though I was a husband to them," says the Lord. "But this is the covenant that I will make with the house of Israel after those days," says the Lord...**

We, the Church of the Lord Jesus, became spiritual Israel; we were grafted in (Romans 11:17). God intended that we would be the descendants of Abraham; Abraham is our father by faith (Romans 4:16). This is what God has to say about us:

> **"...I will put My law in their minds, and write it on their hearts; and I will be their God, and they shall be My people" (Jeremiah 31:33b).**

That's exactly what happened when you received Jesus as Lord and the Holy Spirit came into your spirit. God infuses the presence of the Holy Spirit with His Word – so now your spirit is infused with God's Word, as well. It is "written on your heart."

I love to meditate on this fact: the Holy Spirit didn't forget any of God's Word when He moved into my spirit. Now it's my job to allow Him to get it from my spirit to my head, and to make that connection, that being "transformed by the renewing of the mind," so that I have God's Word both in my spirit and in my mind. That's when the miraculous release of faith happens, when we come to that place of the illumination of the truth of God's Word.

WE HAVE THE MIND OF CHRIST

As amazing as it may seem, the Bible clearly says, "We have the mind of Christ" (1 Corinthians 2:16). Let's take a look at this verse in context. Paul is talking about all the wonderful things that God has prepared for us and says that we have not perceived these things with our senses – our eyes or our ears – but that the Holy Spirit has revealed them to us. The Amplified Bible makes this passage crystal clear:

> **Now we have received, not the spirit of the world, but the [Holy] Spirit who is from God, so that we may know and understand the [wonderful] things freely given to us by God. We also speak of these things, not in words taught or supplied by human wisdom, but in those taught by the Spirit, combining and interpreting spiritual thoughts with spiritual words [for those being guided by the Holy Spirit] (1 Corinthians 2:12,13 AMP).**

> **For who has known or understood the mind (the counsels and purposes) of the Lord so as to guide and instruct Him and give Him knowledge? But we have the mind of Christ (the Messiah) and do hold the thoughts (feelings and purposes) of His heart (1 Corinthians 2:16 AMPC).**

Not only do we have the mind of Christ, but we were also made to be like Jesus in this world. And this happens now, not later when we get to heaven!

1 John 4:17 tells us:

> **Love has been perfected among us in this: that we may have boldness in the day of judgment; because as He is, so are we in this world.**

This is a picture of where the Church has to be: in total dominion. The only way that is going to happen is when believers are baptized with the Holy Spirit and the holy fire. As Spirit-filled believers, we can now stay continuously filled with the Holy Spirit (Acts 13:52 AMPC) and with the fire of God. The final revival before the Lord returns is the revival of the Holy Spirit, holy fire, and dominion.

John says that God has made the way for us, as born-again believers, to have love perfected in our hearts. Because of this, we are bold. We may well be the generation still on earth on the day of judgment. Picture this: as the Lord Jesus is today, seated at the right hand of the Father, with dominion over all life, ruling and reigning the whole universe, so are we in this world. Jesus is in total dominion, in splendor and glory, and so are we, now in this world. There are a lot of Christians who don't walk in this. But it's available to us – so you and I can boldly declare: "As He is, so am I in this world. I'm going to come into that place, having the mind of Christ, walking in dominion, and fulfilling what God has called me to do."

HOW TO RECEIVE AND APPLY WISDOM FOR LONGEVITY

We have covered these verses already, but I want to stress having faith to receive a long and healthy life. Knowing what the Bible promises us is always good, but receiving the promises is better, by far!

> **My son, do not forget my law,**
> **But let your heart keep my commands;**
> **For length of days and long life**
> **And peace they will add to you**
> **(Proverbs 3:1,2).**

God says knowing His Word is going to add length of days, long life, and peace to us. We need to find out how to be able to apply it!

> **Hear, my son, and receive my sayings,**
> **And the years of your life will be many**
> **(Proverbs 4:10).**

There's something about receiving the Word of God and getting it activated in your life that makes the years of your life "many."

> **"The fear of the Lord is the beginning of**
> **wisdom,**
> **And the knowledge of the Holy One is**
> **understanding.**
> **For by me your days will be multiplied,**
> **And years of life will be added to you"**
> **(Proverbs 9:10,11).**

We have seen that evil men live only half of their years, and stiff-necked, rebellious people live only 70 to 80 years. By simply gaining knowledge of God's Word, obeying it, and exercising faith in His promises, days will be multiplied to you and years of life will be added to you.

The fear of the Lord prolongs days,
But the years of the wicked will be shortened
(Proverbs 10:27).

All through the Word of God, we see that following after God's way and His Word causes you to increase your days. Of course, we know that "faith comes by hearing and hearing by the Word of God" (Romans 10:17), so we know that it's the increase of our faith that causes us to live longer and longer.

WHAT NOT TO DO!

The carcasses of you who have complained against Me shall fall in this wilderness, all of you who were numbered, according to your entire number, from twenty years old and above. Except for Caleb the son of Jephunneh and Joshua the son of Nun, you shall by no means enter the land which I swore I would make you dwell in (Numbers 14:29,30).

God pronounced that the complainers would die in the wilderness. He prophesied it, and it came to pass. Remember, Israel all believed the report of the ten spies who said, "We can't go in. We were like grasshoppers in their eyes." Only Joshua and Caleb said, "We are able to take the land because God said we could. If God said we could, we can! Why do you look at the natural things?" So, they were the only two who got to enter the Promised Land.

This is an important principle to receive and apply as God's wisdom for longevity: don't look at the natural things! Abraham didn't:

> **And not being weak in faith, he did not consider his own body, already dead (since he was about a hundred years old), and the deadness of Sarah's womb. He did not waver at the promise of God through unbelief, but was strengthened in faith, giving glory to God, and being fully convinced that what He had promised He was also able to perform (Romans 4:19-21).**

Abraham had many encounters with God, who kept promising him a son. But it clicked when God changed his name from "Abram" to "Abraham" and Sarai's name to "Sarah." Every time Abraham spoke to Sarah, he would call her "Mother of Nations." And every time Sarah spoke to Abraham, she would call him "Father of a Multitude." Also, when they met new people, they changed how they introduced themselves. Words paint a picture, and as they continually called each other these new, God-given names, they began to change how they thought of themselves. They envisioned themselves as parents, even though there was no natural evidence that this could happen. Like Joshua and Caleb, they decided, "If God says we can, we can! It doesn't matter how old we are. We can be parents!" They became fully persuaded.

In the same way, we can envision ourselves enjoying a long, healthy life. If God says we can, we can!

SECTION TWO:

LAYING DOUBTS TO REST

CHAPTER TWELVE

WHAT ABOUT JOB?

MANY TIMES, CHRISTIANS HAVE DOUBTS concern
ing healing because they have a long list of unan-
swered questions which, unfortunately, have come from
erroneous teaching of God's Word. We will take a close
look at the most common of these questions and discover
what the Bible really has to say. We will see that – without
exception – it is *always* God's will to heal. As doubts in this
matter are finally put to rest, you will be able to receive
healing from the Lord.

I don't know why people want to stress the negatives
of the Scripture and try to make an argument for the right
to die young, to be sick, beaten-down, and poor. To them,
it's almost a heresy to say that God wants us to be healthy,
to live long, to be prosperous – even though the purpose of
our longevity is to be fruitful in producing a lot of disciples. We want to have an effect on other peoples' lives for
the gospel's sake.

Some of the following questions may still be in the
back of your subconscious mind – you don't even realize
they are there. The more you meditate on the Word of God,

and the more any bad teaching you may have received is replaced with truth, the sooner you will realize that God has a great plan for you to have a long, healthy life.

WHAT ABOUT JOB?

The story of Job is probably the oldest story of the Bible, which was handed down for centuries by oral tradition. No one knows for sure who wrote it down and when. Some scholars say it was written down by Moses. Others suggest Solomon wrote it.

Job was a contemporary of Abraham and one of the wealthiest men in the Bible. The Bible tells us that Job was "blameless and upright."

There was a man in the land of Uz, whose name was Job; and that man was blameless and upright, and one who feared God and shunned evil (Job 1:1).

Job was "blameless": in God's eyes, he had done no sin. That's because the Law of Moses had not yet been given to define sin. Romans 5:13 tells us:

For until the law, sin was in the world, but sin is not imputed when there is no law.

Romans 7:7b confirms this thought:

I would not have known sin except through the law. For I would not have known covetousness unless the law had said, "You shall not covet."

WHAT WENT WRONG?

So, Job had not sinned against the Lord, and yet we know terrible things suddenly happened to him. I would like to point out that Job had a consuming fear, and this was probably what opened the door to Satan.

Job had seven sons and three daughters. They would go to one another's house and have feasts that would last for days, with eating and drinking. Job didn't know exactly what they were doing, but he had this fear that they were somehow committing sins at these feasts.

> **So it was, when the days of feasting had run their course, that Job would send and sanctify them, and he would rise early in the morning and offer burnt offerings according to the number of them all. For Job said, "It may be that my sons have sinned and cursed God in their hearts." Thus Job did regularly (Job 1:5).**

Some Hebrew scholars say the Hebrew word translated "regularly" here could easily be translated "compulsively." Job exhibited what we would consider compulsive fear: he made burnt offerings for his sons and daughters "regularly"; he was driven by the fear that they had "sinned and cursed God in their hearts."

A LOOK BEHIND THE SCENES

Next, the writer of Job records a behind-the-scenes story, which starts off in Job 1:6-12. Let's take a close look at these verses:

> **Now there was a day when the sons of God came to present themselves before the Lord, and Satan also came among them (Job 1:6).**

The "sons of God" here is a reference to angels. It seems the angels had to report to the Lord, including even Satan, as a fallen angel. It appears God forced Satan to come back and report what he was doing.

> **And the Lord said to Satan, "From where do you come?"**
>
> **So Satan answered the Lord and said, "From going to and fro on the earth, and from walking back and forth on it" (Job 1:7).**

I find it interesting that Satan has to *walk* back and forth through the earth as he seeks someone to devour (1 Peter 5:8), while the eyes of the Lord *run* to and fro looking for someone to bless (2 Chronicles 16:9). That just shows how much better God's ways are!

> **Then the Lord said to Satan, "Have you considered My servant Job, that there is none like him on the earth, a blameless and upright man, one who fears God and shuns evil?" (Job 1:8).**

Some people think God was saying, "Hey, Satan, have you thought about attacking My servant Job?" What God literally said in the Hebrew was: "Have you set your heart upon My servant Job?" Why would God ask that question of Satan? Because God knew that Job's fear had opened a door, and that Satan had already "set his heart" upon stealing, killing, and destroying in Job's life.

God saw this "chink in Job's armor," this breach where Satan could rush in. God pointed out that Job was blameless and upright; Job did everything right - *except* he had this open door of fear, this compulsion of offering the sin sacrifices for his sons and daughters over and over again.

People have a lot of questions about why God gave permission to the devil to attack Job. The next passage of Scripture answers this question, as our behind-the-scenes story continues in Job 1:9-12:

So Satan answered the Lord and said, "Does Job fear God for nothing? Have You not made a hedge around him, around his household, and around all that he has on every side? You have blessed the work of his hands, and his possessions have increased in the land. But now, stretch out Your hand and touch all that he has, and he will surely curse You to Your face!"

And the Lord said to Satan, "Behold, all that he has is in your power; only do not lay a hand on his person."

So Satan went out from the presence of the Lord.

Satan suggested that if God "touched" Job with evil, that things would be different: that Job would curse God to His face. God refused Satan's challenge to harm Job – but simply noted that Job was already in Satan's power. Job had already opened the door through fear.

THE ATTACK ON JOB BEGINS

The attacks began to come: in a single day, Job lost all his herds and flocks and then was told his sons and daughters had all died in a freak windstorm.

Now there was a day when his sons and daughters were eating and drinking wine in their oldest brother's house; and a messenger came to Job and said, "The oxen were plowing and the donkeys feeding beside them, when the Sabeans raided them and took them away – indeed they have killed the servants with the

edge of the sword; and I alone have escaped to tell you!"

While he was still speaking, another also came and said, "The fire of God fell from heaven and burned up the sheep and the servants, and consumed them; and I alone have escaped to tell you!"

While he was still speaking, another also came and said, "The Chaldeans formed three bands, raided the camels and took them away, yes, and killed the servants with the edge of the sword; and I alone have escaped to tell you!"

While he was still speaking, another also came and said, "Your sons and daughters were eating and drinking wine in their oldest brother's house, and suddenly a great wind came from across the wilderness and struck the four corners of the house, and it fell on the young people, and they are dead; and I alone have escaped to tell you!" (Job 1:13-19).

After Job lost everything, he made this statement:

"Naked I came from my mother's womb,
And naked shall I return there.
The Lord gave, and the Lord has taken away;
Blessed be the name of the Lord" (Job 1:21).

Now this sounds really pious: we think, "This guy is totally submitted to the Lord." This sounds so noble, but we know it is *completely wrong*. We have an advantage that Job did not have: we see what was going on behind the scenes, so we know *God* did not take anything from Job.

Next, Satan attacked Job's body as recorded in Job 2:7:

So Satan went out from the presence of the Lord, and struck Job with painful boils from the sole of his foot to the crown of his head.

After Job's whole life collapsed and he lost everything, including his health, Job said:

"For the thing I greatly feared has come upon me, And what I dreaded has happened to me" (Job 3:25).

This statement gives us great insight as to what was going on in Job's heart and mind, even before anything bad happened. His biggest fear was that he would lose his whole family. Job had no sin in his life, but fear is just as much of an open door to the devil to come and attack someone's life as sin can be. Fear takes you out from under the umbrella of God's protection. It wasn't God saying, "Satan, I give you permission to attack my servant Job." Job's fear had put him into the devil's hands.

Proverbs 26:2 AMPC says this:

Like the sparrow in her wandering, like the swallow in her flying, So the curse without cause does not come and alight [on the undeserving].

In other words, just as birds need a place to land, a curse cannot light without a cause. So, every curse that has happened in the life of mankind is because of an open door. Sometimes people were blindsided by what the devil was doing and the curse was able to light. In Job's case, the cause was fear. Sometimes it is stress. I am learning to walk in what I call "the pace of grace." I pray through until I have peace and receive directions from the Lord. Often, He says, "You don't have to do this. It will stress you out." So, I make the adjustments.

Doctors are now telling us how bad stress is for our bodies: when under stress, our bodies release cortisol, which suppresses the immune system.

Jesus knew stress was bad, two thousand years ago! He said:

"Walk with me and work with me – watch how I do it. Learn the unforced rhythms of grace. I won't lay anything heavy or ill-fitting on you. Keep company with me and you'll learn to live freely and lightly" (Matthew 11:29-30 MSG).

Walking in the pace of grace has given me a new motto: "Don't engage!" I don't engage with "the crazy." I stay focused on the Lord.

THE ANGUISH OF HUMAN REASONING

Because Job did not know the behind-the-scenes story, when he lost everything, he thought God took it. He went through the anguish of human reasoning with his limited understanding. Job wanted to die. He said:

"Oh, that I might have my request, That God would grant me the thing that I long for! That it would please God to crush me, That He would loose His hand and cut me off!" (Job 6:8,9).

In other words, "God, just kill me!" It stands to reason: if you lost your possessions, your children, and your health, you would probably be just as depressed as Job! He was also quite confused, because earlier, God had been blessing everything Job put his hand to. Job was blessed immeasurably: he was probably the richest man on the face of the earth at that time. So, Job was wondering, "Why did God stop blessing me? Why are God's blessings all gone?"

Next, Job complained in bitterness:

"Therefore I will not restrain my mouth; I will speak in the anguish of my spirit; I will complain in the bitterness of my soul" (Job 7:11).

Job was sitting in his house in sackcloth and ashes, using a piece of pottery to scrape the boils that covered his body. His three friends were there with him, telling him, "Job, you must have sinned some horrible sin, and now you are lying about it. You're not revealing it, and you're not repenting. That's why God has sent all this trouble your way." It's easy to become bitter if you think all the bad things that have happened to you are the will of the Lord.

Job was trying to defend himself against his friends' mindless accusations. (With friends like this, you don't need enemies! I certainly wouldn't want these three men to comfort me in the midst of trouble, because they had nothing good to say!)

Next, Job tried to justify himself. He said:

**"But I have understanding as well as you;
I am not inferior to you.
Indeed, who does not know such things as
those?" (Job 12:3)**

**"Behold, my eye has seen all this,
My ear has heard and understood it" (Job 13:1).**

In other words, Job thinks he knows everything. Have you ever known a "know-it-all," someone who thinks they know everything, but doesn't? Job's friends were thinking this about Job at this point because he was sounding like a "know-it-all."

Then, Job tried to defend himself to God:

**"Though He slay me, yet will I trust Him.
Even so, I will defend my own ways before
Him"(Job 13:15).**

Starting in Job 15:1 all the way to Job 32:1 - that's seventeen chapters! - are found all the arguments of Job's friends which alternate with Job defending himself to them and to God. We're not even going to read these chapters where Job is repeatedly condemned by his friends.

I'd like to make a statement here: people will tell you, "To really know God, you have to read the entire Bible through once every year." And they will read this endless discussion with back-and-forth accusations and justifications in the book of Job, every year.

Brother Hagin said, "I do 90% of my reading and studying in the new covenant, because that's where we live." I know the old covenant. I've read the old covenant. Those stories were given to us as examples. Once you know the new covenant, you can now read the old covenant and pick out the messages of faith and the principles that stand out. The Old Testament is two-thirds of the Bible and the New Testament is one-third of the Bible. You would be spending all that time studying about where you *don't* live. It's fine to read through the Old Testament a couple of times, but not once a year! If you *do* read your Bible through once a year, *don't read from Job 15:1 to Job 32:1!* Because when these people said the things they said, they didn't know what they were talking about!

ELIHU: SPEAKING UP FOR GOD

Then, in Job 32:2, Elihu began to speak for God - against Job and his friends. Elihu was a young man who had been sitting there listening to Job's older (and supposedly wiser) friends. Elihu did the honorable thing, which was to sit quietly and let each of the older men express everything they want to say first. But he was sitting there boiling, thinking, "You guys don't know God at all!" Elihu must have been very much like Enoch: he was walking with God, he'd been hearing from God, and he knew the justice of God. He ended up being able to speak as a prophet for God, prophesying God's true character. His speech goes from Job 32:2 to Job 37:24. It's a five-chapter dissertation by Elihu, speaking for God.

Elihu pointed out that God is just:

> "Therefore listen to me, you men of
>   understanding:
> Far be it from God to do wickedness,
> And from the Almighty to commit iniquity"
> (Job 34:10).

Job's friends had been blaming Job's problems on God, telling him, "God is the one who did this to you," not recognizing that Satan was the one who did it because there was an open door. Elihu continued:

> "For He repays man according to his work,
> And makes man to find a reward according to
>   his way.
> Surely God will never do wickedly,
> Nor will the Almighty pervert justice"
> (Job 34:11,12).

Elihu was speaking with great wisdom: God does not steal, kill, or destroy. Next, Elihu prophesied what happens to those who obey and serve God and what happens to those who do not:

> "Behold, God is mighty, but despises no one;
> He is mighty in strength of understanding.
> He does not preserve the life of the wicked,

> But gives justice to the oppressed.
> He does not withdraw His eyes from the
>   righteous;
> But they are on the throne with kings,
> For He has seated them forever,
> And they are exalted.
> And if they are bound in fetters,
> Held in the cords of affliction,
> Then He tells them their work and their
>   transgressions –
> That they have acted defiantly.
> He also opens their ear to instruction,
> And commands that they turn from iniquity.
> If they obey and serve Him,
> They shall spend their days in prosperity,
> And their years in pleasures.
> But if they do not obey,
> They shall perish by the sword,
> And they shall die without knowledge"
> (Job 36:5-12).

This reminds me of what God revealed in Deuteronomy 30:19b: "I have set before you life and death, blessing and cursing; therefore choose life." If you obey God, you will have prosperity and pleasure.

> "But the hypocrites in heart store up wrath;
> They do not cry for help when He binds
>   them.
> They die in youth,
> And their life ends among the perverted
>   persons.
> He delivers the poor in their affliction,
> And opens their ears in oppression.
>
> "Indeed He would have brought you out of

dire distress,
**Into a broad place where there is no restraint;
And what is set on your table would be full of
richness" (Job 36:13-16).**

Elihu thoroughly described the true character of God
and how God would respond to anybody who turned to
Him, listened to Him, received correction, and was repen-
tant in their heart. Elihu ended in Job 37 with a stunning
proclamation of God's majesty and wonderful works as
seen in nature. Job and Job's friends were listening to
Elihu, and really hearing him.

GOD ANSWERS JOB DIRECTLY

Suddenly, God answers Job directly and straightens
Job out completely. It takes a little over four chapters,
from Job 38 to the beginning of Job 42.

**Then the Lord answered Job out of the whirl-
wind, and said:
"Who is this who darkens counsel
By words without knowledge?" (Job 38:1,2).**

According to God, the things Job said when he spoke
"darkened counsel by words without knowledge." Some
people say we need to study the words of Job and live by
those words. No, not when God rebuked him, saying the
things he said were not correct. God continued:

**"Now prepare yourself like a man;
I will question you, and you shall answer Me.
Where were you when I laid the foundations
    of the earth?
Tell Me, if you have understanding.
Who determined its measurements?
Surely you know!**

> **Or who stretched the line upon it?**
> **To what were its foundations fastened?**
> **Or who laid its cornerstone" (Job 38:3-6).**

God goes down a long litany designed for Job and his friends to hear the truth from God's side and to realize they were just talking off the top of their heads, and they didn't know anything! Their theology was abysmal and wasn't doing anyone any good.

God's words cause Job to repent - he recognized he had done something wrong. What was it that Job did wrong? He spoke without wisdom, he "darkened counsel without knowledge." He was speaking about God without *knowing* God.

BUT NOW MY EYE SEES YOU

> **"I have heard of You by the hearing of the ear,**
> **But now my eye sees You.**
> **Therefore I abhor myself,**
> **And repent in dust and ashes" (Job 42:5,6).**

If anyone is trying to present their own righteousness, when they come face-to-face with Jesus Christ, they realize their righteousness is as filthy rags (Isaiah 64:6). They realize the holiness and pureness of God. That's what Job encountered: the holiness and pureness of God! Job said, "What was I thinking? Why did I even open my mouth? What an idiot I've been!" And so he repented in dust and ashes. When Job changed his mind, when he stopped blaming God, when he realized that it was *not* the hand of God that had caused this, God turned everything around. God said, "That's all I needed, Job. Now I am able to turn everything around for you and restore everything to double what you had before, simply because you got your heart right."

RESTORATION!

At this point, Job's healing began. Repentance causes release and forgiveness. Job had to forgive his friends because they were "down in the basement with him," digging holes and trying to bury him under their bad theology. God instructed Job to pray for them, and Job's restoration began:

And the Lord restored Job's losses when he prayed for his friends. Indeed the Lord gave Job twice as much as he had before (Job 42:10).

Job received restoration even beyond his greatest expectation, as Paul wrote in Ephesians 3:20 – it was "exceedingly abundantly above all that we ask or think."

God replaced Job's children with seven sons and three daughters (Job 42:13). You may remember that Job's wife came to him and said, "Why don't you just curse God and die?" (Job 2:9). I don't know about you, but I don't think it was *that* wife that he had ten more kids with! I think God gave him one or two more wives! (This was permitted in Old Testament times.)

Job had a full restoration of his family, his heritage, and his health; plus everything he owned was doubled. Job now had twice as much, simply because of a change of heart.

THE LORD GIVES – AND DOES NOT TAKE AWAY

This clears up one of the most common misunderstandings of Job, where people think, "Well, the Lord gives, and the Lord takes away." Although this *is* a scripture and it is an *accurate record* of what Job actually said, we have seen that it is *not the truth*. In fact, this is the biggest lie recorded in the Bible! As Job discovered, the

Lord gives; Satan takes away; then the Lord gives again!

People still use this verse at funerals. When they do, I feel like Elihu: I want to get up and slap them! I was at a funeral once, for a child who died. I was sitting next to the associate pastor's wife, and she said, "Well, we will just never understand why the Lord needed that little boy in heaven and why He took him."

I said, "Jesus didn't kill that little boy!"

She quickly responded, "I didn't say that!"

I replied, "You said, 'God took him.' Isn't that the same thing? 'Jesus needed him, so Jesus had to kill him.'"

I was angry! This lack of understanding can't come from the pulpit anymore. This wrong doctrine needs to get straightened out, or people will always labor under doubt and unbelief. They need to have their theological questions answered in a way that will give them faith to be able to rise up and get victory over the devil! God gives and does not take away!

CHAPTER THIRTEEN

WHAT ABOUT PAUL'S "THORN"?

ANOTHER BIG QUESTION PEOPLE ASK concerning God's will to heal is, "What about Paul's thorn in the flesh?"

And lest I should be exalted above measure by the abundance of the revelations, a thorn in the flesh was given to me, a messenger of Satan to buffet me, lest I be exalted above measure (2 Corinthians 12:7).

People reason, "Paul had a thorn in the flesh. He was a great man of God with a terrible, oozing eye disease. And God didn't heal him." That's what people think this scripture is talking about. They argue for the right to be sick because they think Paul was sick. We'll find out that Paul was *not* sick, and we will see what his "thorn" really was: a messenger of Satan.

FIRST: SOME BACKGROUND

But first, a little background: starting in 2 Corinthians 11, Paul was seeking to reestablish his apostleship to the

Corinthians. Other so-called apostles had come to town in Paul's absence. They were taking advantage of the believers and teaching bad doctrine. Paul wrote to the Corinthians, trying to correct these things. First, Paul defended himself: "Listen, do I still have to prove my apostleship to you? I'm the one who preached the gospel to you from the very beginning." Paul was their father in the faith: he shouldn't have to defend his apostleship. But here he is basically saying, "Okay, I'll go ahead and do it. I'll show you how much of an apostle I am, so you will listen to me and trust me. That way, I can lead you back into truth, and not let you be deceived by these others."

So, Paul lists his credentials, followed by a long list of all the hardships he's gone through as an apostle.

> **Are they Hebrews? So am I. Are they Israelites? So am I. Are they the seed of Abraham? So am I. Are they ministers of Christ? – I speak as a fool – I am more: in labors more abundant, in stripes above measure, in prisons more frequently, in deaths often. From the Jews five times I received forty stripes minus one. Three times I was beaten with rods; once I was stoned; three times I was shipwrecked; a night and a day I have been in the deep; in journeys often, in perils of waters, in perils of robbers, in perils of my own countrymen, in perils of the Gentiles, in perils in the city, in perils in the wilderness, in perils in the sea, in perils among false brethren; in weariness and toil, in sleeplessness often, in hunger and thirst, in fastings often, in cold and nakedness....**
>
> **In Damascus the governor, under Aretas the king, was guarding the city of the Damascenes**

with a garrison, desiring to arrest me; but
I was let down in a basket through a window
in the wall, and escaped from his hands
(2 Corinthians 11:22-27,32,33).

THE ABUNDANCE OF THE REVELATIONS

Then, in chapter 12, Paul began to speak of spiritual
things:

It is doubtless not profitable for me to boast. I
will come to visions and revelations of the
Lord: I know a man in Christ who fourteen
years ago – whether in the body I do not know,
or whether out of the body I do not know, God
knows – such a one was caught up to the
third heaven (2 Corinthians 12:1,2).

Here, Paul was talking about himself: he had been
caught up to the third heaven. Paul is telling them, "I don't
want to boast about these things, but you're making me
tell you how I received this revelation of the things of
God. I'm telling you, it's because I have been to heaven.
That's why I know what I'm telling you. You've been
taught some bad things. Let me get your doctrine corrected again."

And I know such a man – whether in the body
or out of the body I do not know, God knows
(2 Corinthians 12:3).

Paul wasn't sure if he was dead at the time he received
this revelation or not; whether he actually left his body and
went to heaven, or if he was just in the realm of the Spirit
and had a vision. Either way, God was able to show him all
these things. It was so real to Paul that he doesn't know if he
left his body, or not. (Later, we will look at a time when

Paul probably *did* leave his body. That was most likely when he had this vision.) Paul continues:

> ...how he was caught up into Paradise and heard inexpressible words, which it is not lawful for a man to utter (2 Corinthians 12:4).

"Not lawful" is an odd translation. It was not against the Law of Moses for Paul to tell of the things he saw. Here are two other translations that help us better understand the original Greek:

> ...that he was caught away to the paradise, and heard unutterable sayings, that it is not possible for man to speak (2 Corinthians 12:4 YLT).

> ...There he heard words that could not be articulated into language; he understood a conversation that did not originate in human thought (2 Corinthians 12:4 MIRROR).

Paul was saying, "You wouldn't understand these heavenly things. I can't even put them into words. They are so incredible, there's no way I could really describe them and lawfully do any justice to what I saw, but let me share with you the things I can."

LEST I SHOULD BE EXALTED ABOVE MEASURE

> Of such a one I will boast; yet of myself I will not boast, except in my infirmities. For though I might desire to boast, I will not be a fool; for I will speak the truth. But I refrain, lest anyone should think of me above what he sees me to be or hears from me (2 Corinthians 12:5,6).

In essence, Paul was saying, "I'm not trying to exalt

myself so you will think I'm in the category of Christ, or that I'm a supernatural being. I'm a regular human being, anointed by the Spirit of God." We can look at people in the Bible – like Moses and Paul – and say, "Oh my gosh! How could we ever possibly measure up? These guys were superhuman!" But when we get to heaven, we may turn a corner and come face-to-face with Moses for the first time. We're in shock – even more so when Moses greets us by name – without the help of a name badge!

Then Moses might say, "I'm just a person like you. God happened to use me, and it was recorded in the Bible. But He used *you* in *your* generation and it's also recorded in heaven. We've been watching from up here, watching what your generation of believers have been doing. You were doing the same things we did: simply obeying the Lord and flowing in the anointing of the Holy Spirit.

And lest I should be exalted above measure by the abundance of the revelations... (2 Corinthians 12:7a).

In other words, "I had all these revelations, and guess what? By the abundance of these revelations, there was a plan for me to be exalted."

Think about this: who's the one who exalts? The Lord – He is the only one who can exalt. It was *God's* plan to exalt Paul, but *Satan* didn't want Paul to be exalted. Why? Because if Paul were exalted, he would have a bigger platform and be able to reach more people. He would have a larger sphere of influence. Fortunately, Paul realized that Satan was warring against God's plan.

The opposition came to Paul because of his great understanding of the Scripture from the Old Testament and the revelation of the new covenant that the Lord was giving him. Paul received an understanding of all that

Jesus had fulfilled. He understood that the Jews were no longer under the Law contained in ordinances. They were no longer required to make ceremonial offerings, because Jesus was the final offering. Animal sacrifices could never pay for their sins: the animal sacrifices would only "cover" their sins for a year. But Jesus offered Himself: He was the perfect, human sacrifice of the new covenant. Now - for those who receive Him - their sins have been eradicated, done away with, forever. Paul understood this, and that's why he faced such strong opposition.

> **...a thorn in the flesh was given to me, a messenger of Satan to buffet me... (2 Corinthians 12:7b).**

The Greek word for "messenger" here is *angelos*, translated 179 times as "angel" and 7 times as "messenger." Most times, *angelos* refers to one of God's messengers, but sometimes it refers to one of the devil's messengers. Paul clearly said this was a messenger of Satan, a demon spirit - or perhaps a fallen angel - who was assigned to him to stir up the Jews against him.

> **...lest I be exalted above measure (2 Corinthians 12:7c).**

A lot of people think God sent this thorn in the flesh to Paul so he wouldn't get "a big head" and be exalted above measure by all the revelations he received. How stupid would it be for God to give Paul an abundance of revelation and then say, "Now, Paul, I don't want you to get a big head because I gave you all these revelations. I don't want you to be effective in telling people all this truth that I've given you. So I'm going to make you sick and miserable and shut down your ministry." No, God's not a fool! God knows how to get people out preaching the gospel.

He knows how to get them promoted and exalted, because His job is to give them influence so they are able to reach more people.

GOD EXALTS THE HUMBLE

Take a person like Billy Graham: he was probably one of the most humble people on the planet. God was able to exalt him because Billy Graham humbled himself in the eyes of God. God said, "Let Me give you a worldwide platform to preach on, Billy, because I know you will use it right." More people in America were saved under Billy Graham's ministry than anyone else's. Oral Roberts would probably be second, as they were the big television evangelists for so many years and so many people were saved.

Billy Graham lived to be 99 years old. At one point, the doctors thought Billy had Parkinson's disease, but it was a wrong diagnosis. He regained good health, and at 93, he wrote a new book and developed a new evangelistic plan. Praise God! I love it! It fits right in with our longevity teaching!

Someone once asked Billy, "What is the first thing you want to ask God when you see Him face-to-face?"

Billy said, "That's easy! I'm going to ask Him, "Why me? I don't see at all why You would have chosen me, but I'd like to know!" That's humility! The Bible says when you humble yourself in the sight of God, He will lift you up. He will exalt you.

Therefore humble yourselves under the mighty hand of God, that He may exalt you in due time (1 Peter 5:6).

Humble yourselves in the sight of the Lord, and He will lift you up (James 4:10).

By the time Paul wrote the various epistles, he was a humble man. God wanted to exalt him; it was Satan who did not want Paul to be exalted, and who stirred up such tremendous opposition to his ministry.

MY STRENGTH IS MADE PERFECT IN WEAKNESS

Concerning this thing I pleaded with the Lord three times that it might depart from me. And He said to me, "My grace is sufficient for you, for My strength is made perfect in weakness." Therefore most gladly I will rather boast in my infirmities... (2 Corinthians 12:8,9a).

The Greek word for both "weakness" and "infirmities" in the above verse is *astheneia,* which means feebleness, strengthlessness or weakness. It is used 24 times in the New Testament: it is translated 17 times as "infirmity;" 5 times as "weakness; and only 1 time as "disease" or "sickness."

Astheneia comes from a compound word which literally means "without strength." "Infirmity" is not a sickness or disease; it is simply a lack of strength. In this sense, infirmity is common to all humans. It means any kind of weakness that we might experience, when opposition comes our way.

In other words, none of us are totally strong against *everything - all* the time. Brother Hagin used to tell us, "The crisis of life is going to come to everybody." Everyone is going to have some challenges at some point in time. How we handle those challenges all depends on what we believe: what part of God's Word we have meditated upon and come into faith concerning. Then we can pray the prayer of faith, believe, and receive.

As Paul tells us here, we overcome all weaknesses and all opposition with God's grace. God, in His grace and mercy, has given us another way for us to overcome any weakness.

In addition to His Word, God has also given us a secret weapon: praying in tongues. This is how the Holy Spirit helps us in our weaknesses:

> **Likewise the Spirit also helps in our weaknesses. For we do not know what we should pray for as we ought, but the Spirit Himself makes intercession for us with groanings which cannot be uttered. Now He who searches the hearts knows what the mind of the Spirit is, because He makes intercession for the saints according to the will of God (Romans 8:26,27).**

Here, our "weaknesses" are simply the human condition of not knowing how to pray the prayer of faith in every situation. So what do we do? We pray in the Spirit, in tongues: then we know that we're praying the perfect prayer according to the will of God, a faith-filled prayer that will get results.

A DEEPER EXPERIENCE OF THE POWER OF CHRIST

> **...that the power of Christ may rest upon me. Therefore I take pleasure in infirmities, in reproaches, in needs, in persecutions, in distresses, for Christ's sake. For when I am weak, then I am strong (2 Corinthians 12:9b,10).**

Taking pleasure in tough situations is so foreign to human logic and reasoning. We think, "Really, Paul? You take pleasure is hardships? You enjoy them?"

Let's look at this important passage in other translations:

Three times I begged the Lord for it to leave

me, but his reply has been, "My grace is enough for you: for where there is weakness, my power is shown the more completely." Therefore, I have cheerfully made up my mind to be proud of my weaknesses, because they mean a deeper experience of the power of Christ. I can even enjoy weaknesses, suffering, privations, persecutions and difficulties for Christ's sake. For my very weakness makes me strong in him (2 Corinthians 12:8-10 PHILLIPS).

...for when I am weak [in human strength], then am I [truly] strong (able, powerful in divine strength) (2 Corinthians 12:10b AMPC).

So I will celebrate my weaknesses, for when I'm weak I sense more deeply the mighty power of Christ living in me. So I'm not defeated by my weakness, but delighted! For when I feel my weakness and endure mistreatment – when I'm surrounded with troubles on every side and face persecution because of my love for Christ – I am made yet stronger. For my weakness becomes a portal to God's power (2 Corinthians 12:9,10 TPT).

Paul learned to "take pleasure in his weaknesses," to celebrate them. This reminds me of what James wrote in James 1:2:

My brethren, count it all joy when you fall into various trials.

Paul and James were cut of the same cloth! They both realized, "Hey, when we get a lot of opposition, that just means God is getting ready to move, big time! We are going to see great fruit!" They had great expectation when the opposition came. They knew that meant it was time for a big upgrade in miraculous help. They said, "Man, look out! God is getting ready to do miraculous things! I'm happy to go through this opposition because I know the miracles are on the other side of this test and trial!" We will take a detailed look at this passage from James a little later, but for now, we can celebrate with Paul and James, because Satan's plans always backfire on him! Hallelujah!

WHAT IS A "THORN IN THE FLESH"?

Now let's look carefully at the biblical meaning of the phrase, "a thorn in the flesh." We find this phrase or something similar to it throughout Scripture, including: "thorns in the flesh," "thorns in the sides," and "thorns in the eyes."

Moses wrote of them in Numbers 33:55:

"But if you do not drive out the inhabitants of the land from before you, then it shall be that those whom you let remain shall be irritants in your eyes and thorns in your sides, and they shall harass you in the land where you dwell."

God was talking here about people, personalities. If Israel didn't drive these inhabitants out, they would become "thorns in your sides."

Joshua spoke of "scourges on your sides and thorns in your eyes" in Joshua 23:11-13:

"Know for certain that the Lord your God will no longer drive out these nations from before you. But they shall be snares and traps to you, and scourges on your sides and thorns in your eyes, until you perish from this good land

which the Lord your God has given you."

In these two passages, God was giving His people very strong instructions to drive the other nations out of the Promise Land. Israel decided they didn't want to keep fighting; they wanted to compromise on what God told them to do. Joshua prophesied, "Here's what's going to happen: these people will be a problem to you, like a "thorn in the flesh."

An angel spoke of "thorns" in Judges 2:3:

"Therefore I also said, 'I will not drive them out before you; but they shall be thorns in your side, and their gods shall be a snare to you.'"

The angel is talking here about people who served false, foreign gods - those gods would prove to be a snare to Israel.

David wrote of "thorns" in 2 Samuel 23:6.

"But the sons of rebellion shall all be as thorns thrust away, Because they cannot be taken with hands."

In every one of these passages, "thorns" were *personalities,* not diseases. These personalities brought opposition to Israel. In Paul's case, the personality was a demon spirit who continually stirred up the Jews against him. Paul had such a love for the Jews that he would go to the Jews first, in every city he visited. Sometimes a few Jews would believe the gospel, but most rejected his message. Paul would then go to preach to the Gentiles. A demon spirit would stir up the Jews in every place Paul went, and before long, the Jews would start to oppose him - often violently! We will take a deeper look at the reasons for Paul's afflictions of persecution later.

SATAN COULD NOT STOP PAUL

This demon spirit was not able to stop Paul. Even with opposition from the devil, God has a plan to make all things work together for good if you are in God's will and love Him. Paul wrote:

And we know that all things work together for good to those who love God, to those who are the called according to His purpose (Romans 8:28).

God has a way of turning everything back on the devil, making him sorry that he ever opposed us, because he ends up looking like a fool in the long run.

DON'T LET SATAN STEAL GOD'S WORD

Paul said the "thorn" was sent because of the abundance of revelation given to him. This is because Satan always comes to steal the Word.

"The sower soweth the word. And these are the ones by the wayside where the word is sown. When they hear, Satan comes immediately and takes away the word that was sown in their hearts" (Mark 4:14,15).

Satan also tries to steal God's Word from the hearts of those who need healing by distracting them with other things to think about and do, things that he can magnify and make seem so urgent. But we can steadfastly resist him and hold fast to God's Word, meditate on it, let it build faith in us...and get healed every time!

CHAPTER FOURTEEN

WHAT ABOUT PAUL'S "EYE DISEASE"?

IN GALATIANS 4:13, PAUL MENTIONS a "physical infirmity" that he had:

> **You know that because of physical infirmity I preached the gospel to you at the first. And my trial which was in my flesh you did not despise or reject, but you received me as an angel of God, even as Christ Jesus. What then was the blessing you enjoyed? For I bear you witness that, if possible, you would have plucked out your own eyes and given them to me (Galatians 4:13-15).**

DID PAUL HAVE AN EYE DISEASE?

Because Paul mentioned his eyes in this passage, some say Paul's infirmity was a kind of eye problem or disease. Many Bible commentaries say that Paul suffered from a disease called *ophthalmia,* which is highly contagious and results in excessive yellow or green oozing discharge from the eyes. Of course, someone with this condition would be awful to look at. But apparently the Galatians opened their hearts to Paul and were greatly moved with compassion for his condition.

WHAT REALLY HAPPENED

So, did Paul have an eye disease? No! I believe this is what happened. On Paul's first missionary journey, he preached in Galatia, which is a region of Asia Minor which is modern-day Turkey. In the city of Lystra, he was stoned by the Jews and left for dead.

> **Then Jews from Antioch and Iconium came there; and having persuaded the multitudes, they stoned Paul and dragged him out of the city, supposing him to be dead. However, when the disciples gathered around him, he rose up and went into the city. And the next day he departed with Barnabas to Derbe (Acts 14:19,20).**

After the disciples traveling with Paul gathered around him and prayed, "he rose up." The Greek word here is *anistemi.* It is translated "arise," "rise up," and "stand up." It was used many times by Jesus in reference to His own resurrection from the dead, as well as in gospel accounts of people raised from the dead. I believe this is when Paul had his great revelation and was caught up to the third heaven (2 Corinthians 12:2). We mentioned earlier that the experience was so real that Paul didn't know whether he had died or not. I personally believe he actually died and went to heaven and saw the amazing things he later wrote about in his letters to the Ephesians and the Colossians: the "mysteries" of the riches of the inheritance of the saints, the exceeding greatness of the power of God within us, and all the "in Him" realities.

The disciples took Paul back into Lystra to recover.

Then, amazingly, the next day, Paul and Barnabas went to Derbe, which was about 60 miles away! Later, they returned to Lystra, then went back to all the other places they had been and preached the gospel to the rest of Galatia again.

> **And when they had preached the gospel to that city and made many disciples, they returned to Lystra, Iconium, and Antioch, strengthening the souls of the disciples, exhorting them to continue in the faith, and saying, "We must through many tribulations enter the kingdom of God" (Acts 14:21,22).**

In my thinking, some of the same people who stoned Paul to death were still there when he came back to Lystra. People back then knew how to stone people - they knew what they were doing. They were sure they had stoned him to death, but, all of a sudden, he's back! I'm sure they were shocked! I believe this struck the fear of God in them!

His physical appearance after being stoned and left for dead was most likely what Paul referred to as his "physical infirmity" in Galatians 4:13. Someone with this condition would also be awful to look at! Yet here's how the Amplified Bible describes the reaction of the Galatians to Paul:

> **...You know that it was on account of a bodily ailment that [I remained and] preached the Gospel to you the first time. And [yet] although my physical condition was [such] a trial to you, you did not regard it with contempt, or scorn and loathe and reject me; but you received me as an angel of God, [even] as Christ Jesus [Himself]! (Galatians 4:13,14 AMPC).**

I believe the Galatians received Paul "as an angel of God" because he'd been raised from the dead! They received him "even as Christ Jesus Himself"!

So, what about Paul's "eye disease?" He had been stoned to death and had been hit on his face and head, repeatedly, with rocks. I'm sure that his eyes must have still been a bruised and swollen mess. Even though he was raised from the dead, everything about his face must have still been horrible to look at! Yet, people take from this letter that Paul had a contagious eye disease. To me, that's really a stretch, when you think about it.

PAUL HAD A POWERFUL MINISTRY OF FAITH AND HEALING

Paul was not sick with some kind of an eye disease! Paul walked in a strong anointing, and special miracles were wrought through his ministry. How could a man burdened with a painful and disgusting eye disease walk in such a powerful healing ministry? Acts 19:11,12 tells us:

Now God worked unusual miracles by the hands of Paul, so that even handkerchiefs or aprons were brought from his body to the sick, and the diseases left them and the evil spirits went out of them.

If this man had a contagious disease with yellow discharge coming out of his eyes, would you want a handkerchief that's been hanging on his body? You would assume that he had probably been wiping his eyes with it! Yuck! How can people say, "Paul was a miserable, sick man, yet all these healings took place. He could just send his old handkerchiefs to people and everyone would be delivered and healed." It doesn't match up. No, Paul had to walk in great health, in order to survive what he survived: the man was a mighty champion – like a gladiator for the kingdom of God – to survive what he suffered.

Paul was the greatest teacher of all scriptural authors concerning faith in God and the fulfillment of His covenant promises. It would be highly unlikely for the greatest faith teacher of all time – except for Jesus Himself – to be unable to receive healing for his own body. Paul was the man inspired to write Romans 10:8-10:

> **But what does it say? "The word is near you, in your mouth and in your heart" (that is, the word of faith which we preach): That if you confess with your mouth the Lord Jesus and believe in your heart that God has raised Him from the dead, you will be saved. For with the heart one believes unto righteousness, and with the mouth confession is made unto salvation.**

Paul also wrote Romans 10:17:

> **So then faith comes by hearing, and hearing by the word of God.**

The man wrote the book on faith! How could he not have used faith to maintain his own healing and health? It's just such a flimsy theory when you really look at it and unfold the history of what actually happened when Paul was stoned and left for dead.

CHAPTER FIFTEEN

WHAT ABOUT PAUL'S "INFIRMITY"?

A NOTHER TIME PAUL MENTIONS AN "INFIRMITY" is in 2 Corinthians 11:30:

If I must boast, I will boast in the things which concern my infirmity.

The Greek word for "boast" here is used 38 times in the New Testament and is most often translated as "glory" (23 times), "boast" (8 times), and "rejoice" (4 times).

BOASTING ABOUT THE "INFIRMITIES" OF PERSECUTION

Paul makes this statement right after the long list of hardships he had suffered for the gospel that we read earlier in 2 Corinthians 11:23-29. These include being whipped "above measure," being imprisoned frequently, receiving 39 stripes five times, being beaten with rods three times, being shipwrecked three times, being stoned and left for dead, plus being in constant danger as he travelled, often hungry, thirsty, and cold. In context, it's clear to see that Paul was boasting here about the "infirmities" of persecution – not sickness. The Jews believed Paul was teaching against Moses and against the prophets and the Law, so they would run him out of town. Paul eventually caught on and stopped going to the Jews first.

It's interesting that Paul's list includes a lot more hardships than the few recorded in the Book of Acts. Much of the incredible opposition that Paul faced was because he was so entrenched in the leadership of the Jewish nation. To them, he was a total turncoat, a "Benedict Arnold." That's why they opposed him everywhere he went.

We know that Paul went back to Tarsus, his hometown, for a period of time. Paul had been raised and educated to be a member of the Council of the Sanhedrin. His family was wealthy – they bought their Roman citizenship. His father was the ruler of the synagogue in Tarsus and had invested so much in Paul becoming a member of the Sanhedrin. Paul had his own set of scrolls of all the Old Testament Scriptures, and he was a student of Gamaliel, a greatly-respected teacher in Jerusalem. In fact, Paul was one of Gamaliel's premier students, a genius in the Word of God.

Paul had done everything necessary, according to the Law and the traditions, to be on the Council of the Sanhedrin. One of the requirements was to be married. I believe Paul had been married, but when he became a Christian, he was suddenly a total disgrace to the family, and his wife left him because of his faith in Jesus. It is also likely that at least one of the five times Paul received 39 stripes from the Jews happened in Tarsus, by his own father's order.

And yet, Paul was willing to keep preaching the gospel to the Jews. He loved these people! However, God called him to be the Apostle to the Gentiles (Acts 9:15). This is how it came about: Barnabas invited Paul to come to

Antioch (Acts 11:25), where the church was growing rapidly among the Greek population (Acts 11:20-22). Paul accepted Barnabas' invitation and then helped him establish the church in Antioch (Acts 11:26). That's where God later spoke and sent Paul and Barnabas out to take the gospel to the rest of the world (Acts 13:2,3). We have seen how the demon spirit followed them and stirred up trouble for them everywhere they went.

Paul wrote about the toll all these hardships of persecution took on his body:

Therefore we do not lose heart. Even though our outward man is perishing, yet the inward man is being renewed day by day (2 Corinthians 4:16).

If you have experienced all these terrible things, you realize your outward man is perishing! Paul was a scarred man! But he says, "Our inward man is being renewed day by day." He continues:

For our light affliction, which is but for a moment, is working for us a far more exceeding and eternal weight of glory, while we do not look at the things which are seen, but at the things which are not seen. For the things which are seen are temporary, but the things which are not seen are eternal (2 Corinthians 4:17,18).

Paul called these hardships "light afflictions" compared to the "eternal weight of glory" that we would receive. What a perspective! He says it doesn't matter what we go through: we're amassing for ourselves a reward in heaven when we face these trials and press through them all.

PAUL'S DEEP CONCERN FOR THE CHURCHES

Paul continues to talk about his "infirmity" in 2 Corinthians 11:28,29:

...besides the other things, what comes upon me daily: my deep concern for all the churches.

Who is weak, and I am not weak? Who is made to stumble, and I do not burn with indignation?

Paul was interceding through this whole time for every church that he had established, desirous that every one of them would be completely established in the things of God. Paul also deeply sympathized with their feelings: like Jesus, he was "touched with the feelings of their infirmities" (Hebrews 4:15 KJV).

GOD'S GRACE WAS SUFFICIENT FOR PAUL

We have seen that Paul sought the Lord three times to have the demon removed that was oppressing his ministry. Then God said to him:

"My grace is sufficient for you" (2 Corinthians 12:9).

I believe this is what God was saying, "My grace is sufficient for you, Paul. You're going to get this. You're going to figure this out! You will learn to rise up in authority over this demon spirit, and you're going to get the results I have planned for you."

You see, Paul was growing too: as much as he knew, as much as he was already "out there" with spiritual revelations, we can see his spiritual growth in his letters. He just keeps getting more and more insight: it's like faith on steroids! Paul learned to use his shield of faith to quench the devil's fiery darts (Ephesians 6:16).

Paul was becoming such a faith giant that it didn't stop him even when he was imprisoned in Rome: in fact, he wrote his greatest faith letters while he was in prison! At the end of the Book of Acts, we read that Paul was actually under "house arrest," and it only lasted for two years, then he was released (Acts 28:30). Acts does not mention Paul's second Roman imprisonment. We only hear that he was imprisoned there again when he wrote to Timothy in 2 Timothy 1:8:

> **Therefore do not be ashamed of the testimony of our Lord, nor of me His prisoner.**

Later, in that same letter, Paul wrote:

> **I have fought the good fight, I have finished the race, I have kept the faith. Finally, there is laid up for me the crown of righteousness (2 Timothy 4:7,8a).**

At that point in time, Paul was ready to go. He knew he'd accomplished everything God had asked him to do. Years earlier, he had written to the church at Philippi:

> **For I am hard-pressed between the two, having a desire to depart and be with Christ, which is far better. Nevertheless to remain in the flesh is more needful for you. And being confident of this, I know that I shall remain and continue with you all for your progress and joy of faith (Philippians 1:23-25).**

Paul didn't leave early: he kept on until he knew that he had written everything that he was supposed to write, he had been everywhere he was supposed to go, and he was free to go home to be with the Lord. Paul did not die young. He finished his race.

I believe that when you look at all of the evidence, you have to conclude that Paul was not sick. This great faith teacher had enough faith to be able to receive his own healing and walk in divine health. God's grace was sufficient. Paul was able to finish all that God called him to do.

A DUAL MEANING

Here, I would like to point out that the statement "My grace is sufficient for you" has a second meaning for Paul. You see, Paul feared that all of his apostolic work might be in vain. In fact, he mentioned this several times in his letters.

Twice, he mentioned running in vain:

And I went up by revelation, and communicated to them that gospel which I preach among the Gentiles, but privately to those who were of reputation, lest by any means I might run, or had run, in vain (Galatians 2:2).

Do all things without complaining and disputing...holding fast the word of life, so that I may rejoice in the day of Christ that I have not run in vain or labored in vain (Philippians 2:14,16).

Twice, he mentioned laboring in vain:

I am afraid for you, lest I have labored for you in vain (Galatians 4:11).

For this reason, when I could no longer endure it, I sent to know your faith, lest by some

means the tempter had tempted you, and our labor might be in vain (1 Thessalonians 3:5).

Paul was always concerned, wherever he preached the gospel, that believers would be established in their faith. He wanted to make sure that the churches were also established and strong and that they would last, even if he couldn't go back to visit them. Here, God is saying, "Paul, don't worry. My grace is sufficient. Your work will last." Three hundred years after Paul's death, every church that he established was still in existence. I'd say he got the job done!

OUR FAITH IN GOD'S GRACE

The Lord spoke to me while we were in prayer one day and said, "My grace is sufficient for you, and *your faith in My grace* is sufficient for *Me*." I thought about that, and I realized God was letting me know how much our faith means to Him. We put faith in His grace and that's all He needs: it *satisfies* Him. In other words, He was saying, "Thank you for putting faith in My grace. That's all I needed! Now I can do the miracle! Just hide and watch. I'll do wondrous things because you understand what I need: I just need your faith in My grace! That's sufficient for Me." I thought that was a really neat twist on the fulfillment of "My grace is sufficient for you," that His grace is all we need. It's so good to know that our faith in His grace is sufficient for Him. It's what He needs!

THE PROBLEM DOES NOT COME FROM GOD

It's important to realize that our problem or temptation does not come from God. The Bible assures us this is true! Earlier, we saw that James said to be joyful in tough times. Let's look closely at *why* and *how* we do that.

My brethren, count it all joy when you fall into

various trials, knowing that the testing of your faith produces patience. But let patience have its perfect work, that you may be perfect and complete, lacking nothing. If any of you lacks wisdom, let him ask of God, who gives to all liberally and without reproach, and it will be given to him (James 1:2-5).

In other words, you can inquire of the Lord: if you seek the Lord, He will answer you. He wants to talk to you and give you the answers as you go.

Blessed is the man who endures temptation; for when he has been approved, he will receive the crown of life which the Lord has promised to those who love Him (James 1:12).

Guess what? As you go through this life as a Christian, opposing the opposition of the devil, you develop spiritually. You learn to "pass the test": you overcome the devil; you push him back; and you are approved! You get an A+. And then you get an eternal reward for all the opposition you overcame and all you accomplished that the Lord directed you to do.

Let no one say when he is tempted, "I am tempted by God"; for God cannot be tempted by evil, nor does He Himself tempt anyone. But each one is tempted when he is drawn away by his own desires and enticed. Then, when desire has conceived, it gives birth to sin; and sin, when it is full-grown, brings forth death. Do not be deceived, my beloved brethren (James 1:13-16).

Resisting sin is dying to the flesh and that's the one suffering the Lord asks us to do. We resist sin, come out victorious, and receive the "crown of life."

Every good gift and every perfect gift is from above, and comes down from the Father of lights, with whom there is no variation or shadow of turning (James 1:17).

All the good things come from God. All the bad things come from the devil. God cannot be tempted by evil, nor does He Himself tempt anyone. So, run from all the bad things; resist the temptations. God's going to be there, faithfully waiting for you.

THROUGH FAITH AND PATIENCE WE INHERIT THE PROMISES

Hebrews 6:12 says:

Through faith and patience we inherit the promises.

Patience is so important! In walking with the Lord since November 1973, and in the ministry since 1975, I've learned that there's a lot of opposition – but you overcome: over...and over...and over again. Then, God tells you, "I've got a crown of life stored up for you because you keep on going – like the Energizer Bunny! Keep trusting Me from the Word and I'll keep fulfilling all My promises in your life." The fact that we are going to have to exercise patience along with faith shouldn't be a big surprise to us. It just comes with life: it takes patience for some prayers to be answered. It can take awhile before God manifests everything, between when you say, "Amen!" and when you can say, "There it is!" Now, the good thing about believing for healing is that we often see healing manifested quickly. That's why I believe receiving healing is one of the quickest answers to prayer that we can receive.

CHAPTER SIXTEEN

WHAT ABOUT TIMOTHY'S STOMACH?

IN PAUL'S TRAVELS, HE WAS OFTEN ACCOMPANIED by Luke, the physician, and was quite familiar with helpful natural and medical remedies. He told Timothy:

> **No longer drink only water, but use a little wine for your stomach's sake and your frequent infirmities (1 Timothy 5:23).**

Apparently, Timothy was coming down with weaknesses every now and then, so Paul wrote, "Drink some wine also." Note: You will lose the argument that it's not biblical to drink wine: Jesus drank wine and the disciples all drank wine. But when Paul wrote this to Timothy, some people must have started to come up with the idea that believers should abstain from wine. The Bible does say, "Wine is a mocker" (Proverbs 20:1), so, obviously being drunk and becoming an alcoholic is completely negative.

I believe it's probably best if we have an alcohol-free environment for people who are weak in this area. We don't want people who are "on the wagon" to fall "off the wagon"! I have no problem with not being a drinker. I'm just saying you will lose the argument if you want to argue whether or not it's okay for Christians to drink wine.

A NATUROPATHIC REMEDY

As a physician, Luke had mostly naturopathic remedies, using things that were available to them. We now know that, once inside the body, the organic compounds found in wine kill germs. So, wine was probably helpful for a stomach in distress. Paul was careful to give wise counsel concerning spiritual matters and their application and saw no conflict between faith and common sense. Thus, Timothy could be an "example in faith" and also use medicine.

Let no one despise your youth, but be an example to the believers in word, in conduct, in love, in spirit, in faith, in purity (1 Timothy 4:12).

Timothy was a great help to Paul. He accompanied Paul on his second missionary journey and was with him in Corinth, Macedonia, Ephesus, and Jerusalem. Timothy is mentioned as being with Paul when Paul wrote several New Testament letters, including Romans, 2 Corinthians, Philippians, Colossians, 1 and 2 Thessalonians, and Philemon. Paul sent Timothy as his emissary to the churches at Corinth and at Philippi. Later, Timothy pastored the church in Ephesus. We know that Timothy was a champion of faith, just like Paul, his father in the faith.

CHAPTER SEVENTEEN

WHAT ABOUT MARTYRS?

IS THERE A DIFFERENCE BETWEEN DYING for one's faith and dying from illness or an accident? What about someone who is out on the cutting edge, completely in the appointed place where God wants them to be, and they die as a martyr for refusing to deny that Jesus is their Lord?

In recent years, Islamic State of Iraq and Syria (ISIS) rebels, who were trying to overthrow the government in Syria, had terrorists from *Al Qaeda* among them. They attacked one of the Christian towns in Syria and burned down 50 Christian churches, killing thousands and thousands of Arabs who had become Christians, even though they had converted many years before. The *jihadists* killed them all: they called them "infidels." As I write this, the public threat of ISIS has largely subsided. Yet, Christians in Syria are always aware that – on any day – they could be martyred for their faith in the Lord Jesus.

Open Doors Ministries keeps a "World Watch List," which shows the top 50 countries where it is most difficult to follow Jesus. They report that in 2021, the persecution of Christians had reached the highest levels since the

World Watch List began, nearly 30 years ago. They say:

>   Across 76 countries, more than 360 million Christians, 1 in 7 believers, suffer high levels of persecution and discrimination for their faith – an increase of 20 million since last year.

>   An average of 13 Christians are killed every day. That's nearly 400 Christians dying every month. Just because they follow Jesus.

>   These are staggering and sobering statistics.

A GREAT REVIVAL IN IRAN!

Yet, God can bring good out of evil. Dr. Coflin, an LCU professor and Vice President of LCU, was recently on a mission trip with "A Time of Refreshing," a ministry which brings missionaries from Europe and Asia Minor to Switzerland to minister to them for a week. Dr. Coflin got to know a missionary couple who are ministering in Turkey. They asked him, "Do you know where the greatest revival is going on in the earth today? There's a huge underground Church and a huge revival happening in Iran!" They said, "Iran today is like China was, 20 years ago, when the underground Church got so huge in China." (The Chinese Church is still there and still strong, but twenty years ago, they were in the great revival that was bringing huge numbers of people into the Church in China.) These missionaries said, "Iran is going through a huge revival and the people are terribly persecuted for their faith in Christ. They are disowned by their families, and if anybody finds out that they are a Christian, it's merciless." Yet, the Church there continues to grow.

The missionaries in Turkey who told this story have been there for over 30 years, and God has constantly protected them. They relate how they seek His specific guidance, many times, every day. I believe you can go anywhere in the world, when you know, that you know, that you know, that God has told you to go there to do a specific ministry. I thank God that He has not sent me into Arab Muslim countries where I could die for my faith, but I *do* have influence in the lives and ministries of many, many people who are now born again, including former Muslims in Africa, who are being used by God in a mighty way to win people to Jesus, as well as former Hindus and witch doctors in India, who are now pastors there!

SOME MISSIONARIES MAY HAVE DIED UNNECESSARILY

Sad to say, it is possible that some Christian missionaries have acted foolishly or in presumption – rather than in wisdom and true faith – and have died unnecessarily. For example, entering into dangerous areas without hearing directly from the Lord, that they should go there, and that they would be protected. Or, overloading aircraft beyond their capacities, or flying into extreme weather conditions on the erroneous assumption that God has to override natural laws, because they were doing ministry business. I personally know some marvelous men and women of God who have died in these situations.

He who leans on, trusts in, and is confident of his own mind and heart is a [self-confident] fool, but he who walks in skillful and godly Wisdom shall be delivered (Proverbs 28:26 AMP).

IS THERE ALWAYS A WAY OF ESCAPE?

Can a person have enough faith so as not to be martyred? Can they believe God to always provide a way of escape for them? Just like Shadrach, Meshach, and

Abednego, Church history tells us that the Roman emperor Domitian commanded the Apostle John to be boiled to death in oil, but he wasn't harmed. In fact, he continued to preach from within the pot! And, just like Daniel in the lion's den, there were early Christians whom the lions would not harm in the Roman Colosseum. We have seen that Paul was stoned and raised back to life. The murderous actions of satanically-driven men were not effective against these believers. Yet, Stephen was stoned and died, and James, the brother of John, was executed by Herod.

Who is delivered, and who is not delivered, is a mystery.

THERE IS A DIFFERENCE

To sum this all up, yes, there is a difference between dying for one's faith and dying from illness or an accident. I believe this about any true martyr: they have run their race and finished their course, and are choosing not to be delivered, just like Paul, Peter, the other original disciples (except John), and many leaders of the first-century Church. That's *not* the case in cities where *all* the Christians are being killed by radical Muslims. That is mass murder. Still, I believe these Christians qualify to receive a martyr's crown: if they were killed for their faith, they will receive something special in heaven.

The Lord Jesus told the church at Smyrna:

Do not fear any of those things which you are about to suffer. Indeed, the devil is about to throw some of you into prison, that you may be tested, and you will have tribulation ten days. Be faithful until death, and I will give you the crown of life (Revelation 2:10).

And, whether a person is martyred or dying for missing God's will and wisdom, it is not our business to judge.

206

That which is not revealed to us is known only between God and each one of His ministers.

"The secret things belong to the Lord our God, but those things which are revealed belong to us and to our children forever, that we may do all the words of this law" (Deuteronomy 29:29).

There are going to be some mysteries we won't understand, but we *can* have enough understanding and enough wisdom about the Word of God to know that - short of martyrdom - it is God's will for us to be healed and walk in divine health, until we are satisfied (Psalm 91:16).

CHAPTER EIGHTEEN

WHY DOESN'T GOD ELIMINATE ALL SICKNESS?

O NE DAY, GOD WILL MAKE A NEW HEAVEN and a new earth.

> **Now I saw a new heaven and a new earth, for the first heaven and the first earth had passed away. Also there was no more sea. Then I, John, saw the holy city, New Jerusalem, coming down out of heaven from God, prepared as a bride adorned for her husband. And I heard a loud voice from heaven saying, "Behold, the tabernacle of God is with men, and He will dwell with them, and they shall be His people. God Himself will be with them and be their God" (Revelation 21:1-3).**

This is a description of what will happen once all the Christians who have ever been saved are all in the city of God, the new Jerusalem. John saw the city descending and coming to the Lord Jesus, being presented to Him "as a bride." Right now, we're the Body of Christ: He's the head, we are the body. There are analogies made to us being married to Christ, symbolically. One day, we will be standing before Him - all of us together - everybody facing Jesus. Then there's going to be the marriage supper of the Lamb; this is the beginning of the eternal feast in heaven. God is a big partier: He always had all kinds of feasts in the Old Testament, and we'll also have a feast in the New Jerusalem!

At that time, there will be no more suffering:

"And God will wipe away every tear from their eyes; there shall be no more death, nor sorrow, nor crying. There shall be no more pain, for the former things have passed away" (Revelation 21:4).

All these works of Satan - tears, death, sorrow, crying, and pain - will be totally eradicated. After that, no human will be subject to sickness and disease, at all. The only problem is, God must eradicate everything with fire. Everything that Satan has touched and caused, all that will be eradicated with fire. As 2 Peter 3:7 tells us:

But the heavens and the earth which are now preserved by the same word, are reserved for fire until the day of judgment and perdition of ungodly men.

God is going to create a new heaven and a new earth (Revelation 21:1). It might be that God creates this "new" earth out of the same planet and calls it "new" afterward. Either way, the earth is going to be judged by fire - there is no question about it. God must eliminate every work of Satan on the earth.

THE LARGER PICTURE

That sounds so good! But here is the larger picture: to

wipe away all sickness, God would need to wipe out all that had been set in motion, concerning our current creation. That would include sending over 5 billion unsaved people to hell, which God is not in a hurry to do, because of His great mercy. As 2 Peter 3:9,10 says:

> **The Lord is not slack concerning His promise, as some count slackness, but is longsuffering toward us, not willing that any should perish but that all should come to repentance. But the day of the Lord will come as a thief in the night, in which the heavens will pass away with a great noise, and the elements will melt with fervent heat; both the earth and the works that are in it will be burned up.**

We *do* know there will be a final judgment: that's the time all sicknesses will be done away with, but every human who is *not* born again is going to be cast into hell on that day. Everyone who is born again will enjoy the great marriage supper of the Lamb, the feast in heaven. So, we just go by what the Word says. We don't make the rules, God does. It's been revealed in Scripture how this is going to come to pass.

CHAPTER NINETEEN

CAN YOU LOSE YOUR HEALING?

WHY DO SOME PEOPLE GET HEALED and then lose their healing? This is a really good question! Many people get healed through the laying on of hands or through the "gifts of healings," which are mentioned in a list of other such spiritual gifts in 1 Corinthians 12:9:

> **To another faith by the same Spirit; to another the gifts of healings by the same Spirit.**

These people are healed as a result of the agreement of their faith and the faith of the one ministering to them. When their symptoms return, if they have not learned personal faith in God's Word concerning healing, they may give in to the sickness again.

Brother Kenneth E. Hagin gave the best illustration I've ever heard concerning the operation of the gifts of healings. He said when he was ministering, that he operated under a special anointing. One day, he had a vision, and the Lord appeared to him and took His finger and put it on the palms of each of Brother Hagin's hands. Jesus said, "I am giving you a special anointing." Brother Hagin's hands began to burn with fire. He said that whenever he was ministering and he felt that fire in his hands, he knew that special anointing to minister with a special gift of healing was in operation. He said he had marvelous success in ministering to anybody who had any kind of tumor. Whether it was a benign or a malignant tumor, he got tremendous results in getting people healed and delivered.

GO, TEACH MY PEOPLE FAITH

During the great healing revival of the 1940s and 50s, there were around 100 healing evangelists crisscrossing America, doing tent revivals. Some were already evangelists traveling from church to church who began to see healings in their services. Some were formerly pastors who had experienced that, suddenly, *everyone* they prayed for in their churches were being healed. They started ministering outside their churches. Before long, they felt like they needed to get as many people healed as they could, so they all bought tents and started traveling from town to town. All kinds of healings were taking place - it was a great revival move of God. These evangelists were operating in the gifts of the Spirit, and they were seeing tremendous results.

Some of these traveling evangelists had not developed Christ-like character. All of a sudden, they were getting rich and famous. If they had *not* determined - at the beginning of their ministry - that they were *not* going to be moved by fame and fortune, they *were changed* by it, and then they lost the anointing. Some of them died young; one was killed in a car wreck. It's only the ones who built their lives on the Word of God who continued on in ministry.

During this great healing revival, many people told Brother Hagin, "You have the same gifts as these healing evangelists and the most incredible demonstrations of the gifts of the Spirit we've seen. You need to have a tent."

Brother Hagin said, "We will pray about it."

As he prayed, he was called by God to teach the Word, hearing an audible voice from God saying, "Go, teach My people faith." He was instructed to stay in the churches, to teach them faith in the morning and do healing services at night. That's what he started doing. He held extended meetings in various churches, ministering in the night services just like all the other healing evangelists who were traveling and doing tent ministry meetings. He operated in the same gifts of the Spirit as the other healing evangelists. But he also told people, "Come to my day meetings where I'm teaching faith, so that you will be established in faith for your healing. Then, in the night services, we will lay hands on the sick, for you to receive your healing." He wanted them to know how to exercise their *own* faith and *keep* their healing.

BEAT OUT OF LIFE BY LYING SYMPTOMS

Brother Hagin told the story of two different ladies, from two different towns. Both had been diagnosed by their doctors as having terminal, cancerous tumors. But one of the ladies came to *every one* of the *day* service, for three or four weeks. She didn't miss a single service: she heard the Word, she took notes, and she learned God's Word concerning healing. The other lady only came to the *night* services. Both were healed in a night service when Brother Hagin was ministering, and the special gift of the Spirit was in operation. Both ladies got a clean bill of health from their doctors, stating they were completely cancer-free.

Later, the lady who had only attended the *night* meetings started having symptoms again: she started feeling a

Divine Healing & Health

lump. She said, "I guess that old cancer has come back on me again," and she died. The other woman, when she started having the same symptoms and felt a lump in the same place, she said, "Oh, no you don't devil! I'm one up on you now! I know 'By His stripes I was healed.' I have been healed! You're not going to put that back on me! Just get out of here with all your cancer. It's yours, it's not mine!" She refused to receive it...and she lived!

The doctors of the first woman were concerned, because they had confirmed that she been had healed of cancer, but then she suddenly died. So, they did an autopsy on her. As it turned out, *she didn't even have cancer!* She let the devil beat her out of life with lying symptoms. She just laid down and died because she didn't know how to stand by faith, knowing the Word. When the symptoms came again, she died without even having cancer!

TURN BACK THE ATTACK!

That's amazing to me! It's a perfect illustration of why we need the Word of God. We pump the Word into ourselves concerning healing, so we can *receive* divine healing and *keep it.* Then, we come to the place where we can *walk* in divine health.

Everyone comes under attack - there's no question about it - but you can turn sickness back, quickly. You just keep resisting the devil and pushing the lying symptoms away. When I found out I could turn a cold back in a couple of hours, I said, "This is cool. I like being able to do this!"

CHAPTER TWENTY

DOES SICKNESS TEACH, CORRECT, OR PERFECT US?

T HE ANSWER TO THIS QUESTION is "Absolutely no!" Sickness is not our teacher.

THE HOLY SPIRIT IS OUR TEACHER

The Holy Spirit is our teacher: He will teach us all things - everything we need to learn! Jesus said in John 14:26:

"But the Helper, the Holy Spirit, whom the Father will send in My name, He will teach you all things, and bring to your remembrance all things that I said to you."

If Jesus said it's the Holy Spirit who is going to teach you all things, then there's no one else who is going to teach you the things you need to know. It's not going to be sickness and disease that teaches you! It's not by going to the hospital and then praying and reading the Word. You can learn to hear from God without going to the hospital, if you will just get into the Word! Make yourself desperate for the Word - get hungry on your own. Don't do it out of desperation, because you neglected God's Word, and all of a sudden you have a crisis.

I'm starting to get so irate about modern preachers telling other Christians, "If you pray in tongues today, it's from the devil. It's a demonic spirit that's causing you to pray in tongues."

This same thing happened in Jesus' day: the Pharisees said Jesus cast out demons by Beelzebub, the ruler of the demons. Jesus said that calling the work of the Holy Spirit the work of Satan was blasphemy. Let's look at this story in Matthew's gospel:

> **"And if I cast out demons by Beelzebub, by whom do your sons cast them out?...But if I cast out demons by the Spirit of God, surely the kingdom of God has come upon you....He who is not with Me is against Me, and he who does not gather with Me scatters abroad.**
>
> **"Therefore I say to you, every sin and blasphemy will be forgiven men, but the blasphemy against the Spirit will not be forgiven men. Anyone who speaks a word against the Son of Man, it will be forgiven him; but whoever speaks against the Holy Spirit, it will not be forgiven him, either in this age or in the age to come (Matthew 12:27,28,30-32).**

In other words, Jesus was saying, "I cast out demons by the Spirit of God. If you are attributing what the Holy Spirit does to the devil, then you are blaspheming the Holy Spirit. There's no forgiveness for that, not now, or in the future."

We refer to this as "the unpardonable sin." If that is so, then it seems to follow that people will lose their salvation for blaspheming the Holy Spirit. They will not be forgiven now - or later. In Mark's version of this story, Jesus said they were "subject to eternal condemnation" (Mark 3:29). Well, I'm wondering about when modern preachers start attributing speaking in tongues to the devil. I believe that is blaspheming the Holy Spirit!

And what about saying that God is the one putting sickness upon you to teach you something? I'm not sure if that's not also blaspheming the Holy Spirit, since that's attributing the works of the devil to God - or to the Holy Spirit, because He is the one doing God's works here on the earth. God doesn't have any sickness to put upon anybody. Saying such things is dangerous! I want to tell the folks who say these things, "Wake up! Learn the truth of the Word of God. Stop speaking out of spiritual ignorance! Stop saying things that might bring eternal judgment on yourself."

THE ANOINTING OF THE HOLY SPIRIT

We can receive healing because the Holy Spirit is our teacher, and He will bring everything Jesus taught us from the Word to our remembrance. The Holy Spirit will reveal all the truth of God's Word to correct and guide us into the things of the Spirit.

But you have an anointing from the Holy One, and you know all things....But the anointing which you have received from Him abides in you, and you do not need that anyone teach you; but as the same anointing teaches you concerning all things, and is true, and is not a lie, and just as it has taught you, you will abide in Him (1 John 2:20,27).

In other words, the truth that we need spiritually, no

one can teach us. Now, we can listen to teachers teach the Word, but it's the Holy Spirit and the anointing that teaches us the truth out of those words. Otherwise, they are just words that fall on deaf ears! But for people who are hungry for the things of God, the Holy Spirit will cause those words to go into us. Suddenly, we understand it and we believe it. We say, "I've been enlightened to this truth! The illumination has come!"

As we live in the anointing, we live in the presence of the Teacher. He's the one who will teach us everything we really need to know. And yes, there are lots of ways He does that. We've already seen how God gets His Word to us, through the Scriptures themselves, through the voice of the Holy Spirit, and through ministry gifts – apostles, prophets, evangelists, pastors, and teachers.

He has also provided many other ways for us to be impacted by the Word of God. We can put the Word in by listening to Christian music, by singing to ourselves (Ephesians 5:19), or by speaking the Word to ourselves. We have an anointing from the Spirit of God: as the Word goes in, the illumination comes, and we live in this realm of the Spirit. We can also gain the mind of Christ by the Holy Spirit of God (1 Corinthians 2:12-16): He brings us into maturity, teaching us to live by the spiritual man and not the natural man; and He compares spiritual things with spiritual things, so we can live according to the mind of Christ. We have looked at this passage already, but we need to come back to it again and again because we need to be reminded that we've been given the mind of Christ.

IT'S NOT LOGICAL: #1

If sickness and disease was a method by which God taught, corrected, or perfected His children, then we would have to accept them as His perfect will. Think about this: follow the logic here. If sickness was what God used to teach us valuable lessons, we would have to accept sickness and disease as His perfect will.

Conversely, any attempt to get healed from sickness or disease would be an attempt to avoid the perfect will of God. Whether one sought healing through doctors and medicine or through faith and ministry, either would be a sin, as one would be trying to avoid the perfect will of God, instead of submitting to Him, as the Bible commands (James 4:7).

No, it just does not make sense for people to think, "God would send me a sickness to teach me something." Extending that train of thought, one would conclude: "Well then, don't go to the hospital. Pray for a double lesson! If it's a good lesson that you want to learn from the Lord, then get a double lesson. If one cancer can teach one lesson, pray for another cancer, to get a double lesson. Wouldn't it be that much more fruitful?" No, they don't want to go that direction!

IT'S NOT LOGICAL: #2

No, God wouldn't use sickness or disease to teach His children any more than a sane, normal parent would use sickness or disease to teach their children. Just get into the mindset of thinking like a loving parent. Every loving parent would tell you, "Of course, God would not do that! That's insanity!"

Any argument to the contrary would be to accuse God of being more insane than Hitler, for over the history of mankind, God would have killed hundreds of millions of His own children, simply because they failed to learn some lesson He was trying to teach them.

LAY YOUR DOUBTS TO REST IN A GRAVE

God desires to convince you fully that He wants you well, and He is willing to eliminate all your doubts in His compassionate grace and healing mercy, as you meditate on His Word. I like to put it this way:

When all your doubts are laid to rest in a grave,
then your faith will rise to great heights
and your healing and health
will spring forth suddenly.

SECTION THREE:

SEVEN METHODS OF RECEIVING & MINISTERING HEALING

CHAPTER TWENTY-ONE

GOD'S WAYS TO SURROUND US WITH HEALING

IT IS IMPORTANT TO KNOW that everything that we need to be able to receive, we can receive by faith. This includes an understanding of Scripture and scriptural methods, to be able to minister to those you will encounter: whether in family situations, in day-to-day circumstances and situations, or in your ministry. You are going to hear of people who need healing: they are going to come to you, quite often. Be aware of the fact that you might have to back up and take the time to teach them the Word of God. In Jesus' ministry, the people came "to hear and to be healed." As folks hear the Word, it starts building their faith – and *then* you release the healing anointing into their lives.

SEVEN BIBLICAL METHODS FOR HEALING THE SICK

God so desires that we be healed, that He has provided multiple ways to surround us with healing. In fact, there are seven biblical methods by which we may obtain or minister healing. This is not because God hasn't made up His mind about which way is best. It's because He loves us so much, He has provided many ways, so that we can surely receive divine healing and health. Jesus wants to knock the devil out for you. I like the old adage about boxing: "If the right one don't get you, then the left one will!" I believe that's God's approach in knocking out the devil for us: He's trying to make sure that if we don't receive healing one way, we do receive it another way. And, if we receive it one way one time, we're able to receive it another way the next time, until we're able to start turning back sickness when the symptoms first appear.

These seven methods to receive or minister healing often occur in various combinations, but for our study, we will divide them into three basic categories. Here is the overview:

Category 1 - Receiving by Your Own Faith:
- Method #1 - The Prayer of Faith
- Method #2 - Prayer to the Father in Jesus' Name

Category 2 - Healing by Mutual Faith:
- Method #3 - The Laying on of Hands
- Method #4 - The Prayer of Agreement

Category Three - Methods of Ministering to Others:
- Method #5 - Gifts of Healings
- Method #6 - Using the Name of Jesus in Authority
- Method #7 - Anointing with Oil

We will find out, that quite often, several of these methods will be in operation at the same time. Plus, the gifts of the Spirit usually operate in conjunction with these methods, as well. This makes for a great variety of ways to receive and to minister healing: Jesus is an individual, personal Savior, and He ministers to each person individually.

CHAPTER TWENTY-TWO

CATEGORY 1 – RECEIVING BY YOUR OWN FAITH

I CALL "RECEIVING BY YOUR OWN FAITH" the highest level – and some people get offended with that. They ask, "How can you possibly put one level of God's mercy ahead of another?" I say this, because if you need healing, it's good to be able to receive healing for yourself – and not be dependent upon someone else. You won't have to wait for an evangelist who operates in the working of miracles or gifts of healings to come to town for you to be healed. You won't have to wait for your pastor to suddenly be anointed beyond measure.

Although it turns out that most people are healed by joint faith – as God puts us together to pray for one another – that's because He cares for His people. Still, receiving by your own faith is the highest level, simply because you don't have to find someone else to minister to you: you can just go straight to the Lord and receive the healing that you need. Also, those who have received healing by themselves, or learned faith for receiving healing, are better equipped to *keep* their healing, even if they received their healing by mutual faith, through a gift of the Spirit. That's why I feel this category is the most valuable to the individual. I put it like this, "If it were just you and the Lord on a desert island, and you were sick and needed healing, you could get into His Word, get into faith, and receive your healing."

Let's take a look at the first method in Category 1 – receiving by your own faith – which has two methods: the prayer of faith and praying to the Father in Jesus' name.

METHOD 1 - THE PRAYER OF FAITH

We talked about the prayer of faith in the Life Christian University "Principles of Faith" course and learned how we release our ability to receive when we pray the prayer of faith. In other words, we have the ability built into us to receive from God; it's a spiritual ability that comes with the new birth. It comes from being yielded to the Holy Spirit and to the Lord, but there's another aspect to it: I like to visualize the arm of faith that reaches into the promises of God and grabs hold of them – knowing how much God wants to give you these promises – and brings them to you. Jesus already purchased them for you with His own blood, and the Father wants you to have them.

Jesus taught His disciples the prayer of faith in Mark 11:22-25:

Jesus answered and said to them, "Have faith in God. For assuredly, I say to you, whoever says to this mountain, 'Be removed and be cast into the sea,' and does not doubt in his heart, but believes that those things he says will be done, he will have whatever he says. Therefore I say to you, whatever things you ask when you pray, believe that you receive them, and you will have them. And whenever you stand

praying, if you have anything against anyone, forgive him, that your Father in heaven may also forgive you your trespasses."

Jesus was talking here about exercising authority over the devil and speaking to the circumstances. Almost every translation says, "Have faith in God." A few say, "Have the faith of God." Literally, in the Greek it says, "Have God's faith." Human "faith" is so limited: we need *supernatural* faith. We don't have supernatural faith of our own, but once we believe God's Word, He puts His own faith in our heart. In this verse, it's as if He were saying, "Use My faith, not your own!"

The second thing Jesus said to do, once you have God's faith, is take authority over the devil. When it comes to receiving healing and exercising faith, you will be speaking to the mountain of sickness, the mountain of opposition to your body. You are going to call that mountain cursed and removed from your life. There's a tremendous element of authority being used here. We will study this in depth later, but in the original Greek, Jesus told His disciples to "make a demand in My name" (John 14:13,14). We are not demanding from God or Jesus, but from the circumstances, from the mountain.

Third, Jesus tied this in, saying, "Therefore I say to you, whatever things that you ask *when you pray,* believe that you receive them, and you will have them." There's the prayer of faith, right there: *when you pray, you believe.* You are receiving God's replacement to the mountain that you just cast out.

The mountain was a sickness and we're casting that mountain into the sea. Now we say, "Lord, I need the healing power coming in my body, preventing that sickness from coming back or ever taking root again. If there's any vestige of it, I need the healing power coming and running all of it out."

Fourth, Jesus said, "If you have anything against anybody, forgive them." The Amplified Bible says it like this:

And whenever you stand praying, if you have anything against anyone, forgive him and let it drop (leave it, let it go), in order that your Father Who is in heaven may also forgive you your [own] failings and shortcomings and let them drop.

But if you do not forgive, neither will your Father in heaven forgive your failings and shortcomings (Mark 11:25,26 AMPC).

We are to walk in love with everyone, at all times. It takes the anointing of the Spirit of God for you to be able to do that – even as a believer at church, because there are going to be people at church who will try to offend you.

We often "write off" unbelievers who offend us, but at church, we think, "These folks are supposed to be different. They are my family members." We are mostly offended when it's a *Christian* who criticizes us or attacks us in some way. Jesus told us, "You are going to learn how to forgive people. The whole kingdom is built on forgiveness. I forgave you. You must forgive others, and then you have positioned yourself to keep your healing." If there's one way to keep your faith from working, it's unforgiveness; also the way to lose something you've gained by faith is through unforgiveness. So, we have to do all four steps to make sure we hold onto everything we have received.

After you have done these four steps, you realize, "Okay, now I'm waiting for the healing to manifest in my body." Brother Hagin said this, "If you are willing to stand in faith for 20 years, it probably won't take very long. You must have the kind of tenacity that says, 'I don't care if it takes me 20 years, I'm going to receive this.' Then, it will probably show up this week!"

YOU MUST BELIEVE AT THE MOMENT YOU ASK

So, when is it that you believe that you receive what you asked for? When you pray. You don't believe that you receive healing *after* it shows up and manifests in your body. That's too late: that's not faith, that's sight. Faith is asking and believing *at the moment that you asked* – because you're connected to God, who is not bound by space or time. We're connected to Him in the realm of the Spirit. So, spiritually speaking, we're actually seated with Christ in the heavenly places and looking down on the situation. We have access to God's throne. When we pray the prayer of faith, we are in God's throne room. We are asking Him face-to-face, and He is saying, "Yes!" at that point in time. We must believe that we're receiving at the same time that He says, "Yes, I will. Here's your answer," and releases our answer to us, in the realm of the spirit. In other words, we need to catch our answer as it is released, like a wide receiver in football needs to be ready to catch a pass, once it's thrown. Jesus has thrown the pass of healing and health. Catch it!

Now, there may be a little bit of a lag time between the "Amen!" of your prayer and when it manifests in the natural realm, but we've already received it by faith, when we prayed the prayer of faith.

FAITH COMES BY SPIRITUAL HEARING

So then faith comes by hearing and hearing by

the word of God (Romans 10:17).

Fools, because of their transgression, And because of their iniquities, were afflicted. Their soul abhorred all manner of food, And they drew near to the gates of death. Then they cried out to the Lord in their trouble, And He saved them out of their distresses. He sent His word and healed them, And delivered them from their destructions (Psalm 107:17-20).

If, in the Old Testament, God would send His Word and His people would be delivered from their destructions, how much more will *we* be delivered after He sent His Word - who is the Son of God, the second person of the Godhead - as John tells us:

In the beginning was the Word and the Word was with God, and the Word was God....And the Word became flesh and dwelt among us (John 1:1,14a).

This is a reference to God literally sending not only His healing Word that He spoke in the Old Testament, but Jesus Himself, the living Word. Then, Jesus delivered the Word of healing to us, for us to be able to receive from that Word. Now, we can simply meditate on these passages of Scripture and the lights turn on: faith comes alive. We simply find the passages of Scripture that deal with the different issues that we're facing in life. We find covenant promises concerning the provision of the Lord or the overcoming of the opposition. We cover all the many promises for provision of finances, in the Life Christian University course "Biblical Prosperity." In this book, we are looking at all the scriptures concerning divine healing.

As we have already seen, the pattern under Jesus' ministry was: hearing first, healing after. No one could teach faith like Jesus!

However, the report went around concerning Him all the more; and great multitudes came together to hear, and to be healed by Him of their infirmities (Luke 5:15).

Can we minister this message to unsaved people? What if they haven't "heard"? Can they still "be healed"? Yes! We have heard of many missionary evangelists who see large crowds of Muslims, Hindus, and witch doctors healed...and saved. They hear the simple gospel message, which God confirms with signs and miracles. As I write this, we are seeing a revival of the tent evangelists in America, who are holding crusades for the unsaved. Many times, those who won't darken the door of a church will come to an open-air meeting – and God is working miracles among them, and they get saved!

Yet, for the most part, the focus of our teaching ministry will be on the Church. Just as Jesus ministered to His followers, we are going to minister to Christ-followers, the ones who come to us to "hear and be healed." That's because you cannot teach people who won't listen to a message on divine healing! We teach those who have received Jesus, who are part of the community of the family of God. We're going to be together for all eternity.

It disturbs me when I hear some unsaved politician on television trying to quote the Bible to tell all of America how they should think and feel, and they give some unscriptural "opining," attempting to shame everyone. They try to influence everyone that it is our duty to do something that they think is Christian, like all of us should just give all of our money to the poor through our taxes, to make everything equal. What they are now describing is the onset of socialism, which is shared misery for all, except the elite politicians. We were never instructed to become socialists or communists for the benefit of all marginalized people, Christian or not. Without the gospel being included while attempting to meet the physical needs, the people would survive this life, but would still be doomed to hell.

Even under Jesus' ministry, you see the people who followed Him were those who believed in Him, that He was at least a prophet, if not the Messiah. So, He was able to teach them and minister to them, and in some cases, even feed great multitudes of them.

The Church doesn't need systems to feed the whole world. That's not what is in the Bible. In the Bible, the Christians fed those in the Church, those who believed:

Now all who believed were together, and had all things in common, and sold their possessions and goods, and divided them among all, as anyone had need.

So continuing daily with one accord in the temple, and breaking bread from house to house, they ate their food with gladness and simplicity of heart, praising God and having favor with all the people. And the Lord added to the church daily those who were being saved (Acts 2:44-47).

Should we be concerned about all the other people? Yes, absolutely! We want them to get saved! Jesus loves everyone, and He died for everyone. He wants them to be part of our heavenly Father's family. The beauty about being part of this family is, anyone can join us! They can get born again into the family of God, at any time. So, yes, we appeal to the unbeliever and try to get them to respond to the gospel and then come into the full blessing of redemption, but our focus for who we can actually minister to is, obviously, the Church.

YOU HAVE HEARD IT SAID...

People came to hear and be healed. The followers of Jesus followed Him around, they listened to Him, and they received His ministry. He was teaching them as one with great authority. They had never heard anyone teach like this before. He would say, "You've heard it said..." And He would quote the teachers of the Law - who had completely misunderstood the Law. Then, Jesus would say, "But I tell you..." and then He would tell the people the spiritual import *behind* the Law; what God was really trying to get at when He gave the Jews the Law of Moses.

From our New Testament perspective, we realize much of God's message in the Old Testament was, "It's obvious: you can't live up to this high standard, so you need a Redeemer. Until He comes, you need to come to Me for forgiveness and I'll cover your sins over." Basically, people had to put faith in the Messiah who was to come. The Old Testament saints were - in a sense - "saved on credit" for what Jesus was going to do when He came. All of those who died before Jesus came, but who believed in Jehovah, were waiting in Abraham's bosom (Luke 16:33). After the Resurrection, Jesus gathered these Jewish believers together and took them to heaven (Ephesians 4:8). Since then, anyone who dies believing in Jesus Christ, the Messiah, goes directly into the presence of God.

We see that Jesus was very concerned for those who were hungry for the truth. They came to hear the Word of God, to discover the truth, and to get their lives in alignment with God's plan. Then Jesus could minister to them. Quite often, I believe, they had to hear the Word to begin to grow in faith enough so that when Jesus *did* operate in one of the gifts of the Spirit and they were healed, that they had enough faith to be able to resist the devil later on, when he came back with lying symptoms. That's exactly the approach that we're going to have. I've told you the stories of how Brother Hagin tried to get people to come to the day sessions to hear teaching and build them up in faith. Then, he would minister at night with gifts of the Spirit, and wonderful healings would take place there.

In a similar passage, Luke mentions the deliverance of people who were tormented with unclean spirits, who were also healed.

And He came down with them and stood on a level place with a crowd of His disciples and a great multitude of people from all Judea and Jerusalem, and from the seacoast of Tyre and Sidon, who came to hear Him and be healed of their diseases, as well as those who were tormented with unclean spirits. And they were healed (Luke 6:17,18).

In some cases, there are unclean spirits of infirmity that cause sickness. Most sicknesses come simply because Satan was able to pervert things that were here on earth that once were beneficial, but suddenly, they are deadly and horrible. That's how the devil was able to loose all sorts of diseases on the planet. In other cases, there are actually spirits of infirmity behind the sickness. Chemotherapy doesn't work on a spirit of infirmity, so you have to cast the evil spirit out. Then, you will start seeing the success of the medical treatment. Note: I wouldn't recommend that anyone go into any sort of medical treatment without faith in God first, making sure He's going to be working along with the treatment, so that they get the full restoration of the Lord.

METHOD 1 - EXAMPLE #1: A WOMAN WHO WAS DETERMINED TO BE HEALED

Let's look at some examples of our "Method 1," of individuals who received healing by their own faith.

I love the passage in Mark 5:25-34 that tells the story of the woman with the issue of blood. But first, we have to back up concerning this story, because Jesus was on His way to heal someone else, when this woman came up and touched the hem of His garment and received her healing. Just before this, Jesus had delivered the demoniac from the legion of demons and had returned by boat from the Gadarenes. Mark 5:21-24 tells us:

Now when Jesus had crossed over again by boat to the other side, a great multitude gathered to Him; and He was by the sea. And behold, one of the rulers of the synagogue came, Jairus by name. And when he saw Him, he fell at His feet and begged Him earnestly, saying, "My little daughter lies at the point of death. Come and lay Your hands on her, that she may be healed, and she will live." So Jesus went with him, and a great multitude followed Him and thronged Him.

Jairus' daughter was about to die, and Jesus was on His way to minister to her. She actually died before Jesus could get there. First, the huge crowd made it hard to move quickly, and then this woman came along and interrupted everything. I like to say, "She ambushed Jesus!" Jesus was not concerned about this delay, any more than

He was concerned with the fact that Lazarus had been dead for four days by the time Jesus got there. He knew He could raise her from the dead and God would be glorified.

SHE HAD SUFFERED FOR TWELVE YEARS

Now a certain woman had a flow of blood for twelve years... (Mark 5:25).

This issue of blood would have caused her to be considered unclean by the nation of Israel. Under the Law of Moses, she could not mix with the rest of the people or even go into the Temple because of this issue of blood. She had it for twelve years: it was a menstrual issue of blood that just wouldn't stop.

...and had suffered many things from many physicians. She had spent all that she had and was no better, but rather grew worse. When she heard about Jesus, she came behind Him in the crowd and touched His garment (Mark 5:26,27).

What had she heard about Jesus? Obviously, she heard stories about Jesus going about and ministering and that everyone who came to Him was healed. She knew it was unlawful for her to enter into a crowd: that's the reason she didn't want to ask Jesus to pray for her healing. She came in secretly, but she came with the confidence of knowing that Jesus had healing power. I believe she was the first to receive healing by touching the Lord's garment. She probably assumed Jesus would not notice her if she did not touch His body. Obviously, Jesus was thronged about by people all the time, with a lot of people jostling Him or touching Him with a touch of curiosity. But it's different when somebody touches with a touch of faith.

This woman was going to touch Jesus' clothes with a touch of faith. She believed that once she got hold of the hem of His garment, that she was going to be made completely whole and would suddenly be legal. Then, if anyone found her out and said, "I know who you are. You are not supposed to be here!" She could say, "No, it's okay. I'm healed. I'm here legally." Even the priest would be able to examine her and give her a clean bill of health, to be able to be among the people.

IF ONLY I MAY TOUCH HIS CLOTHES...

For she said, "If only I may touch His clothes, I shall be made well" (Mark 5:28).

Greek scholars tell us that "she said" is in a repetitive, continuous tense, meaning "she continually said." She had been saying and saying and saying this ever since she heard about Jesus. Nobody expected Him that day. He had just crossed the lake after delivering the demoniac, and now, here He was, back in her hometown! She had kept saying, "Whenever He comes back to town, if I can get to where He is, if I can just touch His clothes, I can be healed."

In Matthew's account of this event, we see she actually "touched the hem of His garment":

And suddenly, a woman who had a flow of blood for twelve years came from behind and touched the hem of His garment (Matthew 9:20).

I believe she literally got down near Jesus' feet, to the bottom of His robe, and touched it. In other words, she was willing to crawl on her hands and knees through the crowd, to get to the hem of Jesus' garment, to be able to lay hold of that garment, and receive the Lord's healing power flowing into her body. I really believe that's what she did: she crawled on the ground – she totally humbled herself. She had already been totally humiliated in life for twelve years, so what was it to press through the crowd and get to "The Healer," who was like no other prophet before Him? She was so determined to touch His clothes, that she crawled to Him to get her healing.

Immediately the fountain of her blood was dried up, and she felt in her body that she was healed of the affliction (Mark 5:29).

The minute she touched the garment of the Lord Jesus, the healing anointing flowed out of Him through His clothes – because of this touch of faith – right into the woman's body. It brought a complete healing and a cure for her body; she instantly felt the healing power going through her; she felt her body being healed. There was no more pain, no more suffering, and everything was perfectly normal, as it should be.

HEALING POWER FLOWED FROM JESUS

And Jesus, immediately knowing in Himself that power had gone out of Him, turned around in the crowd and said, "Who touched My clothes?" (Mark 5:30).

I've noticed this about the power of God: there are times when the power of God can flow and you wouldn't even know it; you can't sense it. But there are other times when the power of God flows and it's so tangible: it's like electricity and it'll knock you flat on the ground! It is incredible! Jesus was obviously so in tune with the Holy Spirit, that He would know whether a light touch and small amount of anointing was going out of Him or whether it was a huge amount for a big need. In this case, I'm sure He felt a power surge go out of Him, just like someone plugged a cord into a power socket and turned something on. Then, He narrowed it down: He turned to the crowd and asked, "Who touched My clothes?"

But His disciples said to Him, "You see the multitude thronging You, and You say, 'Who touched Me?'" (Mark 5:31).

The disciples were bewildered at His question. They saw what was going on. They asked Him, "You've been touched by hundreds of people as You are moving through the crowd. How can You ask, 'Who touched Me?'"

SHE TOLD JESUS THE WHOLE STORY

And He looked around to see her who had done this thing. But the woman, fearing and trembling, knowing what had happened to her, came and fell down before Him and told Him the whole truth (Mark 5:32,33).

At this point, the woman knew she was busted: when Jesus, the Son of God, the Healer, the Messiah, the Christ, is looking for you, you are found out! Fearing and trembling, she came and fell down before Jesus and told Him "the whole truth." That means everything; the whole story, with every detail! We don't know how long it took for her to tell the story. It might have taken her a long time. It is one of those situations where Jesus stopped to minister to one person: this woman caught His attention by her faith.

YOUR FAITH HAS MADE YOU WELL

And He said to her, "Daughter, your faith has

made you well. Go in peace, and be healed of your affliction" (Mark 5:34).

Jesus said, "Daughter, your faith has made you well." Jesus didn't pray for her; He didn't speak anything over her; He didn't do anything! He didn't even know she was receiving her healing until she pulled the power of God from Him. Even then He didn't say, "Daughter, My anointing has made you well." He didn't say that. He didn't even say anything about her being one of those who came "to hear and be healed." She just heard *about* Him. There was no indication she ever heard a single one of His messages. She just knew that He was a healer, a prophet, maybe the Messiah, and that if she could touch His clothes, the healing power of God would flow into her. She got exactly what she was believing God for. Whenever Jesus points out someone's faith, that is something notable to remember and meditate on as a pattern concerning how to be healed.

Next, Jesus told her, "Go in peace, and be healed of your affliction." Earlier, we saw that the Hebrew word for peace, *shalom*, also means wholeness. Jesus was telling this woman, "Be absolutely whole, never to experience this affliction again."

HE DIDN'T SAY A WORD

Remember Jairus? He was probably freaking out! He was surely thinking, "My daughter is at the verge of death. Jesus was on His way to minister to her, and I need to get Him there *now!* But this woman is taking up so much of His time!"

Mark 5:35,36 tells us:

While He [Jesus] was still speaking, some came from the ruler of the synagogue's house who

said, "Your daughter is dead. Why trouble the Teacher any further?"

As soon as Jesus heard the word that was spoken, He said to the ruler of the synagogue, "Do not be afraid; only believe."

In the face of this devastating news, Jesus told Jairus, "Don't fear." And all of a sudden, this man didn't fear. Jesus said, "Only believe." It was the perfect place for this father to cry out or fall down or have a panic attack. Instead, Jairus was silent; he didn't say a word. He simply followed Jesus – and watched as Jesus went in and raised his daughter from the dead. Jairus would not have gotten this miracle if he had not obeyed Jesus' word, "Don't fear. Don't panic. Only believe."

The words "don't fear," "don't be afraid," and other slight variations appear 167 times in the Word of God. It must be important! We said this earlier, but it bears repeating: It would be unfair for Jesus to command us to stop the fear, if we couldn't. If Jesus told Jairus not to fear in the *worst* of circumstances, we can *also* choose not to fear no, matter what we face. As born-again, Spirit-filled Christians, God has given us the ability to stop the fear.

I like what Jairus said after Jesus told him, "Don't be afraid." Jairus said nothing! He had expressed his faith when he first told Jesus, "Come and lay Your hands on her, that she may be healed, and she will live." His faith declaration had been spoken and he said nothing new to cancel it. This is good for us to remember when the crisis of faith comes to us. Keep believing your faith statement, and all will be well. Jairus was silent the rest of the way as he went with Jesus to the house. And of course, Jesus raised his daughter from the dead.

I found it interesting what Jesus did to the people who mocked Him when He said, "The child is not dead, but sleeping." He put them all outside (Mark 5:40). I've heard people say, "Jesus had to get all the doubt and unbelief out of the room." I wondered about that, so I asked the Lord, "You raised Lazarus from the dead, in the midst of a whole crowd of people. I don't think You had to get the doubting unbelief out of the room. Why did You only take those three disciples in with You and You put everybody else out?"

He told me, "Those three disciples were the only ones who qualified to see a manifestation of God's glory on that level."

My heart cried out, "Lord, don't ever let me be disqualified from seeing a manifestation of Your glory. Keep me walking with You and hearing from You, all the way."

METHOD 1 - EXAMPLE #2: A BLIND MAN WHO WOULD NOT BE QUIET

Another wonderful story about a person who received healing using their own faith is the story of blind Bartimaeus, which happened in Jericho. I have always been fascinated with this story. I've been to the city of Jericho. It's under Arab rule right now; it's a part of the land that Israel gave to the Palestinians. It is a town that's filled with palm trees: they are everywhere, so the city is well-shaded, which makes it very unique in that part of the world. Remember the history of Jericho: this was the place where Israel first came into the Promised Land. The walls of the city were so wide, they could do chariot races on top of the walls around the city, and yet, those were the walls that crumbled and fell when the nation of Israel encircled the city for seven days (Hebrews 11:30). Jericho was a very historic place. You would think that because this city was so important, that Jesus was going to do some major ministry there, but look what happened:

> **Now they came to Jericho. As He went out of Jericho with His disciples and a great multitude, blind Bartimaeus, the son of Timaeus, sat by the road begging (Mark 10:46).**

Notice, Jesus came to Jericho and went out of Jericho in the same verse. There is no record of Him ministering there. Obviously, nothing notable happened, and we don't know why: was it doubt and unbelief like what kept Jesus from healing people in Nazareth (Mark 6:5)? For whatever reason, it seemed they were just not ready to receive. So, Jesus came to Jericho and then left Jericho on the other side, with a great multitude of people following Him. As He was leaving town, blind Bartimaeus was sitting by the side of the road, begging. He sat there every day, because it was a busy city with lots of people coming and going. Bartimaeus had no other way to make his living because he was blind. Blind beggars had a special coat they would wear, that identified them as a beggar, so everyone would know it was lawful for them to be there asking alms, and people would give to them. So, Bartimaeus was sitting there with his beggar's robe on.

HAVE MERCY ON ME!

> **And when he heard that it was Jesus of Nazareth, he began to cry out and say, "Jesus, Son of David, have mercy on me!" (Mark 10:47).**

The word got out about Jesus – His fame went everywhere (Mark 1:28, Matthew 4:24). He was famous, as the prophet who came and healed everyone.

Bartimaeus began to cry out, "Jesus, Son of David, have mercy on me." Obviously, the man had some knowledge of Scripture, because he knew that the Messiah was going to be the Son of David: he had more knowledge of who Jesus was than the theologians of that day. Here, we see a huge, noisy crowd of people following Jesus. As they came by Bartimaeus, he started screaming out. He couldn't see where Jesus was; he just knew there was a big crowd. He heard Jesus was the reason for the crowd, so he was screaming at the top of his lungs, to the point where all the people around him - many of them Jesus' own disciples - are telling him, "Shut up!"

> **Then many warned him to be quiet; but he cried out all the more, "Son of David, have mercy on me!" (Mark 10:48).**

I love this guy! He had such faith - just like the woman with the issue of blood - she knew if she could get to Jesus, she would be healed, even if she had to crawl on her hands and knees through the crowd, to touch the hem of His garment. Bartimaeus knew if he could get Jesus' attention, he could receive healing for his blind eyes, so he kept screaming out while everyone was telling him, "Shut up. Don't bother Him."

JESUS STOOD STILL

> **So Jesus stood still and commanded him to be called.**

> **Then they called the blind man, saying to him, "Be of good cheer. Rise, He is calling you." (Mark 10:49).**

Jesus heard him. Jesus stopped and commanded

Bartimaeus to come to him. It's amazing to watch how everybody suddenly changes their tune. When Jesus pays attention this man, suddenly, they would like be part of this miracle, to be recognized as helping this man get his healing. They go from saying, "Shut up, He's not interested in you. He doesn't want to heal you," to "Oh! It's okay! Be of good cheer! Yes! We'll get you right to Jesus." They told Bartimaeus, "Rise, He is calling you." Jesus must have still been so far away that Bartimaeus couldn't hear Jesus calling him.

And throwing aside his garment, he rose and came to Jesus (Mark 10:50).

Remember, this is the beggar's garment that identified him as a blind man, who has no other way to make a living. Bartimaeus knew when Jesus called for him, it was time to get rid of the beggar's garment. He is ready to be shed of that thing. He got up and came to Jesus.

So Jesus answered and said to him, "What do you want Me to do for you?" (Mark 10:51a).

Picture this: here comes blind Bartimaeus, without his beggar's robe. He is standing before Jesus - totally blind - and Jesus asks him what he wants. What happens next is interesting! I think it has something to do with Jesus needing us to say what we believe. In the story of the woman with the issue of blood, she kept saying over and over again to herself, "If I can only touch His clothes, I will be well." Jesus needed to hear the words out of Bartimaeus' own mouth: that's why He asked, "What do you want Me to do for you?" Wouldn't it have been weird for blind Bartimaeus to say, "Jesus, I know that You have been blessing people. I'd like to be the richest blind beggar in all of Jericho." No, Jesus already knew what Bartimaeus needed, but Jesus wanted the man to say it, so that out of his own mouth, he was professing his wholeness.

THAT I MAY RECEIVE MY SIGHT

The blind man said to Him, "Rabboni, that I may receive my sight" (Mark 10:51b).

Bartimaeus had been acting on his faith. He called out to Jesus because he knew that if Jesus ministered to him, he would receive his sight. He threw away his beggar's garment because he knew he would not have to beg anymore. Now, out of his mouth, Bartimaeus boldly proclaimed, "That I may receive my sight."

GO YOUR WAY; YOUR FAITH HAS MADE YOU WELL

Then Jesus said to him, "Go your way; your faith has made you well." And immediately he received his sight and followed Jesus on the road (Mark 10:52).

Jesus saw Bartimaeus' faith. Jesus spoke out in response to the man identifying exactly what he was believing Jesus for. Jesus said to him, "Your faith has made you well": it was Bartimaeus' faith. There's no indication of the disciples being involved here: no other people prayed for Bartimaeus. It was his faith in Jesus alone. In these places, you see how vital it is to put faith in Jesus and have Him say, "Your faith has made you well." These stories grip our hearts - we see the faith of the person and the compassion of Jesus.

METHOD 1 - EXAMPLE #3: THE TENTH LEPER

Now it happened as He went to Jerusalem that

He passed through the midst of Samaria and Galilee. Then as He entered a certain village, there met Him ten men who were lepers, who stood afar off. And they lifted up their voices and said, "Jesus, Master, have mercy on us!" (Luke 17:11-13).

The ten lepers knew they couldn't come into the crowd, so they were standing "afar off" from the rest of the people. But they called out loudly, just like blind Bartimaeus did, and said, "Jesus, Master, have mercy on us!"

AS THEY WENT, THEY WERE CLEANSED

So when He saw them, He said to them, "Go, show yourselves to the priests." And so it was that as they went, they were cleansed (Luke 17:14).

It doesn't say Jesus got close enough to touch them, but He must have gotten close enough that He could speak to them, without having to yell. When He saw them, He told them, "Go show yourselves to the priest." We talked about this before: even though Jesus was ushering in the new covenant, He was still ministering under the old covenant. He told the lepers to do what was required by the Law of Moses, because He hadn't yet done away with the Law of commandments contained in ordinances. He could only do away with the Law after He had fulfilled the Law. He said, "Do not think that I came to destroy the Law or the Prophets. I did not come to destroy but to fulfill" (Matthew 5:17). But after Jesus fulfilled it, the Bible says that He abolished it:

...having abolished in His flesh the enmity, that is, the law of commandments contained in

ordinances (Ephesians 2:15a).

"Abolished" means to render it null and void, inoperative, inactive, annulled, as though it had never been. It was no longer needed because Jesus came and replaced it by fulfilling it all.

For now, Jesus told these men, "Go show yourself to the priest." In the Old Testament, people would be healed of leprosy as the prophets ministered to them. In those cases, the Law of Moses required them to go show themselves to the priests so that they could be examined, be declared clean, and be able to return to society.

All ten lepers obeyed Jesus, turned around, and went to show themselves to the priest. As they took this step of faith, while they were walking, all the leprosy died in their body. They were completely cured of leprosy. Now, the problem with being cured of leprosy is that other horrible things happen with leprosy. People might lose their fingers, toes, ears, or lips. People are affected to different degrees: these ten lepers might have lost different parts of their body to this horrible, disfiguring disease. But all ten were at least healed of the disease itself as they went.

ONLY ONE OF THEM RETURNED

And one of them, when he saw that he was healed, returned, and with a loud voice glorified God, and fell down on his face at His feet, giving Him thanks. And he was a Samaritan (Luke 17:15,16).

One man, when he saw that there was no more white, leprous skin, and that it was all normal, he returned to where Jesus was, and with a loud voice, he glorified God. Maybe he did it from a distance, but as he turned back, he glorified God with a loud voice. Or, maybe he got all the way up to Jesus, but he was just so excited about his healing, he just glorified God with a great, loud voice. When he got close enough to Jesus, he fell down on his face at Jesus' feet, thanking Him. Why did his healing mean so much more to this man than it did the other lepers? We will never know, but this man was so very thankful, and he glorified God.

> **So Jesus answered and said, "Were there not ten cleansed? But where are the nine? Were there not any found who returned to give glory to God except this foreigner?" (Luke 17:17,18).**

Here, Jesus was speaking to His disciples who, are all around Him. He was always using every opportunity of ministry to teach His disciples something. He asked His disciples, "Were there not any found who returned to give glory to God except this foreigner?" Jesus points out to His disciples, "I know this man is a foreigner, a Samaritan." It could be that the others were Jews: they were all just part of the leper colony, and it didn't matter if you were a Samaritan or a Jew, you were not part of the rest of society.

YOUR FAITH HAS MADE YOU WHOLE

> **And He said to him, "Arise, go your way. Your faith has made you well" (Luke 17:19).**

In the Greek, it doesn't say, "Your faith has made you *well.*" It's very accurate in the King James Version, where this is translated as "Your faith has made you *whole.*" This is hugely different than just the leprosy dying in this man's body. When he was made whole because he came back to glorify God and thank Jesus, he was made *completely* whole. In other words, everything that had been lost because of the leprosy was restored! So, perhaps, all of his fingers and toes and his ears grew back - a creative miracle - right in front of everybody. People ask, "Can God really do that?" Are you kidding me? God can do anything. "Does God really *want* to do that?" Yes!

I believe we can see the pattern here of how God will do everything for those who truly revere Him, who are really thankful for everything He does. It was faith coupled with worship: honoring God and His Son as the true healers. These people get the entire package of the blessing of the Lord. That's why I wanted to point out this tenth leper and how his healing was different from the other nine: it was *his* faith that took him from being *healed* to being *made completely whole.*

METHOD 1 - EXAMPLE #4: THE CENTURION

Let's take a look at the story of the centurion in Matthew 8. This is another example of a person receiving by their own faith. I will spend extra time on this story, because it is really foundational for what we will cover later, concerning the different methods of ministering healing to others because the centurion received healing for another person. It is good to be able to operate in faith for yourself for healing - once that is established, it opens up the door for ministering healing to others.

RECEIVING HEALING FOR ANOTHER
PERSON – BY FAITH

This story takes place in Capernaum, on the northern part of the Sea of Galilee, which is also known as Lake Tiberius.

Now when Jesus had entered Capernaum, a centurion came to Him, pleading with Him, saying, "Lord, my servant is lying at home paralyzed,

dreadfully tormented."

And Jesus said to him, "I will come and heal him."

The centurion answered and said, "Lord, I am not worthy that You should come under my roof. But only speak a word, and my servant will be healed" (Matthew 8:5-8).

Now, the centurion must have known what the Law of Moses said: a Jew could not enter the house of a non-Jew. This was a Roman centurion, but he loved the nation of Israel and built the people of Capernaum a synagogue (Luke 7:5). He obviously believed in the power of God. Jesus was more than willing to go to his house.

I UNDERSTAND THE CHAIN OF COMMAND

Then the centurion said:

"I also am a man under authority, having soldiers under me. And I say to this one, 'Go,' and he goes; and to another, 'Come,' and he comes; and to my servant, 'Do this,' and he does it" (Matthew 8:9).

The centurion was describing what he understood about the chain of command: he was under the authority of Rome and could tell other people to do things because he had been given authority by his Roman commander. Commanding others was part of his job. Here, he was basically saying, "I know how the chain of command works. And, Jesus, I know You are under the authority of God, and that whatever You say, God backs it up, in the same way Rome backs me up. All You have to do is say the Word, and I know that my servant will be healed."

I HAVE NOT FOUND SUCH FAITH IN ALL OF ISRAEL

When Jesus heard it, He marveled, and said to those who followed, "Assuredly, I say to you, I have not found such great faith, not even in Israel!" (Matthew 8:10).

Jesus was making a point here: "I haven't seen this kind of faith in any person from Israel - there's not one single Jew who has the kind of faith this centurion has!" That's why I want to emphasize this story so strongly: the centurion understood how faith works - it is by the authority that we have in the name of Jesus. Because we are submitted to Jesus, and Jesus is submitted to the Father, and we are flowing with the Holy Spirit - when we use that authority, we get the same anointing of the Holy Spirit to do the same things in our lives and ministries as the Holy Spirit did in Jesus' life and ministry and in the disciples' lives and ministries.

"And I say to you that many will come from east and west, and sit down with Abraham, Isaac, and Jacob in the kingdom of heaven" (Matthew 8:11).

Jesus was telling the Jews around Him things they were not yet ready for. Even His disciples didn't yet understand that Jesus was dying for the *whole world*, even though Jesus had already told them, "God so loved the *world* that He gave His only begotten Son" (John 3:16). There are many other teachings in the Old Testament that also allude to this. For example, God told Abraham:

"In your seed all the nations of the earth shall be blessed, because you have obeyed My voice" (Genesis 22:18).

God based it on the faith and obedience of Abraham: this was the method by which all people were going to come into one family through Christ. Jesus pointed out that this Roman centurion stood head and shoulders above all the Jews who weren't getting it. He was saying, "This centurion will be part of the kingdom of heaven. People are going to come from all over - everyplace besides Israel and every belief besides Judaism - because I'm making the way for them to come into the kingdom of heaven, and *they* are going to sit down with Abraham, Isaac, and Jacob."

"But the sons of the kingdom will be cast out into outer darkness. There will be weeping and gnashing of teeth" (Matthew 8:12).

Jesus was describing the fact that the people who should have accepted Him and His message, didn't. The Bible tells us:

"He came to His own, and His own did not receive Him" (John 1:11).

Israel should have received His message, but they didn't.

To me, the centurion's story is a wonderful illustration of pure faith - totally separate from the Law of Moses and totally separate from the lineage of the house of Israel - just faith in Jesus alone. And it got the job done!

AS YOU HAVE BELIEVED,
SO LET IT BE DONE FOR YOU

Then Jesus said to the centurion, "Go your way; and as you have believed, so let it be done for you." And his servant was healed that same hour (Matthew 8:13).

Jesus recognized the centurion's faith and released the Word of healing. "Go your way; as you have believed, so let it be done for you" is the same thing as "Your faith has made you well." Jesus' words caused the centurion's servant to be healed at that same time. What a great example of being able to receive healing for someone else by one's own faith.

METHOD 1 - EXAMPLE #5: NO MORE SICK DAYS

After God called me to the ministry, it was only two weeks later that I was a student at Rhema. It was a real quick thing! I never actually heard Brother Hagin minister before I was sitting in class - I had just heard that he was a great faith teacher. I vividly remember the first time I heard him say, "I haven't had a sick day in over fifty years." He literally meant not one sick day, not even one aspirin! I was blown away by the concept that you can walk in faith and ward off sickness and that Brother Hagin was able to give that testimony. I said to myself, "I will say that one day!"

When I first got to Rhema, I spent all my time studying really hard. But after just a couple of weeks, the Lord spoke to me and said, "That's not the reason I sent you here. I want you to go to healing school." In our morning class, Brother Hagin was teaching on healing, but I found out that in the *afternoon,* Rhema also had a "Healing School," conducted by Brother Hagin. A lot of sick people would come, and Brother Hagin would minister to them - while also using that time as an opportunity to train up his students. It was a great place to go, to sit and learn. I got so charged up, I told my friends, "Gosh! Brother Hagin is demonstrating everything he is teaching us in class! I'm watching people be healed as he lays hands on them. It's amazing!"

So, I sat there in the front row, just ten feet from Brother Hagin, being spoon-fed the Word of God, by the prophet of God. I came to the place where I knew, that I knew, that I knew: I was going to have a testimony like Brother Hagin. I really believed that I had faith enough to never get sick again!

THE TRYING OF MY FAITH

Then came the month of November. There was a flu epidemic going through Tulsa and it also swept through Rhema, the Word of Faith school. Students there were supposed to be built up in faith, but a whole bunch of them were out sick! Lester Sumrall was coming for a seminar the following week, and I didn't want to miss a single bit of that seminar! I just knew I would be fine. I went to a restaurant for lunch, and they seated me right by the door. The temperature had dropped, and it was really cold. When people came in and out, the wind blew great gusts of freezing air in through the door, and I got so chilled! But I went on to Healing School and afterwards, went home. I thought, "Even though I got chilled, I probably haven't been exposed to any flu viruses." Ha! Those germs were everywhere!

Later, I was reading the book for my course on healing, *Christ the Healer.* Before long, I started getting all the symptoms of flu: I ran to the bathroom and started throwing up; I got diarrhea; I broke out in the sweats. I thought, "This can't be happening! I *know* I've got faith!" I prayed the prayer of faith: "I believe that I receive *right now* the healing of my body from this flu." And I expected all the symptoms just to go, right then. But instead, the symptoms kept going on and on. Finally, I got to the point where I couldn't read *Christ the Healer* anymore, everything was so blurry! At 4 in the morning, I was still struggling and battling. I couldn't understand why my prayer of faith wasn't working. You see, I wasn't really thinking about *all* of Mark 11:23 and 24, about the part on using my authority and saying to the mountain, "Be removed and go away." What I needed to do was take authority over the devil, but that didn't dawn on me until then.

PUT THE PLAGUE GERMS IN MY HAND

About that time, I remembered a story about John G. Lake when he was ministering in Africa. They were experiencing the bubonic plague, and many were dying. He was ministering to people who were really sick, but he never got sick himself. When the ships from England finally came with the necessary medicine, the doctors told him, "You must take our medicine."

John G. Lake said, "I won't need that."

They asked him, "What are you taking?"

He replied, "I'm taking the law of the Spirit of life in Christ Jesus, who set me free from the law of sin and death. So, the law of sin and death can't work against me."

Then, he told the doctors, "Listen, if you want to do an experiment, I'll show you how the law of the Spirit of life in Christ Jesus works. Take the foam from the mouth and nose of someone who died from the plague, and put it under a microscope. You will see that the germs are alive."

The doctors did that. Then, John G. Lake said, "Now take the foam and put it in the palm of my hand."

The doctors did that. John G. Lake continued, "Now take the foam from my hand and look at it under your microscope. You will see that all the germs are dead."

Sure enough, they looked at it and said, "We've never seen anything like this! What is it?"

John G. Lake replied, "I told you: it is the law of the Spirit of life in Christ Jesus. I won't need any of your medicine."

SATAN, TAKE YOUR HANDS OFF MY BODY!

As I remembered that story, I realized I had not used my authority and had not spoken to the devil. A righteous indignation came over me! I jumped up in the middle my bed 4 o'clock in the morning. Suddenly, I was so angry at the devil, I yelled at him: "Satan, take your hands off my body! It is the temple of the Holy Ghost!" When I said that, it was like the anointing of the Spirit of God rushed all over me. It settled down over my head and coursed through my body. I was suddenly really sleepy, so I lay down and went to sleep.

At that time, I had trained myself to listen to my spirit to wake up at 7 in the morning, without using an alarm clock. That morning, like always, I woke up at 7 - just three hours later - completely and totally healed!

Well, I was really excited about being able to turn back the flu. I was so used to having the flu every year that it seemed like I had faith for the flu! It usually lasted a week, so to have it turned around so quickly was just amazing! I can now testify that the last time I have ever had the flu was in November 1980.

After this experience, I really believed I had this sickness thing completely handled. I went to school the next day and told my friends, "I was sick as a dog! Here's what I did, and I received healing from the flu!" I was thinking, "Now I'll be able to say, 'I haven't had a sick day since November 1980.'"

METHOD 1 - EXAMPLE #6: A SLOW LEARNER?

As it turned out, about two weeks later, my faith was tested again. My roommate and I were single guys at the time. We'd buy our own groceries and put them in the refrigerator, and sometimes we would forget which food belonged to who, and how long it had been there. I remembered one morning, I poured myself a glass of orange juice. I didn't even think to smell it first, but after two or three gulps, I realized it was bad. I couldn't reverse it because it was already in me. I thought, "Well, it tasted bad, but I'll probably be okay." I went to class, then Healing School, then came home.

I can testify that food poisoning feels exactly like the flu: I was just as sick as I was with the flu! I went through the entire scenario again - I prayed the prayer of faith and stood against the symptoms. I don't want to say I was a slow learner, but it wasn't until 4 in the morning that it dawned on me again: I haven't taken authority over the devil! I stood up in the middle of my bed and said, "Satan, get your hands off my body! It is the temple of the Holy Ghost!" I was able to lay down and sleep, and I woke up at 7, completely healed.

Since that time, I have been able to give testimony that since November 1980, I never had a sick day. Now, I've had six days that I stayed at home to receive the manifestation of my healing - it seemed better to do that than to come to the office - but I wasn't really all that sick. I just didn't want to be around everybody, plus I wanted to focus on standing my ground and receiving my healing. But mostly, these were basically minor things along the way. There was one exception to this in February 2012, but we will cover that later, as it applies to a different method of healing.

METHOD 1 - EXAMPLE #7: IT'S NOW OR NEVER!

Another time I received a supernaturally fast manifestation of healing happened in Grand Cayman. A good friend of mine pastors a church and we had a campus there. Once, when we were visiting, we went out to dinner. While at the restaurant, the symptoms of food poisoning suddenly came upon me. While the others were still eating, I spent most of the time in the restroom. Several times I tried to go back out to join them, but it just didn't work. Not only did I miss dinner, but I was also supposed to minister at the church service that night!

As we finally left for the church, my friend, Brother Ron, said, "Listen, we have an apartment upstairs. Why don't you go up there and rest?" At that time, my son D.J., who is now an adult, was just a toddler. He was kind of fussy and needed a nap, so we went upstairs and were laying down. Church started, and I could hear the worship. My son woke up crying. I finally got him calmed down, but he would not go back to sleep.

I still didn't feel any better, but I thought, "Well, *I* won't be able to sleep if *he* doesn't go to sleep. We'll just go down and slip into the back of the church, and enjoy the service." As worship ended, Brother Ron looked back at me and said, "I see that Dr. Wingate has joined us. He's bringing the Word to us tonight, now that he's feeling better." I took my son to my wife, who was sitting on the front row. I was thinking, "Okay, Lord, this is it. It's now or never! Five minutes into the message, I don't want to have to run to the restroom." Then I said, "Lord, I'm going to minister on healing. I know the people here probably need healing, and I know I do, so I'm going to focus on healing."

I started teaching on healing - although it wasn't the message I had planned to deliver. I ran through a number of healing scriptures. Three minutes into that message, the power of God hit me, from the top my head, to the soles of my feet. I received that instant manifestation of healing - and then we had a healing service that was awesome! The anointing was so strong, because when you *were* feeling like death warmed over, then suddenly you're feeling *great,* it's easy to believe for others!

Receiving healing by your own faith is real. It's available. I am here to testify to that, and you'll also hear many, many ministers testify to the same thing. It's important to experience healing by your own faith as a foundation for the other categories of healing we will be covering.

METHOD 2 - PRAYER IN JESUS' NAME

Method 2 - Prayer in Jesus' Name is still in the category of receiving by your own faith. It includes both prayer to the *Father* in Jesus' name and prayer to *Jesus* in His name. It uses the prayer of authority and couples it with what we have seen in Mark 11:23 about speaking to your mountain, taking authority over it, and moving that problem out of your life.

ASK THE FATHER IN MY NAME

"And in that day you will ask Me nothing. Most assuredly, I say to you, whatever you ask the Father in My name He will give you. Until now you have asked nothing in My name. Ask, and you will receive, that your joy may be full" **(John 16:23,24).**

Here, in context, Jesus is specifically talking about praying for your own needs: asking the Father to answer your prayer and receive something for yourself. It's important to know that Jesus was changing the whole dynamic of prayer. He was giving us authority to go to the Father in His name, so that the Father would answer our prayer just like He answers Jesus' prayers. This was a new way to be able to receive whatever we needed.

Jesus wants us to be connected to the Father. His purpose was to reveal the love of the Father, and to get everyone's picture of God changed, because they were seeing

God as an austere judge. Jesus demonstrated love and compassion wherever He went. He told people He only did what He saw the Father do (John 5:19) and only said what He heard the Father say (John 8:28). Basically, He was saying, "You must understand this: it's the Father's great love and great compassion for you that you are seeing extended through Me." He told Philip, "He who has seen Me has seen the Father" (John 14:9).

Jesus is identifying here that *all* the answers come from the Father. Before Jesus left the planet, He wanted His disciples to switch over from asking Him, to asking the Father. He is instructing His disciples to go directly to the Father for themselves: "Ask, and you will receive that your joy may be full." God wants us to have our life full of joy by having all our prayers answered, which means we will receive a lot of miracles!

MAKE A DEMAND
ON THE COVENANT PROMISES IN MY NAME

"Most assuredly, I say to you, he who believes in Me, the works that I do he will do also; and greater works than these he will do, because I go to My Father" (John 14:12).

Jesus was talking about authority here – He said we will be ministering these works to other people, using the authority He gave us: we will "cast the mountain into the sea," and because we believe when we pray, we are going to receive exactly what we pray. Then, He said we will do even greater works than the works He did, "because I go to My Father."

Many people wonder, "What are the 'greater works'?" For one: just getting people saved! Because no one could be saved before Jesus was crucified.

These works are certainly greater in number because God has poured out the anointing on the whole body of Christ. If we will receive it and walk in it, then we can have that anointing for healing, as well. In addition, with modern technology such as radio, television, and the internet, we can reach more people in more places at one time than Jesus could in His earthly ministry. We also see in the Book of Acts, how the early Church extended these "greater works" to include folks being healed by Peter's shadow (Acts 5:15) and Paul's handkerchiefs (Acts 19:12).

"And whatever you ask in My name, that I will do..." (John 14:13a).

There are five Greek words that are sometimes translated as "ask" – the word used here is *aitoe* (Strong's number 154). *The New Strong's Concise Dictionary of the Words in the Greek Testament* gives the shades of meaning for each of these five words in the entry for *punthanomai* (Strong's number 4441). Here's what it says:

> **4441**...to question, to ascertain by inquiry (as a matter of information merely); and thus differing from **2065**, which properly means a request as a favor; and from **154**, which is strictly a demand for something due; as well as from **2212**, which implies a search for something hidden; and from **1189**, which involves the idea of urgent need (78).

In this verse, the Greek word translated "ask" is "strictly a demand for something due." But the translators were too skittish to put the word "demand" in John 14:13, because they thought, "We're not supposed to be demanding anything of God!" No, we're not arrogant enough or foolish enough to be demanding anything of God: we are making a demand on His Word, that He gave us as a promise. In other words, Jesus was saying, "Put a demand on My covenant promises." As we do this, Jesus says, "I will do it." We're demanding the circumstances to change. We are demanding that the mountains that the devil has put in our lives be cast into the sea. The promise is, "Whatever you demand in My name, that I will do."

"...that the Father may be glorified in the Son. If you ask anything in My name, I will do it" (John 14:13b,14).

Jesus wants all the glory to go to the Father - whether we ask the Father in Jesus' name as in John 16:23 and 24, or whether we demand something in His name and use His authority to minister to other people - all is done so that the Father is glorified. These are Jesus' words: they are in red! "If you demand anything from the Word - a covenant promise - I will do it, and I will prove that the Father should be glorified, as He gave Me the authority to bring this to pass." Jesus is the one who performs the ministry when we step out in authority to minister to other people.

TWO FAR-REACHING COVENANT PROMISES

Let's look at two covenant promises that are especially far-reaching and all-encompassing!

Christ has redeemed us from the curse of the law, having become a curse for us (for it is written, "Cursed is everyone who hangs on a tree"), that the blessing of Abraham might come upon the Gentiles in Christ Jesus, that we might receive the promise of the Spirit through faith (Galatians 3:13-14).

First, we see we are redeemed from the curse of disobedience. There is a long, long list of these curses in Deuteronomy 28:15-45, including sickness, poverty, confusion, broken relationships, and defeat in war. Verse 45 sums it up:

"Moreover all these curses shall come upon you and pursue and overtake you, until you are destroyed, because you did not obey the voice of the Lord your God, to keep His commandments and His statutes which He commanded you."

The good news is: those curses no longer pursue us. We are redeemed from every single one of them, because Jesus became a curse for us!

Next, Galatians 3:14 declares our blessing. Most of us are Gentiles (non-Jews), but if we are in Christ Jesus, we receive the blessing of Abraham. We already saw that "the promise of the Spirit through faith" was both the promise of receiving the Holy Spirit *and* the promise of *everything* the Holy Spirit promises, based on the Word of God. We can "make a demand" on any and all of these promises, and they will be delivered to us, with the presence of the Holy Spirit. It's the free gift of God, but you can only access it by faith in His Word.

This next covenant promise is equally all-encompassing:

For the law of the Spirit of life in Christ Jesus has made me free from the law of sin and death (Romans 8:2).

What exactly is "the law of sin and death"? Some say it is the law of cause and effect, mentioned throughout the Old Testament. Ezekiel sums it up in Ezekiel 18:20:

"The soul who sins shall die."

Sin has consequences, including sickness and death. But Jesus has removed the curse from us, breaking the cycle of sin and death. For those who are in Christ, the law of the Spirit of life is *much stronger* than the law of sin and death. It sets us free from what *should happen naturally,* as John G. Lake demonstrated. Because of the law of the Spirit of life, the plague germs died when they touched his body! Someone might sneeze or cough in our face, but we will not get sick, because of the law of the Spirit of life. You can tell those you are ministering to, "The healing power in *me* is more contagious than any sickness in *you.* In fact, Jesus said if I lay hands on the sick, they will recover!"

METHOD 2 - EXAMPLE #1: PAUL & SILAS MADE A DEMAND ON JESUS' NAME

Now it happened, as we went to prayer, that a certain slave girl possessed with a spirit of divination met us, who brought her masters much profit by fortune-telling. This girl followed Paul and us, and cried out, saying, "These men are the servants of the Most High God, who proclaim to us the way of salvation." And this she did for many days.

But Paul, greatly annoyed, turned and said to the spirit, "I command you in the name of Jesus Christ to come out of her." And he came out that very hour (Acts 16:16-18).

Demons obeyed Jesus when He walked the earth. Before the Cross, demons "were subject" to the disciples in His name (Luke 10:17). Here, after the Resurrection, a demon obeyed a command made "in the name of Jesus." Nothing has changed: demons still obey that name today!

CHAPTER TWENTY-THREE

CATEGORY 2 – HEALING BY MUTUAL FAITH

CATEGORY 2, GIVING AND RECEIVING HEALING by joint or mutual faith, has two methods: the laying on of hands and the prayer of agreement. Mutual faith is how most healing is accomplished. Brother Hagin often said that in his 65 years of ministry, most of the healings he saw manifest in people's lives were because of joint or mutual faith. In other words, it required faith on the individual's part and somebody else agreeing with them in prayer and ministering to them.

METHOD 3 - THE LAYING ON OF HANDS

The first method we will look at in this category is Method 3 - The Laying on of Hands, to give and receive through mutual faith. Mutual faith is activated when the person comes to you and says, "If you lay hands on me, I will be healed."

And He said to them, "Go into all the world and preach the gospel to every creature. He who believes and is baptized will be saved; but

he who does not believe will be condemned. And these signs will follow those who believe: In My name they will cast out demons; they will speak with new tongues; they will take up serpents; and if they drink anything deadly, it will by no means hurt them; they will lay hands on the sick, and they will recover" (Mark 16:15-18).

THOSE WHO BELIEVE IN MY NAME

As an aside: when Jesus said, "These signs shall follow those who believe," it's important to remember that the original Greek has no punctuation. The punctuation came in as translators made some assumptions about where the punctuation should go. The translators wrote, "These signs shall follow those who believe" - then a colon. Jesus went to say, "In My name they shall cast out demons; they will speak with new tongues," etc. We know that we're to do these things in His name. But we also know that these signs don't follow everyone who believes in Jesus! In my opinion, this sentence should be punctuated like this: "These signs shall follow those who believe in My name" - then the colon, followed by the list of signs, because these signs certainly don't follow those who limit their belief to salvation alone.

This makes a huge difference! There are many who are born-again Christians - they believe - but they're nowhere close to believing the kind of things we're talking about here, for example, that God is still a healer. They are told from the pulpit, "God is not in the healing business anymore. And you would be arrogant to think that we could possibly come to God and ask for healing."

I believe that Jesus meant, "These signs shall follow

those who believe in all the authority that is in My name, and all the covenant promises that are in My name." The list that follows are the activities of the Church, the signs of those who believe fully in His name. We've exposed ourselves to the blessing of Abraham that He wants to deliver to the children of God, and we know it comes in the name of Jesus.

METHOD 3 - EXAMPLES #1, #2, & #3
FROM JESUS AND THE APOSTLES

Let's look at several examples of miraculous signs and wonders, given through the laying on of hands. The person laying hands on someone *must* believe that when they lay hands on someone, that an anointing is released, *and* that there's power in the prayer of agreement. Brother Hagin said that the laying on of hands and the anointing that is transferred seems to operate by what he called the law of contact and transmission. Something happens when we put our hands on someone: the power of God is able to flow through us. Notice that God is not telling us to do miracle incantations or anything, just the simple act of putting our hands on someone. But we believe that when we pray the prayer of faith and we lay hands on someone, that the power of God, and the anointing, *plus their faith* will make it happen. Most likely, people who ask us to lay hands on them have *some* faith that it's going to work. They want to be healed, and they believe the laying on of hands is effective.

The following is an example of when people received healing through the hands of Jesus:

> **When the sun was setting, all those who had any that were sick with various diseases brought them to Him; and He laid His hands on every one of them and healed them (Luke 4:40).**

Jesus laid His hands on everyone there and healed them. There were many times when Jesus actually laid hands on every person in the crowd - it could have been thousands! Other times, He just spoke the Word to people, and they were healed.

In the Book of Acts, the apostles laid hands on people - just as they had seen Jesus do - and many signs and wonders were done.

And through the hands of the apostles many signs and wonders were done among the people (Acts 5:12).

Therefore they stayed there a long time, speaking boldly in the Lord, who was bearing witness to the word of His grace, granting signs and wonders to be done by their hands (Acts 14:3).

METHOD 3 - EXAMPLE #4: THE WOMAN WHO WAS HEALED ON ACCIDENT

We have no way to explain what God's going to do and how He is going to do it! Once, I was scheduled to minister in a weeklong seminar on biblical prosperity, sponsored by our LCU campus in Norway. When the Campus Host Pastor picked me up at the airport, he said, "Someone donated a tent to our church, and for the last two weeks, we've been doing tent meetings in downtown Tonsberg. We can be there in time for you to preach tonight, if you want to." My body was tired after the 15-hour international flight, but my spirit was "ready in season and out of season" (2 Timothy 4:2). I was ready to go and minister!

We made it to the tent meeting in time for worship.

Then, as I began to teach, for some reason, the Lord had me tell my "tie story." You see, my favorite part of wearing a suit has always been the tie. The Lord told me that if anybody complemented me on a favorite tie, I should give it to them. (It was one of those things God does to make sure that we don't have any covetousness.) This had already happened a number of times. That night, the pastor's adult son was translating for me. As I told the story of how the Lord said to give my tie to anyone who complemented me on it, he translated that to the crowd. Then he looked right at me and said, "Wow! I REALLY, REALLY like your tie!" Everyone laughed. I said, "Well then, it's yours!" and I took it off and gave it to him.

Well, something about that exchange hit the crowd, and the next thing we knew, they were laughing hysterically. The joy of the Lord swept into the place - just as many of us have experienced in revival meetings. At times like these, I have learned to step back and see what the Lord wants to do. Suddenly, the Lord quickened to me to do a healing line while everyone was experiencing the joy of the Lord, in the presence of the Lord. I told the pastor, "People need healing. The Lord said to do a healing line."

The tent was in a parking lot - a gravel parking lot. I looked around, thinking, "Lord, You said to do a healing line. I'll lay hands on people, but surely the ushers are not just going to lay the people in the gravel." But that's what happened: as I laid hands on people, if they fell under the power of the anointing, the ushers were laying them down - in the gravel!

SHE WAS A WALKING SKELETON
- JUST SKIN AND BONES

As I went down the healing line, I got to a woman who looked like she had already died: she was a walking skeleton – just skin and bones. Then I noticed her arms: she actually had the ports and wrappings for IVs in her arms! I thought, "Oh my gosh! She really needs a healing." I didn't know the whole story then, but it turned out she had leukemia and she was a drug addict, so she was in terrible physical condition. Someone had brought her to the service two nights earlier, where she got born again. On this night, the doctors had released her from the hospital, even though they thought she may die at any time.

I didn't know all of this: I simply laid hands on her and prayed. I felt a powerful anointing go into her. I was thinking, "Certainly the ushers are not going to lay *her* down in the gravel!" But, sure enough, they did! At least, they covered her up afterwards, with someone's jacket. After I prayed for her, I went on down the healing line, thinking, "Okay, Lord, I trust You for everything." I didn't hear anything more about what happened to her.

The next day, I taught the seminar on biblical prosperity at the church. The first night was good. The second night, this same woman showed up! They had released her from the hospital – completely healed of everything! She was not on drugs anymore, and she was completely healed from leukemia! Her color was starting to come back: she looked so much better! It was just one of those God things! I refer to this story as "The Woman Who Was Healed on Accident," because I wasn't supposed to be preaching that night. But the Lord sets up these divine appointments.

This is a stunning example of someone receiving a healing miracle by mutual faith, through a simple laying on of hands and believing God. It proves miracles still happen: even today we get wonderful results as we use God's biblical methods.

METHOD 3 - EXAMPLE #5: HEALING THE MAGISTRATE'S FATHER

And it happened that the father of Publius lay sick of a fever and dysentery. Paul went into him and prayed, and he laid his hands on him and healed him. So when this was done, the rest of those on the island who had diseases also came and were healed (Acts 28:8,9).

This happened on the island of Malta, where Paul was shipwrecked. Earlier that day, he was bitten by a poisonous snake, which he shook off into the fire. When he didn't die, the natives decided he was a god. Then Paul discovered that the father of the magistrate was sick. Paul laid hands on him and prayed. This was the start of a great revival on the island.

METHOD 3 - EXAMPLE #6: PAUL'S HANDKERCHIEFS

Now God worked unusual miracles by the hands of Paul, so that even handkerchiefs or aprons were brought from his body to the sick, and the diseases left them and the evil spirits went out of them (Acts 19:11-12).

In Method 3, we are discussing healing through the laying on of hands. Paul's handkerchiefs are a very interesting and unique situation. This is an extension of what is available through the laying on of hands - laying hands on cloths and sending them out.

Paul surely heard the stories from Jesus' earthly ministry, for example, how the woman with the issue of blood pressed through the crowd and laid hold of Jesus' garment - just the cloth - and the anointing in it flowed out to her. After this woman was healed, many others got similar results:

> **Wherever He entered, into villages, cities, or the country, they laid the sick in the market-places, and begged Him that they might just touch the hem of His garment. And as many as touched Him were made well (Mark 6:56).**

Paul must have somehow understood that cloth could carry the anointing. Then he got the idea of laying hands on handkerchiefs or aprons, to transfer the anointing to those who could not come to him in person. He probably held the cloths close to his body, prayed for them, and then sent them out to those who needed healing.

This passage goes on to say the diseases left and the evil spirits went out of them. If there was a spirit of infirmity causing the sickness, they were delivered from the spirit of infirmity and *then* they were healed.

METHOD 3 - EXAMPLE #7: A MODERN-DAY HEALING CLOTH

Today, the Church has picked up on sending out anointed cloths as a method of healing, saying, "Why not? Let's give it a whirl! If it worked for Jesus and for the Apostle Paul, let's do it!" When I was ministering in Norway the following year, a young man came forward. While we were in the meeting, he had received a call. He told us, "I have to leave. My grandmother is in the hospital back in Helsinki, Finland, and they told me, 'Get here quickly if you want to see your grandmother before she goes.' Can we pray for her?" The doctors said she had terminal cancer, and there was nothing else they could do for her. We had some prayer clothes nearby: I laid hands on a cloth and anointed it with oil, and the man took it back to his grandmother in Helsinki. That same week, I was still ministering at the conference, when the call came that the grandmother was completely healed and released from the hospital! The doctors gave her a clean bill of health! You can't get a better report than that!

I don't know why these things happen on the foreign field more than they do here. But whenever God opens a door, run through it, and watch the Lord do these wonderful things! This gave me a chance to get experience for this teaching, because God proved this scripture to be true to me.

THE LAYING ON OF HANDS IS A FUNDAMENTAL DOCTRINE

Therefore, leaving the discussion of the elementary principles of Christ, let us go on to perfection, not laying again the foundation of repentance from dead works and of faith toward God, of the doctrine of baptisms, of laying on of hands, of resurrection of the dead, and of eternal judgment (Hebrews 6:1,2).

The laying on of hands is an important, fundamental doctrine, on par with the other doctrines listed. Brother Hagin liked to point this out, because a lot of Christians have discounted the idea of the laying on of hands. You don't find it practiced in a lot of churches. They practice different things they call sacerdotal ordinances, such as baptism, but not the laying on of hands. If we're going to be scriptural, we need to see this as a foundational doctrine, and practice it.

Let's quickly examine these foundational doctrines, one at a time:

· Dead works and faith towards God: For the gospel to go to the Jews, they had to first repent of the dead works that weren't getting them anywhere. The keeping of the Law of Moses did *not* give them the new birth *nor* the infilling of the Spirit of God.

- Baptisms: Notice there is not just one baptism, but several: baptism into Christ at the new birth, baptism in water, baptism in the Holy Spirit, and baptism in holy fire.

- Laying on of hands: Right smack in the middle of these other foundational doctrines, we find the laying on of hands.

- Resurrection of the dead: It's foundational for us to understand that believers will all be raised from the dead and be given glorified bodies so we can live eternally in heaven.

- Eternal judgment: It's foundational to know what's going to happen to all the people who live on the planet – believers are going to be with Christ and the family of God, while those outside of Christ will end up in hell.

LAYING ON OF HANDS FOR SEPARATION INTO MINISTRY

Laying on of hands is also used for separation into ministry. In Acts 6, the apostles told the members of the early Church to choose seven deacons to serve them. Then the apostles anointed them for ministry.

Whom they set before the apostles; and when they had prayed, they laid hands on them (Acts 6:6).

These men were ready to step out into ministry, so the apostles laid hands on them. Our next example is the sending out of Paul and Barnabas.

Now in the church that was at Antioch there were certain prophets and teachers: Barnabas, Simeon who was called Niger, Lucius of

**Cyrene, Manaen who had been brought up
with Herod the tetrarch, and Saul. As they ministered to the Lord and fasted, the Holy Spirit
said, "Now separate to Me Barnabas and Saul
for the work to which I have called them."
Then, having fasted and prayed, and laid
hands on them, they sent them away. So, being
sent out by the Holy Spirit, they went down to
Seleucia, and from there they sailed to Cyprus
(Acts 13:1-4).**

How did the Holy Spirit speak? Through one of the
gifts of the Spirit operating through one of the prophets.
This prophecy launched Barnabas and Paul out on their
first missionary journey, and much of what follows in the
Book of Acts revolves around the missionary journeys of
Paul and Barnabas and, later, Paul and Silas.

Notice that after the church leaders fasted and
prayed, they laid hands on Paul and Barnabas and sent
them away. It seems there was an impartation of a special
equipping to be able to do what God had called them to
do, through the laying on of hands. I believe that because
of the presence of the Holy Spirit inside our spirit, that
everything we need is there. But there's something that
happens with the laying on of hands that breaks it open to
be released to the outside. I don't believe the endowment
comes at that point in time, rather it's released at that
point in time. But it seems to require the anointing from
the laying on of hands to get this special equipping to start
flowing and be in operation.

LAYING ON OF HANDS FOR SPECIAL ENDOWMENTS

Special endowments of miraculous faculties may be
released as well, as we see in 1 Timothy 4:14:

Do not neglect the gift that is in you, which was given to you by prophecy with the laying on of the hands of the eldership.

There was a point in time when several elders laid hands on Timothy. Paul was pointing out here that Timothy should not neglect the gift that was opened up, to be released through him when the elders prayed. Later, Paul himself laid hands on Timothy, who began operating in special giftings.

Therefore I remind you to stir up the gift of God which is in you through the laying on of my hands (2 Timothy 1:6).

Whenever you have an opportunity for an anointed minister with a gift that you deeply respect to lay hands on you, get in that line, and let the Lord impart to you. Over the course of time, Brother Hagin has laid hands on me for impartation several times, Brother Kenneth Copeland several times, as well as a number of other people, whom I deeply respect.

METHOD 3 - EXAMPLE #8: AN IMPARTATION FROM SMITH WIGGLESWORTH

A friend of mine, Desmond Frey, who currently pastors a church in Switzerland, told me the following story. His grandmother had been an intern of Smith Wigglesworth in South Africa. As Desmond found out more about her ministry, he felt led by the Lord to go and visit her. He wanted to get her to lay hands on him, to impart whatever anointing God wanted to impart to him, because of that ministry. Brother Hagin said it had been documented by different ministers that Brother Hagin knew, that 23 people were raised from the dead under Wigglesworth's ministry. When Wigglesworth ministered in South Africa, they saw all kinds of miracles.

Desmond found out that his grandmother, after having been an intern for Wigglesworth, had seen seven people raised from the dead under *her* ministry. Now he had a lot of questions! When his uncle picked him up at the airport, Desmond discovered that this same uncle was the first one raised from the dead under his grandmother's ministry! Desmond started to hear all of these incredible stories. He said, "I really, really want to get Grandmother to lay hands on me and pray for me for an impartation."

When Desmond finally got to talk to his grandmother, he told her, "I want to talk to you about the ministry, because I'm in ministry now."

Grandmother said, "The day you were born, the Lord spoke to me and said that of all of my thirteen grandchildren, you were the one who was called by God, to take His power into your generation."

He asked, "Grandmother, why didn't you ever tell me anything about this?"

She said, "If I told you, you would have thought it was a call from *me* and not from the *Lord.* Once you knew you were called in ministry, I knew you would show up, and I would be able to minister to you then."

ANOINTED TO RAISE THE DEAD

Next, she said, "Let me tell you a story about being an intern with Smith Wigglesworth. He was training all of us, and we would go to the meetings with him. As we got to this one meeting in a small church, he picked four or five of us out of a crowd of interns and said, "Come with me."

Smith Wigglesworth had been a plumber and was a big, gruff kind of guy. He had all these incredible miracles, but quite often he was rough with people, because, as he put it, "I'm dealing with the devil, not with the people." He would do things like punch somebody in a goiter and they would pass out. People watching this would be upset at first, but then suddenly, the person would jump up and start running around the place, completely healed! The goiter was gone! Then, people would understand.

Grandmother said, "Wigglesworth, in his gruff way, said, 'Come! Come! Come! Get in the room!' We walked into the room, and there sat a big box, on top of a table. He grabbed each one of us by the shoulder and took us around to exactly where he wanted us to stand. We didn't understand why. Then he got on the other side of the table and pulled off the top of the box: there was a dead 14-year-old girl laying in there! He said to us, 'You are about to see the greatest demonstration of the love of God that you will ever see. You will never be the same after this night.'

"Then, Wigglesworth grabbed the girl by the lapels of her jacket, pulled her up, and started commanding the power of God back into her body. He commanded her to live and not die. All of a sudden, she just woke up! She looked at everybody and said, 'Hello.' Wigglesworth helped the girl get out of the box and down from the table."

Grandmother continued, "I was never the same after that – and that is why I have this ministry."

Desmond said, "Grandmother, I want you to pray for me."

She said, "No, I want you to pray for me first. I've walked in faith all these years, but I've got this chest congestion and I've not been able to get rid of it. My prayer of faith has not been working on it, and no gift of the Spirit has been working on it. I want you to pray for me. Just lay your hand right here on my chest." Desmond laid his hand on her chest and started praying, thanking the Lord for her life and ministry.

Then Desmond told me, "The weirdest thing in the world happened. While I was praying for her, with my eyes closed, I felt the anointing - it was the most intense electrical power flowing out of my arm. Then it started pressing my hand down. I felt like my hand suddenly dropped through her chest. It was so real, I was afraid to open my eyes in case it really had! I felt my hand touch her heart. All of a sudden, the power started flowing back up into my arm and into my body. I realized I was getting flooded with this incredible anointing from my grand-mother."

I WANT THAT SAME ANOINTING!

As he told me this story, I said, "Brother, I know how this thing works! You take that hand right now and put it on my head. You pray. I want that same anointing!"

We don't really understand how these things work; we just know it's part of the doctrine of laying on of hands. The anointing is transferable, and the law of con-tact and transmission opens us up to God doing certain things by the anointing. Sometimes, the gifting of the Spirit of God to move us into other areas of ministry is released through this process.

BLESSINGS FLOW IN AND OUT

Once, when I was meditating on these scriptures about the laying on of hands, the Lord quickened this to me: "A deep understanding of the Word, along with being yielded to the Holy Spirit and His various anointings, will keep you in the blessing flow - in and out - that which needs to flow *into* your life and that which needs to flow *out of* your life." In other words, if you are immersed in the Word and saturated with the Holy Spirit, you can stay in the flow of the blessing of the Lord and that blessing can flow into your life to give what you need and can flow *out of* your life when you're ministering to other people.

Proverbs 27:17 NIV says, "As iron sharpens iron, so one person sharpens another." Something happens when we are in contact with people. When I have been asked to pray for somebody in the hospital who didn't want me to pray in the name of Jesus, I just leaned on the Word, which says, "Lay hands on the sick and they shall recover." I greet them and shake their hand, and then I put one hand on them and say, "I hope that you will be really blessed and healed." To me, I'm releasing my faith for God to do something in their life. By doing this, I've seen several people healed and come out of the hospital.

If we are conscious of this and we release our faith for it, whenever we shake hands with a born-again believer, we can give and receive from them. They each have various anointings, based on how the Lord uses them. There might be something operational in *their* life that we might need flowing in *our* life and something in *our* life that they might need in *their* life.

Now, every time I shake a Christian minister's hand, I put my faith out there and pray silently, "Lord, I give and receive the anointing that produces the blessing." That's a hand they use to lay hands on other people, to let the anointing flow, and your hand is one that you use to lay hands on other people, to let the blessing flow. You can also do this as an exercise with a group of people: instead of just greeting one another and shaking hands, have them intentionally release blessings and anointings into one another's lives.

LAYING ON OF HANDS AND
THE BAPTISM OF THE HOLY SPIRIT

In the Bible, the baptism of the Holy Spirit was given through the laying on of hands, as seen in the following verses:

Then they laid hands on them, and they received the Holy Spirit. And when Simon saw that through the laying on of the apostles' hands the Holy Spirit was given, he offered them money (Acts 8:17,18).

And Ananias went his way and entered the house; and laying his hands on him he said, "Brother Saul, the Lord Jesus, who appeared to you on the road as you came, has sent me that you may receive your sight and be filled with the Holy Spirit" (Acts 9:17).

And when Paul had laid hands on them, the Holy Spirit came upon them, and they spoke with tongues and prophesied (Acts 19:6).

Still today, the laying on of hands is used quite frequently in ministering the baptism of the Holy Spirit to people.

THIS YOUNG MAN WILL LAY HANDS ON YOU

Right after I graduated from Rhema, international evangelist and church planter Bill Basansky was ministering at the Spirit-filled Methodist Church that I had attended before going to Rhema. I went to the service the first night; the next morning, Brother Basansky started the service by saying, "We're going to have a healing service this morning, like I told you. But the Lord told me to have this young man (he was pointing to me!) lay hands on you, and the same anointing that's on me is going to be on him."

Then, Brother Basansky called me up to the platform and laid hands on me. And, sure enough, as I started laying hands on everyone, I could feel the power of God going into people, and all of a sudden, they were being healed! Hallelujah!

I used to joke about people who had just graduated from Bible school, then suddenly were holding healing services. But this experience changed how I thought about this. The Lord told me, "I can launch you into the healing ministry any time I want to." It just took a word from another man of God, who understood this. Brother Basansky was helping me, as a young minister, get started. It released an anointing to heal the sick that gave me a jump-start in the healing ministry.

A lot is accomplished through the laying on of hands: signs and wonders of healing, separation for ministry, the impartation of special endowments, as well as the baptism of the Holy Spirit. It is obvious that the laying on of hands is important to the Lord, even if so much of the Church sees no value in it.

METHOD 4 - THE PRAYER OF AGREEMENT

Method 4 - The Prayer of Agreement is still in the category of giving and receiving, through joint or mutual faith. The prayer of agreement happens when your faith joins together with someone else's faith for receiving of healing. Jesus said:

"Again I say to you that if two of you agree on earth concerning anything that they ask, it will be done for them by My Father in heaven" (Matthew 18:19).

To come into agreement means to be on the same page, going in the same direction, coming into total alignment concerning the promises of God. Amos 3:3 says:

"Can two walk together, unless they are agreed?"

We understand it's this spiritual agreement, this alignment that makes the miracles happen. Remember, Brother Hagin said the vast majority of the healings he saw were through joint or mutual faith. So, praise God, we want to use all the tools of joint and mutual faith, including the prayer of agreement! This is something that married couples should be able to use concerning praying for any need to be met.

METHOD 4 - EXAMPLE #1: ANOTHER LAME MAN LEAPED

An example of an individual who received by mutual faith is found in Acts 14:8-10:

And in Lystra a certain man without strength in his feet was sitting, a cripple from his mother's womb, who had never walked. This man heard Paul speaking. Paul, observing him intently and seeing that he had faith to be healed, said with a loud voice, "Stand up straight on your feet!" And he leaped and walked.

I don't know *how* Paul saw that the man had faith to be healed. Maybe he saw the spark in his eyes as he heard Paul's words and faith came alive on the inside of him. We don't see the laying on of hands here; we see the alignment, the agreement of faith. Paul had the faith for the man to be healed and when Paul saw the lame man had faith to be healed, Paul simply spoke to him, just like Jesus did. Paul said, "Stand up straight on your feet," and the man did! Wow! It's awesome to see that kind of manifestation!

METHOD 4 - EXAMPLE #2: TOXEMIA REVERSED

Years and years ago, when we first started the University, I pastored a church. For the first five years, Dr. Deb Smith was a youth pastor with us. Her daughter Marchant had been a student at LCU. When Marchant was pregnant with her second child, she was having problems in the pregnancy. Then she got toxemia: her whole system was toxic, and it was getting very urgent. I didn't realize how urgent it was until Deb called me at 3 o'clock in the morning saying, "Come to the hospital and pray! Marchant is really in trouble."

I called my associate pastor, Brother Terry Popp, and asked, "Can you go to the hospital with me?" When we got there, Marchant had tubes in her nose and down her throat. They had her all wired up to a monitor to watch her contractions, which were really consistent. She was only five months pregnant, so this was way too early for the baby to come, but she was basically going into labor because of the toxemia. The doctors were trying to pump poison out of her stomach with the tube, but nothing was coming out.

FIRST, LOCATE WHERE THEY ARE SPIRITUALLY

Before we prayed for Marchant, I remembered a bit of wisdom from Brother Hagin. He said, "It's really good before you pray for somebody for healing, that you locate where they are spiritually, where *their* faith is, what is it *they* believe about the healing power of God, because we're talking about the prayer of agreement." He said he would always ask people, and then he would know more specifically how to pray. So, I asked Marchant, "Tell me how you want me to pray. Do you want me to pray that everything the doctors are doing is going to work and that it will all be fine? Or, do you want me to pray that Jesus would just heal you and that the doctors will be amazed? I need to know where your faith is."

Marchant said, "Jesus is my Healer. I pray that Jesus just heals me right now."

I said, "Okay!" So, we laid hands on her and we prayed. We felt the anointing of God fill room. My associate had not been on a lot of hospital visits and felt squeamish seeing all the tubes in Marchant. He almost passed out; he fell backwards and slid down the wall to the floor. I thought, "Oh, great! Now I need to minister to him while I'm still trying to minister to Marchant." But I knew we had laid hands on her and prayed, we connected with her faith, and we were in that place of agreement.

WE WATCHED AS THE MACHINES RECORDED THE MIRACLE!

I went over to Brother Terry, who said, "Help me stand up." So, I helped by pulling him up the wall. Marchant happened to glance at Terry when he came up the wall – and all of a sudden, she had a vision of Jesus! She reached her hands out to Him and said, "It's Jesus!" We watched the machine that was trying to pump poisons out of her suddenly kick in, pumping all this toxic fluid out of her system. We looked at the monitor showing her contractions, and all of a sudden, this monitor flatlined: the contraction just stopped. Hallelujah!

This was the only time I've ever prayed for somebody and been able to watch the healing actually be recorded by medical instruments, as the healing completely manifested. We were all amazed at being able to see the entire miracle unfold. For the prayer of agreement, it was so important for Marchant to verbalize "Jesus is my Healer. I believe Jesus is going to heal me, and this is going to amaze the doctors." And we got exactly what we were praying for: the doctors were quite shocked! With the crisis was over, Marchant was able to go the full nine months and had a totally healthy baby girl, who now looks like a fashion model and has served in the Air Force for several years.

IT TAKES AN AGREEMENT OF FAITH

It's extremely important that we come to that place where we carefully follow the methods that God uses. When we see a prophet of God with a healing ministry – like Brother Hagin – taking steps to be sure that he was in true agreement with the faith of the one he was ministering to, we need to do the same things. We need to teach people the Word; we need their faith to be developed so they can be in agreement with us. We need to locate the other person's faith so we can meet them where they are. And we need to be in faith ourselves: if we have been healed or we've seen anybody else healed when we prayed for them, that encourages our faith that God will just keep doing it.

It's not rocket science! God is just asking for us to show up, pray in the name of Jesus, lay hands on the sick, and watch Him heal them. Our part is simple: we put our hand on them and pray. He does the miracle part: we get to watch it happen. Yes, it happens by the anointing: we have that anointing in us, and where two people are connected in their faith and agree, there's no telling what can happen! Only God, in the realm of the Spirit, knows.

What does God do when He recreates body parts for people? We will never get an explanation of that – one we can understand – until we get to heaven. If He would explain it to us now, it would be far beyond us to understand the biology of all of it. I'm sure it's beyond our best doctors to be able to grasp an explanation from God, of what He does when He performs His miracles. But, praise God, He *is* the miracle-working, healing God, the God that we serve!

CHAPTER TWENTY-FOUR

CATEGORY 3 – METHODS OF MINISTERING TO OTHERS

IN CATEGORY 3, THERE ARE THREE METHODS of ministering healing to others: the gifts of healings, using the name of Jesus in authority, and anointing with oil.

METHOD 5 - GIFTS OF HEALINGS

But the manifestation of the Spirit is given to each one for the profit of all: for to one is given the word of wisdom through the Spirit, to another the word of knowledge through the same Spirit, To another faith by the same Spirit, to another gifts of healings by the same Spirit, to another the working of miracles, to another prophecy, to another discerning of spirits, to another different kinds of tongues, to another the interpretation of tongues. But one and the same Spirit works all these things, distributing to each one individually as He wills (1 Corinthians 12:7-11).

These are the nine gifts of the Holy Spirit given to the Body of Christ, as the Lord wills and as the Holy Spirit wills. These gifts are given for various purposes. In the Old Testament, there were only seven gifts of the Spirit available, as tongues and the interpretation of tongues were not given until the Day of Pentecost. Jesus operated in all seven of the gifts available to Him. He was instantly ready to use every gift that the Holy Spirit had for Him to use. We know He didn't do anything the Holy Spirit didn't show Him to do. Sometimes, the Father pointed someone out, or someone called to Him and the Holy Spirit said, "Now is the time!"

We will be focusing here on the gifts of healing, but I want to mention the other two power gifts, which would include the working of miracles and what I call "special faith." This is not the "general" kind of faith that we gain through the hearing of the Word of God, that can increase all the time by our meditation on the Word. This is something that God gives as a special gifting. It was described by Smith Wigglesworth as a faith that would come down and wrap itself around his faith. It just took over. He said, "When that faith was in operation, I could believe for anything, any miracle that needed to happen." The gift of special faith usually works in conjunction with one of the other power gifts: working of miracles or gifts of healings. Special faith is also used for a minister to be able to receive from the Lord, for example, in the Old Testament, we quite often see prophets receive miracles of provision, through special faith.

SACRED ENDOWMENTS

Every gift that God gives us should be approached and considered as a sacred endowment because it is an endowment from God the Father. We should value it highly and desire that we would be obedient and yielded to the Lord, so that if He would like to use us in any way with a special gifting, that we would freely move in it in ministry.

Notice that it's the gifts of healings; both words are in

the plural form. The reason there are multiple gifts is there are so many people. I believe everybody can have a gift of healing, if they will simply step into what God has for them. Different ministers have different specialties. After many years of ministry, Brother Hagin said, "I found out that my particular specific gift of healing was for healing any tumor – whether it was benign or malignant. When I ministered in this area, I almost always saw success. The tumors would just wither in people's bodies – they would dry up and be gone!" Other people find that almost everybody who is deaf is healed when they pray.

Let's look at two examples of Method 5 - the gifts of healings in operation.

METHOD 5 - EXAMPLE #1: THE MAN AT THE POOL OF BETHESDA

Now there is in Jerusalem by the Sheep Gate a pool, which is called in Hebrew, Bethesda, having five porches. In these lay a great multitude of sick people, blind, lame, paralyzed, waiting for the moving of the water. For an angel went down at a certain time into the pool and stirred up the water; then whoever stepped in first, after the stirring of the water, was made well of whatever disease he had (John 5:2-4).

Healing angels are powerful. Ever since 1999, whenever I've held a healing service, the healing angels have been there; they are always on assignment.

In this story, a healing angel would come and get in the pool and stir up the water. It wasn't the stirring or the water that healed people, it was the healing angel indicating he was there, by moving the water. Why God did this, we don't know - it was a sign and a wonder. It became well- known that healing would take place at the pool of Bethesda, so many sick people would gather, waiting for the angel to show up and stir the water. Whoever got into the water first, made contact with the healing angel, and they were suddenly and completely healed.

Now a certain man was there who had an infirmity thirty-eight years. When Jesus saw him lying there, and knew that he already had been in that condition a long time, He said to him, "Do you want to be made well?" (John 5:5,6).

Jesus saw the man lying there and knew - by a word of knowledge - exactly how long this man had been like this. Jesus asked, "Do you want to be made well?" Jesus asked him this question to elicit a response from him, hoping he would speak - by faith - exactly what it was that he was believing for.

The sick man answered Him, "Sir, I have no man to put me into the pool when the water is stirred up; but while I am coming, another steps down before me" (John 5:7).

His first statement was about the fact he's waiting for the opportunity to get into the pool of water. As far as he knew, Jesus was just another bystander, asking him a question that should be obvious to everybody. He's thinking, "Of course I want to be healed. That's why I'm sitting here wanting to get in the water." He told Jesus, "I don't have anyone to help me. While I'm coming, someone else gets there before me." Because he was crippled, he couldn't get up and get in the water. Somebody beat him to it - every time. Maybe it was the blind people who were beating him: they could hear the water moving and could dive right in! Or maybe it was the deaf people. He simply couldn't move fast enough to be the first one in.

Jesus was looking for a statement of faith, that the man wanted to be made well. Instead, he described how every time he tried, healing escaped him: he was not *able* to receive his healing, but he *wanted* it.

Jesus said to him, "Rise, take up your bed and walk." And immediately, the man was made well, took up his bed, and walked (John 5:8,9a).

Jesus was operating in one of the gifts of the Spirit. There was no indication here that the man himself had faith, like when Paul saw that a crippled man had faith to be healed (Acts 14:8-10). As soon as Jesus said, "Rise, take up your bed and walk," instantly, the man was healed. He must have immediately felt in himself that he was healed and *could* get up. He instantly tried to do something that he couldn't do before: he began to walk!

METHOD 5 - EXAMPLE #2: PETER RAISES DORCAS FROM THE DEAD

Peter raised Dorcas from the dead after Jesus went to heaven. Peter did what he had seen Jesus do, and he got the same results.

At Joppa there was a certain disciple named Tabitha, which is translated Dorcas. This woman was full of good works and charitable deeds which she did. But it happened in those days that she became sick and died. When they had washed her, they laid her in an upper room. And since Lydda was near Joppa, and the disciples had heard that Peter was there, they sent two men to him, imploring him not to delay in coming to them.

Then Peter arose and went with them. When he had come, they brought him to the upper room. And all the widows stood by him weeping, showing the tunics and garments which Dorcas had made while she was with them. But Peter put them all out, and knelt down and prayed. And turning to the body he said, "Tabitha, arise." And she opened her eyes, and when she saw Peter she sat up. Then he gave her his hand and lifted her up; and when he had called the saints and widows, he presented her alive (Acts 9:36-41).

I'm sure those widows did some serious rejoicing!

WHAT IT TAKES TO RAISE THE DEAD

The gifts of the Spirit were in operation in Peter: in the case of raising somebody from the dead, it usually requires at least two power gifts, most often three. First, their spirit has already left their body. Special faith is involved in calling somebody's spirit back. Second, working of miracles is needed for their body to come back to life. Third, gifts of healings are in operation to heal them from whatever it was that killed them, so they don't just instantly die again.

All of the seven gifts of the Spirit were in operation when Jesus raised Lazarus from the dead, in John 11.

· Word of wisdom and word of knowledge: When Jesus heard Lazarus was sick, He said, "This sickness is not unto death, but for the glory of God, that the Son of God may be glorified through it" (John 11:4). Later Jesus said plainly, "Lazarus is dead." Jesus was operating by the word of knowledge, as He knew that Lazarus had gone from being sick, to dying. Jesus was also operating in a word of wisdom: He knew that He planned to raise Lazarus from the dead.

• Gift of prophecy: Jesus said to Martha, "I am the resurrection and the life. He who believes in Me, though he may die, he shall live. And whoever lives and believes in Me shall never die. Do you believe this?" (John 11:25,26). This is a prophetic exhortation. New Testament prophecy is to speak by sudden inspiration of the Spirit, for edification, exhortation, and comfort. Jesus was prophesying to Martha to encourage her.

• Discerning of spirits: Jesus was at the grave, about to call Lazarus forth. As men rolled back the stone, Jesus lifted up His eyes and said, "Father, I thank You that You have heard Me. And I know that You always hear Me, but because of the people who are standing by I said this, that they may believe that You sent Me" (John 11:41b,42). Jesus was seeing the Father in the realm of the Spirit. That's what discerning of spirits is: to be able to see into the realm of the spirit.

• Gift of faith: This is the special faith that it would take to call Lazarus' spirit back into his body, as he had already departed and was now in Abraham's bosom. Jesus could see Lazarus as a spirit in the realm of the Spirit. Jesus knew He had to call Lazarus' spirit back into his body. Jesus spoke to Lazarus in the realm of the Spirit with a loud voice, saying, "Lazarus, come forth!" (John 11:43).

• Gifts of healings: Lazarus' body was still riddled with whatever sickness killed him. That had to be healed at the same time his spirit was being placed back in his body.

• Working of miracles: This had to be in operation to

be able to raise Lazarus from the dead, to cause his heart to start beating and all his organs to start functioning again.

So, all seven gifts of the Spirit were in operation when Jesus raised Lazarus from the dead. I'm not sure that in every other case when Jesus raised the dead, that He used all seven, but we know that all three of the power gifts are in operation when someone is raised from the dead.

Who gets to raise people from the dead? We don't know, but Jesus said we are supposed to pray for people who died to be raised from the dead (Matthew 10:8). I've prayed for three people to be raised from the dead so far. I haven't seen anyone raised from the dead yet, but I'm three closer to my first one! One thing is for sure: if you never pray for someone to be raised from the dead, you'll never see anyone raised from the dead! It's important to take this step.

Maybe you're like me and you've seen different gifts of the Spirit in operation in your life. I've seen all nine gifts of the Spirit in operation in my life at one time or another. At any point in time that God wants to activate whatever gifts are necessary to raise someone who has died, I'm ready!

I'll still pray for a young Christian to be raised from the dead, but I've kind of given up trying to get an older Christian to come back, because once they go into the presence of Jesus, how are you going to compete? What is there to come back to, compared to being in glory and seeing Jesus face-to-face? Sometimes Jesus says they have to come back because they haven't finished their race. In the case of someone who *didn't* know the Lord, I would be more than happy to pray for them. Finding themselves so close to the gates of hell, they will most certainly want to come back! They can get saved and healed at the same time - so they can stay raised from the dead. Keep this in mind if you happen to come into a situation where you're called on to pray for someone who may have just passed away.

THE NIGHT I RECEIVED THE GIFT OF SPECIAL FAITH

This happened right after we started Life Christian University, in 1995. I began having chest pains that kept me up in the middle of the night. I was way too young to be having any kind of problem with my heart. I prayed the prayer of faith, and I tried standing in faith, but didn't see any change. This went on for about two weeks, when it got so bad, I finally came to the place where I said, "I am not going to be foolish and not go to the doctor because I'm trying to prove that I can walk by faith, if there's something medically that can be done." I needed to at least get a diagnosis and find out what was going on. I had been walking in divine health since November 1980, and hadn't had any problems all that time. I hadn't told my wife anything about this, but I decided that the next day I would tell her, then go to the doctor.

I was sitting in my prayer chair, and I rocked back a little too far and knocked a book off the shelf. It was Howard Carter's book on the gifts of the Spirit. Brother Hagin said he got all his knowledge and understanding about the gifts from this book. As I picked it up, it suddenly fell open to a section on special faith. I read "in many cases special faith manifests on a regular basis for the man or woman of God to be able to receive something of their own."

Immediately, I heard the voice of the Father say, "Son, your faith is not working on this chest pain is it?"

I said, "No, Lord." I felt awful because I felt like I'd failed a test of faith. I started weeping. I was so apologetic: I said, "I'm so sorry, Lord. I'm so sorry! I don't know what to do. I've done everything I know to do, but I haven't been able to receive my healing."

Then, in the most compassionate voice I've ever heard, the Father said, "It's okay, Son. I'm giving you special faith for this." All of a sudden, I felt the presence of God come over me, from the top of my head to the soles of my feet. The pain was lifted off my chest. I jumped up. I knew I was healed. I thought, "How cool is that?" It happened miraculously enough: I knocked a book off the shelf, and it opened to exactly the little nugget that I needed.

A NEAR HEART ATTACK – FROM AN INFECTED ROOT CANAL!

When I turned 50, I started really taking care of myself, working out in, conjunction with eating right. That way, I wasn't working against the anointing for healing and divine health. Then, after I turned 62, there were a couple of months when I couldn't go to the gym. When I went back, I got on the elliptical and suddenly started having a pain right in the center of my chest. It was so bad, I had to get off the elliptical and sit out for minute. The pain went away, so I finished the rest of my workout. I thought maybe it was a bronchial infection or something. A couple of days later, I got back to the gym and got on the elliptical and the same thing happened – a real burning pain. I thought, "Maybe I need to go see if I need an antibiotic or something."

The next day, I woke up in the morning and the chest pain was back. I broke out in a cold sweat. I decided it was time to go to the hospital. I told my wife, "I need you to drive the kids to school today. I feel okay, other than this pain, but I need to be checked out. Tell the kids I'm going to an early doctor's appointment." I took a shower and drove myself to the hospital.

When you walk into the emergency room and tell

them you're having chest pains, they stick a wheelchair under you and immediately start running all kinds of tests. Then they told me, "The cardiologist can't see you until tomorrow. We want to admit you." My wife stayed with me until it was time to go pick up the kids. Later, all five of us were sitting in the room, chatting. Suddenly, the cardiologist walked in and announced, "We see what looks like a restriction in your heart. We want to do a laparoscopic procedure that would go in through the veins in your arm and take a look at your heart. If there's any problem, we will just fix it while we are in there. Everything will be fine."

I asked, "When do you want to do this?"

He said, "Within the hour."

The plan was to do a laparoscopic view first, then put a stent in, if there was any restriction of a blood vessel. The nurses told me, "It takes only about 5 minutes to do this. The prep takes longer than the procedure." Then they gave me a shot of something that made me pray in tongues.

I was kind of groggy and I asked, "Are you going to do this?"

They said, "It's already done!"

The doctor showed me on a fluoroscope: "Here was your heart before the procedure – here is your heart after. See this restriction? It is now completely open. You had a spike in your blood pressure and it caused this artery in your heart to stretch. And then it actually collapsed. We put a couple of stents in there and it's going to be like new. That particular blood vessel, the lateral anterior descending artery, is known as the widow maker. I'm really glad you came in when you did."

I said, "Boy, I am glad I did, too!"

I told you how I went for 31 years without a sick day other than a few days when it was better to stay at home, to receive full manifestation of my healing. Then this happened: the official "sick day and two nights" when they kept me in the hospital.

Later, I found myself going through what seemed to be a faith crisis. I said, "Okay, Lord, I'm doing everything that I know to do: walking in faith, eating right, and exercising. You have to let me know what would cause this. I need to know what's going on here." My wife and I prayed for wisdom.

The next morning, she got an email from Dr. Mercola, which said, "97% of all women who have breast cancer have had this procedure done." It told how having an infected root canal can have disastrous effects on your health.

The morning after we prayed, the Lord revealed the source of the problem! It turns out, I had a root canal done years before and it had gotten infected - and infected root canals can cause your blood pressure to go crazy. I had the tooth with the infected root canal taken out right away and a bridge put in. In my research I read, "Does any doctor tell you that it's okay to keep any part of your body in your body after it dies? No! But your dentist will tell you it's okay to keep a dead root in there." As we researched it further, we found out that infected root canals are a common problem. I want to put out a clarion call to anyone who may be suffering because of an infected root canal - see "Resources for Healing and Health" at the back of this book for more information.

God does so many miraculous things - even if it's to direct us to the knowledge we need in the natural realm. The healing power of the Lord was there, and has provided divine health for me ever since then, I just needed to have something addressed in my body that was infected.

SPECIAL FAITH TO MINISTER
THE BAPTISM OF THE HOLY SPIRIT

When the gift of special faith is operating, you can also help people receive the baptism of the Holy Spirit. I was leading a Sunday service at my home church, when the Lord said, "There are five people here who need to be baptized in the Holy Spirit."

I said, "Okay, Lord." I stopped everything and announced, "We are doing an altar call. There are five people who need to be baptized in the Holy Spirit. Come on up here." I was getting ready to give them some instruction from the Word, when the Lord said, "Why don't you use the gift of faith?"

I asked, "What? The gift You gave me for the healing of my chest pain?"

He said, "My gifts and callings are without repentance. If I give you a gift, use it when I say use it."

I realized it would work for this, so without giving them any instruction, I told them, "When I lay hands on you, you are instantly going to pray in tongues." I grabbed a microphone and stuck it in front of each one of them, and sure enough, each of them prayed in tongues out loud, as I went down the row. I thought that was awesome, and I said, "Lord, let that happen every time!" Well, it doesn't happen every time: it's as the Holy Spirit wills. But as you make yourself available to the Lord, walk in the Spirit, in faith and uprightly before the Lord, these things can happen.

METHOD 6 - USING THE NAME OF JESUS
IN AUTHORITY

The name of Jesus is so powerful. The disciples had a history of using the name of Jesus even before Jesus died on the Cross.

And when He had called His twelve disciples to Him, He gave them power over unclean spirits, to cast them out, and to heal all kinds of sickness and all kinds of disease (Matthew 10:1).

When the disciples went out and used the name of Jesus, they saw all sorts of healings take place. They reported, "Even the demons are subject to us in Your name." They didn't know how it worked, but they obeyed and saw incredible, miraculous things happen.

And Jesus came and spoke to them, saying, "All authority has been given to Me in heaven and on earth. Go therefore and make disciples of all the nations, baptizing them in the name of the Father and of the Son and of the Holy Spirit, teaching them to observe all things that I have commanded you; and lo, I am with you always, even to the end of the age" (Matthew 28:18-20).

The disciples operated in authority and power: we can operate in the same authority and power when we speak out and make a demand on the power of God, in the name of Jesus. It is just like when Jesus was moved with compassion: it was His spirit yearning to meet the person's need that put a demand on the power of God...and miraculous things happened!

We have looked closely at John 14:13,14 where Jesus told us to make a demand on the covenant promises of God, in His name. Jesus was basically saying, "My name won't work unless you put a demand on it." It's like making a demand on the power in the power socket, by plugging something into it. Jesus said, "Plug in here, use the power, and get the job done." He is telling us how to minister in His name, to get people healed.

Jesus is giving us the commission. He is the one telling us that we are authorized to use His name. This is very much like the authority that a law enforcement officer has, to be able to stand in the middle of the intersection and direct traffic. He can't direct traffic with his hand alone. He couldn't stop a car with his hand alone. But the drivers stop because the officer has authority to write a ticket or to arrest them. There's a lot more behind that badge and that hand being held out than just the power of that individual officer. It's life-changing to realize that the kind of authority that backs us up is infinitely greater!

METHOD 6 - EXAMPLE #1: PETER AND JOHN HEAL A LAME MAN

The disciples continued to use the name of Jesus after the Resurrection. Here is an example of an instant healing that happened when Peter and John used the name of Jesus with authority and power.

> **Now Peter and John went up together to the temple at the hour of prayer, the ninth hour. And a certain man lame from his mother's womb was carried, whom they laid daily at the gate of the temple which is called Beautiful, to ask alms from those who entered the temple; who, seeing Peter and John about to go into the temple, asked for alms (Acts 3:1-3).**

The lame man was expecting Peter and John to hand him some money.

> **And fixing his eyes on him, with John, Peter said, "Look at us." So he gave them his attention, expecting to receive something from them. Then Peter said, "Silver and gold I do not have..." (Acts 3:4-6a).**

Why didn't Peter and John have any silver and gold? They weren't poverty-stricken! Remember how, in the chapter before, it told how the disciples in Jerusalem had all things in common, how they sold their possessions and goods and divided them among all the believers, as anyone had need (Acts 2:44,45)? Peter had no cash on him at the time, but he had something far better. He said:

"...but what I do have I give you: In the name of Jesus Christ of Nazareth, rise up and walk" (Acts 3:6b).

Peter and John were doing exactly what Jesus told them to do when He sent out all of the disciples to heal the sick - they had a consistent pattern of using His name - they were experienced at using it. Here they're going out and doing the same thing *after* the Resurrection.

And he took him by the right hand and lifted him up, and immediately his feet and ankle bones received strength (Acts 3:7).

Because this was an instant healing, probably one or more of the supernatural gifts of the Spirit were in operation at the same time Peter used the name of Jesus.

So he, leaping up, stood and walked and entered the temple with them – walking, leaping, and praising God. And all the people saw him walking and praising God. Then they knew that it was he who sat begging alms at the Beautiful Gate of the temple; and they were filled with wonder and amazement at what had happened to him.

Now as the lame man who was healed held on to Peter and John, all the people ran together

to them in the porch which is called Solomon's, greatly amazed. So when Peter saw it, he responded to the people: "Men of Israel, why do you marvel at this? Or why look so intently at us, as though by our own power or godliness we had made this man walk?

"The God of Abraham, Isaac, and Jacob, the God of our fathers, glorified His Servant Jesus, whom you delivered up and denied in the presence of Pilate, when he was determined to let Him go. But you denied the Holy One and the Just, and asked for a murderer to be granted to you, and killed the Prince of life, whom God raised from the dead, of which we are witnesses" (Acts 3:8-15).

I love that! Peter preached the entire story of Jesus' resurrection to the people who were guilty of demanding that Jesus be crucified. And then Peter used the name of Jesus:

"And His name, through faith in His name has made this man strong, whom you see and know" (Acts 3:16a).

It's all in the name of Jesus: everything backs up that name - Jesus' glory, all of His power and majesty and splendor - it's all behind His name. It's not a magic wand, but when you use His name with faith, believing in the authority behind His name, these are the results that you get.

"Yes, the faith which comes through Him has given him this perfect soundness in the presence of you all" (Acts 3:16b).

It's marvelous to see God backing up His Word - the preaching of the gospel - with the name of Jesus. That name is above every other name: it's above lameness, it's above sickness, it's above cancer, it's above heart disease, and it's above joint disease. It's above everything that mankind faces. That name is able to eradicate everything that stands against us! God wants people to receive healing and receive deliverance from oppression.

This healing resulted in a situation where Peter could preach the gospel a second time to a big crowd of people and thousands more got saved. Acts 4:4 says:

Many of those who heard the word believed; and the number of the men came to be about five thousand.

HE OBTAINED A MORE EXCELLENT NAME

We gain faith in Jesus' name by looking at all that His name represents and the power behind His name. Whole books have been written on the name of Jesus and it's always a blessing to read these. Here are some of the scriptures that are covered in these books:

God, who at various times and in various ways spoke in time past to the fathers by the prophets, has in these last days spoken to us by His Son, whom He has appointed heir of all things, through whom also He made the worlds (Hebrews 1:1-2).

Throughout all eternity, the Trinity was the Father, The Word, and the Holy Spirit. The Father thought things; Jesus was the one who spoke and made the worlds; and the Holy Spirit enforced the word spoken by Jesus and did the work of creation.

...who being the brightness of His glory and

the express image of His person, and upholding all things by the word of His power, when He had by Himself purged our sins, sat down at the right hand of the Majesty on high; Having become so much better than the angels, as He has by inheritance obtained a more excellent name than they (Hebrews 1:3-4).

Jesus became much greater than the angels by His work on the Cross. He inherited a more excellent and glorious name than the angels. Jesus has the highest name in the universe, by His conquest.

For to which of the angels did He ever say: "You are My Son, Today I have begotten You"? And again: "I will be to Him a Father, And He shall be to Me a Son"? But when He again brings the firstborn into the world, He says: "Let all the angels of God worship Him" (Hebrews 1:5-6).

Jesus is the only begotten Son; all the angels of God worship Him.

JESUS HAS PREEMINENCE

He has delivered us from the power of darkness and conveyed us into the kingdom of the Son of His love, in whom we have redemption through His blood, the forgiveness of sins. He is the image of the invisible God, the firstborn over all creation.

For by Him all things were created that are in heaven and that are on earth, visible and invisible, whether thrones or dominions or

principalities or powers. All things were created through Him and for Him (Colossians 1:13-16).

Jesus was The Word who spoke it all into existence. It was all created for Him. The universe and all the angelic realm of power were created for Him.

And He is before all things, and in Him all things consist (Colossians 1:17).

All things exist in Christ; it is His power that holds everything - all of creation - together.

And He is the head of the body, the church, who is the beginning, the firstborn from the dead, that in all things He may have the preeminence (Colossians 1:18).

Since Jesus has the preeminence - the first place in the universe - and everything was created for Him and through Him, you can see why His name is above every other name, and why there's so much authority in His name. In fact, the more we look at everything that backs up the name of Jesus, the more confidence we have. When we use that name, all the devils start quaking: the angels are ready do the Word of God, according to what we pray, because of that name, the one who is preeminent over all.

JESUS WAS BEGOTTEN OF GOD BY RESURRECTION

There was an additional thing that God says about His resurrection.

God has fulfilled this for us their children, in that He has raised up Jesus. As it is also written in the second Psalm: "You are My Son, Today I have begotten You" (Acts 13:33).

Jesus is the *firstborn* from the dead (Colossians 1:18, Revelation 1:5); He is also the *first begotten* from the dead (Revelation 1:5) and the *only begotten Son* of the Father (John 1:14). His name carries resurrection power, the same power that heals our bodies.

JESUS HAS A NEW NAME

Jesus has now been given a new name. It says in Revelation 3:12:

> **"He who overcomes, I will make him a pillar in the temple of My God, and he shall go out no more. I will write on him the name of My God and the name of the city of My God, the New Jerusalem, which comes down out of heaven from My God. And I will write on him My new name."**

So, the name Jesus - in Hebrew, *Yehoshua*, which means *"Jehovah* is salvation" - the name that we're familiar with, will not be what we call the Lord when we get to heaven. He's got an even newer name that's above that name. It's a name that we've never even heard, but we're going to know, as soon as we're there. In fact, He will write His new name on us!

JESUS GIVES US A NEW NAME

It's interesting that Jesus also gives *us* a new name. It says in Revelation 2:17:

> **"He who has an ear, let him hear what the Spirit says to the churches. To him who overcomes I will give some of the hidden manna to eat. And I will give him a white stone, and on the stone a new name written which no one knows except him who receives it."**

So, when you get to heaven, Jesus will give you a brand-new name! You will still be known by your earthly name to other people: only Jesus and you will know the special name that only He calls you. I mean, how specific and individual is that? However many billions of people are going to be in heaven, Jesus still has that individual relationship with each one of us. Hallelujah! I believe our new name will somehow include the idea that we are healed, whole, and glorified.

THE NAME OF JESUS IS ABOVE ALL NAMES

The name of Jesus is above all names. Philippians 2:9-11 says:

> **Therefore God also has highly exalted Him and given Him the name which is above every name, that at the name of Jesus every knee should bow, of those in heaven, and of those on earth, and of those under the earth, and that every tongue should confess that Jesus Christ is Lord, to the glory of God the Father.**

Even the unbelievers who see Jesus after they die, will have to acknowledge that Jesus has the preeminence. They will see the one they rejected and didn't want to listen to, and they will know that He really was who He said He was. At this point, it will be too late: they won't be able to profess Jesus as Lord and gain salvation. At this point in time, they will have to bow in judgment, acknowledging that Jesus is Lord of All.

1 Corinthians 2:6 speaks about Jesus' complete authority over the works of darkness and the rulers of this age:

> **However, we speak wisdom among those who are mature, yet not the wisdom of this age, nor**

of the rulers of this age, who are coming to nothing (1 Corinthians 2:6).

I like what a couple of other translations say about these rulers of this age. Moffat's translation says:

Not the wisdom of this world or of the dethroned powers who rule this world (1 Corinthians 2:6b).

The powers that are actually ruling this world have been dethroned, they've been cast down, they have no spiritual authority in the heavenlies. Now they only have authority here on this earth when people give it to them, through doubt and unbelief or ignorance.

LIQUIDATED!

Kenneth Wuest was one of the best Greek scholars ever. This is what he said about these dethroned powers of darkness:

Who are in the process of being liquidated (1 Corinthians 2:6b WUEST).

Wuest says that the dethroned powers that are "coming to nothing" are actually in the process of being liquidated. You know what a liquidation sale is: it's when you break everything down to its parts, then sell everything off - there's nothing left afterwards. That's what God is doing with Satan's kingdom: He's liquidating it! God is in the process of breaking down the devil's kingdom, leaving nothing whatsoever!

A lot of people think that Satan is getting more powerful because the world is getting worse and worse. Did you ever think you'd see the whole planet "celebrating" Sodom and Gomorrah, homosexuality, and transgenderism? Did

you ever think that we would have a global pandemic trying to kill everyone on the planet? No, Satan is not getting
more powerful: he's getting more frantic! He knows his
time is coming up. We're coming to the end of the end of
the age and his judgment is near. So he is kicking up more
dust – more activity – than ever.

As God is liquidating the devil's kingdom, He is giving
us power and dominion over the forces of darkness. We're
going to see the greatest display of God's glory in the last
of the last days. There'll be a revival that will culminate in
the return of the Lord and the rapture of the Church. This
revival will combine the workings of the power of every
revival we've ever seen: Azuza Street and the Pentecostal
Revival, the Healing Revival of the 1940s and 50s, the
Charismatic Renewal, the Brownsville Revival of the
presence of God, the Toronto Blessing Revival, the
Revival of Joy in Rodney Howard-Browne's meetings and
Kenneth E. Hagin's Holy Ghost meetings, as well as missionary evangelism with healings in T.L. Osborn's and
Reinhard Bonnke's miracle crusades. God is in the process
of pushing down the powers of darkness, no matter how
frantic they get, and raising up the power being manifested in the body of Christ.

We're going to see more miracles than we've ever even
imagined! It's going to be a time and a place where God will
shine a spotlight on the Church. Where the Church has
always been looked upon with disdain, it is suddenly going
to be the envy of the world. All of a sudden, the Church is
going to be having such manifestations of healing, that sin-
ners who have been told by their doctors, "We can't do anything else for you," are going to come in, hoping they could
be healed and not die. When they experience the power of
God, they will turn their lives over to the Lord. It will be a
revival that's flat-out amazing! And it's not going to be in

just one place: it will spread throughout the entire earth. So, who is God going to use in this revival? He will use the churches that are contending for the whole counsel of God's Word and for the presence of the Holy Spirit. Suddenly, the power of God will be in full manifestation in these churches. We will see a sweeping move of God, with several billion people coming into the kingdom.

DON'T UNDERESTIMATE THE GOOD
THAT YOU ARE DOING IN HIS NAME

Don't underestimate the good that you are doing in Jesus' name. Whether you have come to this place of using His name in full authority or not, everything you are doing, you're doing in the name of Jesus. It is making an everlasting difference in the lives you touch.

While we are going about and doing good, ministering for the Lord, we are continuing to grow in our ability to walk in the authority in the name of Jesus, through the knowledge of all that is behind His name. Every time we pray for people in the name of Jesus – and see the powerful results – we get a bigger picture of all the authority of the universe that God created, and beyond that universe, all the power of heaven itself. That's what's behind the name of Jesus. Hallelujah!

We can have an increase in the awareness of the presence of the Lord and His power in our lives, all the days of our lives. And should Jesus tarry, some of us may be asked by God to live to be 120. Kenneth Copeland committed to it. God asked him, "Will you commit to live to be 120 if I demand it of you?" Brother Copeland said, "My life is Yours to command, Sir."

Then God said, "You're going to change some things to make it so."

Brother Copeland tells the story: "Every time I went into my little gym, I'd say, 'Oh, I hate this.' And then I realized, 'I can't say that anymore.' Now I walk in there and say, 'I love this because I love what's good for me. It improves my health and extends my life.'"

We learn to take care of ourselves: we exercise – plus we realize we can have a Thanksgiving meal and pumpkin pie sometimes, but not every day! We learn what vitamins and supplements to put in our bodies to help them work best. Of course, the key element is going to be our faith. Faith, exercise, rest, and nutrition are all working together toward our healing, our well-being, and the longevity to be able to go the distance.

METHOD 7 - ANOINTING WITH OIL

The final method of ministering healing to others is simply anointing them with oil. This method is underused, but it is so powerful. Our key scripture for this method was written by James, the half-brother of the Lord Jesus. In the early days of the Church, James became the head of the Church of Jerusalem. The other apostles would go out on mission trips, then come back and report to James. They honored his authority and respected his words and insights, and so should we!

Is anyone among you sick? Let him call for the elders of the church... (James 5:14a).

I believe anyone can lay hands on the sick and anyone can anoint with oil, but this passage is specifically saying, "If you're a member of a church and you are sick and you need healing, don't hesitate. Call on the *elders* of the church." God has empowered the leaders of the Church: every local assembly has people who are mature – whether they are official elders or not – people who can minister healing. That's who James is talking about here: someone who understands the power, the anointing, and the authority that's in the name of Jesus.

> **...and let them pray over him, anointing him with oil in the name of the Lord (James 5:14b).**

Anointing oil had been used throughout the Old Testament: whenever they anointed a priest or king, they poured the oil over the top of their head and it ran down their beard and garment. They had a special anointing oil used by the Levitical priesthood. The elders at the Church of Jerusalem were probably copying that same oil. They had a lot of olive oil in Israel, but for us today, any oil will do.

I personally like using anointing oil that comes from Israel: they use the same formula as the Levitical anointing oil, it's got frankincense and myrrh, and it smells wonderful! So, I use that whenever someone asks for prayer. I also use this anointing oil whenever we lay hands on a cloth, pray for someone, release our faith, and send the cloth out. There's nothing magic in the oil: it's simply a representation of the Holy Spirit and His presence. As we're praying, we recognize the power and the anointing of the Holy Spirit and so we symbolically anoint with oil and release our faith. God's Word says to do it, so we do it...and it works!

> **And the prayer of faith will save the sick, and the Lord will raise him up. And if he has committed sins, he will be forgiven (James 5:15).**

This verse indicates that, in some cases, people may have been the source of their own sickness. They may have opened the door; they have unrepentant sin in their life. This verse is saying you should tell them, "Here's a great opportunity to make sure the sickness doesn't come back. Let's make sure you shut every door. Repent of any sin that God is highlighting to you right now and believe God for the power of His grace to overcome." It's important to help them to *really* access the grace of God. That's where they not only get forgiveness, but they get the empowerment of the grace of God to walk free from anything that entangled them before.

This is brilliant: the entire salvation package is available for somebody who calls for the elders of the church to come and anoint them with oil – they get healed, forgiven, delivered from sin, and empowered to walk free. Let's get the Church doing the job of the Church!

METHOD 7 - EXAMPLE OF ANOINTING WITH OIL FOR HEALING

An example of anointing with oil for ministering healing to others is found in Mark's gospel. The Lord Jesus must have demonstrated anointing the sick with oil, because when He sent the twelve disciples out to heal the sick, that is what they did.

So they went out and preached that people should repent. And they cast out many demons, and anointed with oil many who were sick, and healed them (Mark 6:12-13).

When we minister to the sick, we are calling on the Lord, in compassion, to heal them. We lay hands on them as a point of contact. There's a transfer of the anointing for healing – sometimes we can perceive the power of God go into them through the laying on of our hands.

We take authority over sickness, like casting the mountain into the sea, and we pray the prayer of faith in the name of Jesus. At the same time we're anointing them with oil, symbolic of the Holy Spirit. The Holy Spirit is the one doing all of this: He enforces the covenant promises of God's Word and causes healing to happen.

CONCLUSION

GOD WANTS YOU WELL

WITH THE MANY METHODS GOD HAS PROVIDED for both receiving healing and ministering healing to others, we can see a picture of the great compassion of God and His desire to surround us with His healing power.

God wants you well! He wants to take care of the body of Christ. He wants us to be able to run our race all the way to the finish line. He has given us so many ways to do so.

Is there any condemnation for those who died before a ripe old age, who didn't run their full race? No. We're no one's judge. The Lord Himself will say, "I'll reward you according to whether or not you were yielded to Me." It all really comes down to us: once we get saved, are we going to yield to everything the Lord wants to do in our lives? Are we going to be consecrated to His will - or are we going to continue on with our own agenda?

YOU ARE IN THE HEALING MINISTRY

If you've ever been healed by the power of God, guess

what? You are in the healing ministry, because you are an eyewitness to the healing power of God. Whenever people question my testimonies of supernatural healing and ask me, "How do you know you were healed by God?"

I answer, "Because I was there when it happened. I know I was touched by the hand of God; I've experienced how real it is. So, therefore I cannot be quiet about this."

I know God has already healed everyone through the work of Jesus – and He wants to bring everyone's healing into manifestation. It sometimes takes awhile for that to completely sink in; that's why I suggest people read this book multiple times, going back and meditating on the scriptures concerning healing, over and over again. Read any other faith-filled book on healing that you possibly can. Listen to recordings of healing scriptures. Let the message of healing surround you. You'll find that whatever you meditate on, that's where you will receive greater faith. So, if you're meditating on things concerning divine healing and divine health, then you end up getting greater faith for that.

It's the same principle that works if you meditate on supernatural provision and prosperity: the more you study that, believe it, and work God's system, the more you'll find the favor of God working – the right jobs come, the promotions come, and the increase comes. You will see God's Word at work.

SLOWING THE AGING PROCESS

As we apply these principles to healing, we find we can keep getting healthier and healthier as we go. This is important to know, because there comes a point in the aging process where the going gets tougher. We believe what is promised in Psalm 103:5, that our youth will be renewed like the eagles. Even so, I have come to realize we're not going to be able to use our faith to completely stop the aging process, but we can slow it down. Paul says, "...our outward man is perishing..." (2 Corinthians 4:16b). That means the outward man is growing older. Paul goes on to say, "...yet the inward man is being renewed day by day." That means, in the realm of the Spirit, we can be built up in faith. On the outside, we can't use faith to keep from going gray or going bald, we can't stop the wrinkles from coming, and now it takes a little longer exercising to get back into optimum condition. Plus, we have to become more careful to prevent any kind of injury; if we fall, it seems to take a little longer to heal. It's just a natural thing. That's why it's important for us to constantly be renewed in our inner man as we age, because it takes that much more faith to walk in health on the outside.

Do I believe we can walk in health and overcome everything that would come against us - all the way to our last day? Absolutely! This is true, even for those who have the faith to go to 120, if they feel that's their assignment. We saw that in Psalm 91:16 that we can keep going until we are satisfied with life.

In the process of living, we learn a lot about the right way to take care of ourselves - the right exercise, rest and sleep, and nutrition to work in conjunction with everything that we are learning concerning faith. The knowledge of the Word of God is the most important, but we don't want to work against divine healing and health as we're applying this Word. We want to work in conjunction with it. I believe God has graced us with great scientific discoveries and learning of how the body works. In the section "Resources for Healing and Health" at the end of this book, you will find our favorite resources for meditating on the Word concerning healing as well as for nutritional tips and other life-style changes.

If people would take the time to learn and apply these discoveries, their lives could definitely be tremendously changed. That's what we're hoping for - for the best for everyone who wants to serve the Lord - that their lives would be full of energy, and they would have longevity and joy in serving the Lord all of their days.

MY PRAYER FOR YOU, THE READER

I'M GOING TO PRAY A PRAYER OF HEALING for my readers, because I know that the Lord can touch you right where you are. I believe the Lord is raising the level of your faith to where you are realizing. "I can connect with the prayer of faith being prayed over me, without being touched."

When you receive on your own, it proves to you, "My faith is doing the job." Your confidence in God always meeting your needs rises up. So, let's close with this prayer, believing the Lord will touch your body - directly - with His healing hand.

Father, in Jesus' name, we thank You so much for all of Your Word. You sent Your Word to heal us. And Your Word, of course, was Jesus. You sent Your only begotten Son, who became flesh and dwelt among us. He taught, He ministered, and then, at the whipping post, He bore, in His own body, those physical stripes, as well as those spiritual stripes that purchased our healing. He went to the Cross and there He did the miraculous exchange for us: eternal life for our sin-

fulness and our sinful condition, bringing healing, deliverance, righteousness, and provision.

He bore everything for us so we don't have to bear any of it. Lord Jesus, any time any one of us is under attack, help us envision those stripes that You bore. You paid the price - and You are not asking us to pay the price again. So, Lord Jesus, I'm asking right now that the anointing of Your Holy Spirit who heals, delivers, transforms, and sets free, would rest upon each one of us.

And Lord, that with the presence of Your Spirit to receive everything that we need right now, we also receive the anointing to carry Your healing power to others.

NOW, MAKE THIS DECLARATION:

Father, I come to You in the name of Jesus, and I declare that everything Jesus paid for me is mine: salvation, the infilling of the Holy Spirit, all the power, all the healing, all the provision, all the peace that passes all understanding. I receive it right now into my life, in full measure. Lord, touch me now; manifest healing, provision, balance, wholeness, and peace in my life. In Jesus' mighty and matchless name. Amen. Praise God!

I wanted to lead you in your own prayer of receiving from the Lord, because then Satan can never steal health from you. He can never put any sickness upon you, because you realize you've got the authority, in the name of Jesus, to resist him, steadfast in the faith.

He is going to come along and try. It's like Brother Hagin said, "I have had many marvelous opportunities to be sick, but I passed them all up." You will also be able to pass sickness up, to walk in divine health. Life just keeps getting better and better, as the anointing and the presence of God in your life keeps increasing.

After the Lord asked Brother Copeland if he would be willing to live to be 120, God said, "I've got a new anointing for you for every decade." At the time, Brother Copeland was coming up on his 80th birthday. He said, "I started calling myself 80 when I was 79 because, man, I knew that increase was going to come. And, sure enough, it came. Now I can hardly wait for the nineties' anointing. And then I can hardly wait for the hundreds' anointing!"

The Lord told me, "Anyone who goes the distance and steps into age 110, they receive the Moses anointing." I don't know what God's going to ask *you* to do once *you* reach 110, but it's going to be glorious, because you're going to be walking in some mighty power by then!

So Father, in Jesus' name, we thank You for this book, for the opportunity to continue to learn everything that we need to know. You're the source of all the knowledge. All knowledge that man has discovered, it was in Your mind, first. We're only discovering things that You created. You created us and we want to work in agreement with You, Father, with the way You made us and the way You heal us, how You make us whole and strong.

We declare we shall be healthy and strong and fulfill our days and bring glory and honor to the name of Jesus Christ. We give You praise and thanksgiving for the anointing and for success. We shall apply every truth to our lives and to our ministry to those who You call us to minister to. We give You praise and thanksgiving for it, in Jesus' mighty and matchless name. Amen. Hallelujah!

BIBLIOGRAPHY

Charisma Magazine. "Mario Murillo's Tent Crusades Spark Revival That Is Spreading like Wildfire." Published Jan. 19, 2022. Accessed 06-21-2022. https://charismamag.com/revival/mario-murillo-s-tent-crusades-spark-revival-that-is-spreading-like-wildfire/

Edgar, Julie. "Billy Graham, 'America's Pastor' Dies at 99." WebMD. Last modified February 21, 2018. https://www.webmd.com/a-to-z-guides/news/20180221/billy-graham-americas-pastor-dies-at-99/.

Forbes. "One in Seven Christian Minorities under Threat in 2022." Forbes. Published Jan. 20, 2022. Accessed 06-1-2022. https://www.forbes.com/sites/ewelinaochab/2022/01/20/one-in-seven-christian-minorities-under-threat-in 2022/?sh=54fcfc077d2d/

Hagin, Kenneth E. Seven Things You Should Know about Divine Healing. Broken Arrow, OK: Faith Library Publications, 1979.

Kennedy, D. James. Evangelism Explosion, 4th ed. Carol Stream, IL: Tyndale House Publishers, Inc., 1996.

Kenneth Hagin Ministries. "History of the Ministry – History 1949-1965." No publishing date available. Accessed 06-1-2022. https://www.rhema.org/index.php?option=com_content&view=article&id=9:history-of-the-ministry&catid=174&showall=&limitstart=2. .

Maffucci, Michael. *No Darkness at All: A Biblical Defense for Word of Faith Theology*. Meadville, PA: Christian Faith Publishing, Inc., 2021.

Mosher, Dave. "Wine: Kills Germs on Contact." Livescience.com. Last modified July 5, 2007. Accessed 6-21-2021. https://www.livescience.com/7326-wine-kills-germs-contact.html.

Open Doors USA. "13 Christians Murdered for Following Jesus – Every Day." Published Jan 18, 2021. Last modified March 2, 2021. Accessed 06-1-22. https://www.opendoorsusa.org/christian-persecution/stories/13-christians-killed-every-day/.

Strong, James. *New Strong's Exhaustive Concordance*. Nashville, TN: Thomas Nelson Publishers, 1996.

WHO (World Health Organization). *Coronavirus (COVID-19) Dashboard*. Accessed 04- 6-2022. https://covid19.who.int/.

BIBLES USED

The Amplified Bible AMP. Copyright © 2015 by The Lockman Foundation, La Habra, CA 90631. Used by Permission.

The Amplified Bible, Classic Edition AMPC. Copyright © 1954, 1958, 1962, 1964, 1965, 1987 by The Lockman Foundation, La Habra, CA 90631. Used by Permission.

Bibliography

J.B. Phillips New Testament. The New Testament in Modern English PHILLIPS. Copyright © 1960, 1972 by J. B. Phillips. Administered by The Archbishops' Council of the Church of England. Used by Permission.

The Message MSG. Copyright © 1993, 2002, 2018 by Eugene H. Peterson. Used by Permission.

The Mirror Study Bible MIRROR. Copyright © 2012 by Francois du Toit. mirrorword.net. Used by Permission.

The New Testament: An Expanded Translation by Kenneth S. Wuest. Copyright © 1961. Wm. B. Eerdmans Publishing Co. All rights reserved.

The New King James Version of the Bible, Copyright © 1982 by Thomas Nelson, Inc. Used by permission. All rights reserved.

The Passion Translation TPT. Copyright © 2017, 2018, 2020 Passion and Fire Ministries, Inc. ThePassionTranslation.com. Used by Permission.

Young's Literal Translation YLT. Public Domain.

RESOURCES FOR HEALING & HEALTH

Healing Scriptures for Meditation:

Larry Hutton Ministries Website: larryhutton.org

Larry Hutton's Scripture Recordings:

Heaven's Health Food

Dr. Hutton quotes Healing Scriptures from many translations in a unique way that will truly make God's Word come alive to you! With soft, beautiful piano and string music in the background, you will be blessed as you build your faith to be healed, or to walk in divine health from now on!

Many have been healed after having their faith built up, while listening to this CD.

Larry Hutton Scripture Confession Cards:

Your Prescription for Health

52 cards with scriptures on one side, and a powerful declaration of faith on the other.

Nutrition and Life-Style Changes:

Dr. Mercola's Website: Mercola.com

Root Canal Information:

Price Pottenger Website: price-pottenger.org

Do a search for "Root Canals" or use this link to see a variety of resources: https://price-pottenger.org/?s=root+canals